AAT
INTERACTIVE TEXT

Intermediate Unit 7

Reports and Returns

In this May 2000 edition

- Layout designed to be easier on the eye – and easier to use

- Icons to guide you through a 'fast-track' approach if you wish

- Thorough reliable updating of material to 1 May 2000

FOR 2000 AND 2001 DEVOLVED ASSESSMENTS

BPP Publishing
May 2000

First edition May 1998
Third edition May 2000

ISBN 0 7517 6214 8 (Previous edition 0 7517 6158 3)

British Library Cataloguing-in-Publication Data
A catalogue record for this book
is available from the British Library

Published by

BPP Publishing Limited
Aldine House, Aldine Place
London W12 8AW

www.bpp.com

Printed in Great Britain by W M Print
Frederick Street
Walsall
West Midlands WS2 9NE

We are grateful to the Lead Body for Accounting for permission to reproduce extracts from the Standards of Competence for Accounting, and to the AAT for permission to reproduce extracts from the Mapping and Guidance Notes.

Page

BPP
PUBLISHING

HOW TO USE THIS INTERACTIVE TEXT

Aims of this Interactive Text

To provide the knowledge and practice to help you succeed in the devolved assessments for Intermediate Unit 7 *Preparing Reports and Returns*.

To pass the devolved assessments you need a thorough understanding in all areas covered by the standards of competence.

To tie in with the other components of the BPP Effective Study Package to ensure you have the best possible chance of success.

Interactive Text

This covers all you need to know for devolved assessment for Unit 7 *Preparing Reports and Returns*. Until you are ready to tackle assessment style questions at the end of your course, you only need to take this book to class. Icons clearly mark key areas of the text. Numerous activities throughout the text help you practise what you have just learnt.

Devolved Assessment Kit

When you have understood and practised the material in the Interactive Text, you will have the knowledge and experience to tackle the Devolved Assessment Kit for Unit 7 *Reports and Returns*. This aims to get you through the devolved assessment, whether in the form of the AAT simulation or in the workplace. It contains the AAT's sample simulation for Unit 7 plus other simulations.

Recommended approach to this Interactive Text

(a) To achieve competence in Unit 7 (and all the other units), you need to be able to do **everything** specified by the standards. Study the text very carefully and do not skip any of it.

(b) Learning is an **active** process. Do **all** the activities as you work through the text so you can be sure you really understand what you have read.

(c) After you have covered the material in the Interactive Text, work through the **Devolved Assessment Kit**.

(d) Before you take the devolved assessments, check that you still remember the material using the following quick revision plan for each chapter.

   (i) Read through the **chapter learning objectives**. Are there any gaps in your knowledge? If so, study the section again.

   (ii) Read and learn the **key terms**.

   (iii) Look at the **devolved assessment alerts**. These show the sort of things that are likely to come up.

   (iv) Read and learn the **key learning points,** which are a summary of the chapter.

   (v) Do the **quick quiz** again. If you know what you're doing, it shouldn't take long.

   This approach is only a suggestion. You college may well adapt it to suit your needs.

BPP PUBLISHING

Remember this is a **practical** course.

(a)   Try to relate the material to your experience in the workplace or any other work experience you may have had.

(b)   Try to make as many links as you can to your study of the other Units at Intermediate level.

(c)   Keep this Text - you will need it as you move on to Technician, and (hopefully) you will find it invaluable in your everyday work too!

INTERMEDIATE QUALIFICATION STRUCTURE

The competence-based Education and Training Scheme of the Association of Accounting Technicians is based on an analysis of the work of accounting staff in a wide range of industries and types of organisation. The Standards of Competence for Accounting which students are expected to meet are based on this analysis.

The Standards identify the **key purpose** of the accounting occupation, which is **to operate, maintain and improve systems to record, plan, monitor and report on the financial activities of an organisation**, and a number of **key roles** of the occupation. Each key role is subdivided into **units of competence**, which are further divided into **elements of competences**. By successfully completing assessments in specified units of competence, students can gain qualifications at NVQ/SVQ levels 2, 3 and 4, which correspond to the AAT Foundation, Intermediate and Technician stages of competence respectively.

Whether you are competent in a Unit is demonstrated by means of a Devolved Assessment (where competence is judged by an Approved Assessment Centre to whom responsibility for this is devolved).

Below we set out the overall structure of the Intermediate (NVQ/SVQ Level 3) stage, indicating how competence in each Unit is assessed. In the next section there is more detail about the Devolved Assessments for Unit 7.

BPP PUBLISHING

Intermediate qualification structure

NVQ/SVQ **Level 3 - Intermediate**

All units are mandatory

Unit of competence   **Elements of competence**

Unit 5   Maintaining financial records and preparing accounts

Central *and* Devolved Assessment

5.1	Maintain records relating to capital acquisition and disposal
5.2	Record income and expenditure
5.3	Collect and collate information for the preparation of financial accounts
5.4	Prepare the extended trial balance account

Unit 6   Recording cost information

Central *and* Devolved Assessment

6.1	Record and analyse information relating to direct costs
6.2	Record and analyse information relating to the allocation, apportionment and absorption of overhead costs
6.3	Prepare and present standard cost reports

Unit 7   Preparing reports and returns

Devolved Assessment *only*

7.1	Prepare and present periodic performance reports
7.2	Prepare reports and returns for outside agencies
7.3	Prepare VAT returns

Unit 21   Using information technology

Devolved Assessment *only*

21.1	Obtain information from a computerised Management Information System
21.2	Produce spreadsheets for the analysis of numerical information
21.3	Contribute to the quality of the Management Information System

Unit 22   Monitor and maintain a healthy, safe and secure workplace (ASC)

Devolved Assessment *only*

22.1	Monitor and maintain health and safety within the workplace
22.2	Monitor and maintain the security of the workplace

UNIT 7 STANDARDS OF COMPETENCE

The structure of the Standards for Unit 7

The Unit commences with a statement of the **knowledge and understanding** which underpin competence in the Unit's elements.

The unit of Competence is then divided into **elements of competence** describing activities which the individual should be able to perform.

Each element includes:

(a) A set of **performance criteria** which define what constitutes competent performance

(b) A **range statement** which defines the situations, contexts, methods etc in which competence should be displayed

(c) **Evidence requirements**, which state that competence must be demonstrated consistently, over an appropriate time scale with evidence of performance being provided from the appropriate sources

(d) **Sources of evidence**, being suggestions of ways in which you can find evidence to demonstrate that competence. These fall under the headings: 'observed performance; work produced by the candidate; authenticated testimonies from relevant witnesses; personal account of competence; other sources of evidence.' They are reproduced in full in our Devolved Assessment Kit for Unit 7.

The elements of competence for Unit 7: *Preparing Reports and Returns* are set out below. Knowledge and understanding required for the unit as a whole are listed first, followed by the performance criteria and range statements for each element. Performance criteria are cross-referenced below to chapters in this Unit 7 *Reports and Returns* Interactive Text.

Unit 7: Preparing Reports and Returns

What is the unit about?

This unit relates to the preparation of reports and returns from information obtained from all relevant sources. The candidate is required to calculate ratios and performance indicators and present the information according to the appropriate conventions and definitions to either management or outside agencies, including the VAT office. The unit is also concerned with the communication responsibilities of the candidate which include obtaining authorisation before despatching reports, seeking guidance from the VAT office and presenting reports and returns in the appropriate manner.

Knowledge and understanding

The business environment

- Main sources of relevant government statistics (Elements 7.1 & 7.2)

- Awareness of relevant performance and quality measures (Element 7.1)

- Main types of outside organisations requiring reports and returns: regulatory; grant awarding; information collecting; trade associations (Element 7.2)

- Basic law and practice relating to all issues covered in the range statement and referred to in the performance criteria. Specific issues include: the classification of types of supply; registration requirements; the form of VAT invoices; tax points (Element 7.3)

- Sources of information on VAT: Customs and Excise Guide (Element 7.3)

- Administration of VAT: enforcement (Element 7.3)

- Special schemes: annual accounting; cash accounting; bad debt relief (Element 7.3)

Accounting techniques

- Use of standard units of inputs and outputs (Element 7.1 & 7.3)

- Time series analysis (Element 7.1)

- Use of index numbers (Element 7.1)

- Main types of performance indicators: productivity; cost per unit; resource utilisation; profitability (Elements 7.1 & 7.2)

- Ratios: gross profit margin; net profit margin; return on capital employed (Elements 7.1 & 7.2)

- Tabulation of accounting and other quantitative information (Elements 7.1 & 7.2)

- Methods of presenting information: written reports; diagrammatic; tabular (Elements 7.1 & 7.2)

The organisation

- Understanding of the ways the accounting systems of an organisation are affected by its organisational structure, its administrative systems and procedures and the nature of its business transactions (Elements 7.1, 7.2 & 7.3)

- Understanding of the purpose and structure of reporting systems within the organisation (Element 7.1)

- Background understanding that a variety of outside agencies may require reports and returns from organisations and that these requirements must be built into administrative and accounting systems and procedures (Element 7.2 & 7.3)

- Background understanding that recording and accounting practices may vary between organisations and different parts of organisations (Elements 7.1, 7.2 & 7.3)

- An understanding of the basis of the relationship between the organisation and the VAT office (Element 7.3)

Element 7.1 Prepare and present periodic performance reports

Performance criteria	Chapters in this Text
1 Information derived from different units of the organisation is consolidated into the appropriate form	9
2 Information derived from different information systems within the organisation is correctly reconciled	9
3 When comparing results over time an appropriate method, which allows for changing price levels, is used	7
4 Transactions between separate units of the organisation are accounted for in accordance with the organisation's procedures	10
5 Ratios and performance indicators are accurately calculated in accordance with the organisation's procedures	9, 11
6 Reports are prepared in the appropriate form and presented to management within required timescales	2 – 6, 8

Range statement

1 Information: costs; revenue

2 Ratios: gross profit margin; net profit margin; return on capital employed

3 Performance indicators: productivity; cost per unit; resource utilisation; profitability

4 Methods of presenting information: written report containing diagrams; table

Element 7.2 Prepare reports and returns for outside agencies

Performance criteria	Chapters in this Text
1 Relevant information is identified, collated and presented in accordance with the conventions and definitions used by outside agencies	2, 8
2 Calculations of ratios and performance indicators are accurate	9
3 Authorisation for the despatch of completed reports and returns is sought from the appropriate person	1
4 Reports and returns are presented in accordance with outside agencies' requirements and deadlines	2, 8

Range statement

1 Ratios: gross profit margin; net profit margin; return on capital employed

2 Reports and returns: written report; return on standard form

BPP PUBLISHING

Element 7.3 Prepare VAT returns

Performance criteria	Chapters in this Text
1 VAT returns are correctly completed using data from the appropriate recording systems and are submitted within the statutory time limits	12,
2 Relevant inputs and outputs are correctly identified and calculated	12, 13,
3 Submissions are made in accordance with current legislation	13
4 Guidance is sought from the VAT office when required, in a professional manner	13

Range statement

1   Recording systems: computerised ledgers; manual control account; cash book

2   Inputs and outputs: standard supplies; exempt supplies; zero rated supplies; imports; exports

ASSESSMENT STRATEGY

This unit is assessed entirely by means of *devolved* assessment.

Devolved Assessment (*more detail can be found in the Devolved Assessment Kit*)

Devolved assessment is a means of collecting evidence of your ability to carry out **practical activities** and to **operate effectively in the conditions of the workplace** to the standards required. Evidence may be collected at your place of work or at an Approved Assessment Centre by means of simulations of workplace activity, or by a combination of these methods.

If the Approved Assessment Centre is a **workplace**, you may be observed carrying out accounting activities as part of your normal work routine. You should collect documentary evidence of the work you have done, or contributed to, in an **accounting portfolio**. Evidence collected in a portfolio can be assessed in addition to observed performance or where it is not possible to assess by observation.

Where the Approved Assessment Centre is a **college or training organisation**, devolved assessment will be by means of a combination of the following.

(a) Documentary evidence of activities carried out at the workplace, collected by you in an **accounting portfolio.**

(b) Realistic **simulations** of workplace activities. These simulations may take the form of case studies and in-tray exercises and involve the use of primary documents and reference sources.

(c) **Projects and assignments** designed to assess the Standards of Competence.

If you are unable to provide workplace evidence you will be able to complete the assessment requirements by the alternative methods listed above.

Part A
Preparing reports and returns

Chapter 1 The organisation, accounting and reporting

Chapter topic list

1   Organisations and their structure

2   Accounting practices in different parts of the organisation

3   Internal and external reports

Learning objectives

On completion of this chapter you will be able to:

	Performance criteria	Range statement
• understand that authorisation for the despatch of completed records and returns is sought from the appropriate person	7.2.3	7.2.1
• *understand the ways the accounting system of an organisation are affected by its organisational structure, its administrative systems and procedures and the nature of its business transactions*	n/a	n/a
• *understand that recording and accounting practices may vary in different parts of the organisation*	n/a	n/a
• *understand the purpose and structure of reporting systems within the organisation*	n/a	n/a
• *understand that the accounting systems of an organisation are affected by its organisation structure, its administrative systems and procedures, and the nature of its business transactions*	n/a	n/a
• *understand that a variety of outside agencies may require reports and returns from organisations and that these requirements must be built into administrative and accounting procedures*	n/a	n/a

Italicised objectives are areas of knowledge and understanding underlying the elements of competence for Unit 7.

1 ORGANISATIONS AND THEIR STRUCTURE

Organisations

1.1 There are many different kinds of organisation, from an aircraft manufacturer to a bank to a government department to a hospital to a corner shop.

1.2 It is possible to distinguish organisations from each other in a number of ways, so that the many different types of organisation can be fitted into a number of categories. Ways of classifying and distinguishing organisations include the following.

(a) **By type of activity**. Here are some examples.

- Retailers (eg greengrocer, supermarket chain)
- Manufacturers (eg of painkillers, ballbearings, cars)
- Service organisations (eg restaurants, schools)
- Contractors (eg building power stations)

(b) **By size of business**. A large supermarket would have more in common with another large organisation than with a small grocer's shop.

(c) **Profit orientated or non profit orientated**. An organisation in existence to make a profit seeks to **maximise the difference between what it receives in revenue, and what it pays out in expenses**. The surplus, or profit, is distributed to the owners to do with as they please. A charity, on the other hand, is a **non profit making organisation**. Public sector organisations are funded from general taxation to provide services, not, generally speaking, to make a profit.

(d) **Legal status and ownership.**

(i) The business affairs of **sole traders** are not distinguished from their personal affairs in the eyes of the law.

(ii) A **partnership** is an agreement (normally documented) between two or more individuals, but the partners are still personally liable for the debts of the business.

(iii) A **limited company**, on the other hand, is a **separate legal personality** in the eyes of the law, and is a **separate legal entity** from its owners (shareholders). (A UK limited company can be identified by the words Limited or public limited company, or the letters Ltd or plc after its name - there are equivalents for Welsh companies.)

(iv) Some organisations (eg hospitals) are owned and funded by central or local government. These are **public sector organisations**.

(v) **Unincorporated associations,** such as sports clubs and societies are very common. They are not separate legal bodies from the members who make them up even though that membership is always changing. They are managed by **committees**.

(vi) **Charities** are registered with the Charity Commissioners and have trustees.

Organisation structure

1.3 Organisations are often so large that there have be **formal** and **defined relationships** between the persons within the organisation. This is because of the following reasons.

(a) There is a large number of **tasks** that have to be done, involving several people, and these activities have to be coordinated in some way.

(b) There is often a large number of **people** who have to be coordinated and motivated.

1.4 Many large organisations have a **person** or **committee** at the head who is responsible, ultimately, for the **direction** the organisation takes and its **policies** and **strategies** (for example, what to sell and which countries to trade in). An individual might be called **Chief Executive**, or **Managing Director**. A committee might be called a **Board of Directors** or an **Executive Committee**.

1.5 In a large organisation, the Board's decisions will 'cascade' down for detailed implementation, and **information** about performance will rise up. Each person at the top will have a number of people reporting to him or her, and in turn these other people will have their own **subordinates**, and so on. This is the **management hierarchy**, in which a person's position and responsibilities are defined in relation to other people's positions and responsibilities.

1.6 Another aspect of **organisation structure**, which depends on its size as much as anything else, is how it is arranged.

(a) For example, say you work for an organisation which manufactures a range of cars and buses. These are both manufactured and sold in Europe and Asia. The company has its head office and most of its research facilities in the UK. It is a UK registered company, and has no shareholders outside the UK. The company employs 20,000 people. If you work for a large organisation, you will be familiar with the fact that some people work in, for example, marketing and selling, others work in production and still more in finance and administration.

(b) Such a company is likely to be quite complex. There is bound to be a central committee of top executives in charge of the overall running of the business, but how about the rest of the business? There are a number of ways by which it could be organised.

(i) Would the business be structured **geographically**, like this?

In this **geographical organisation structure** the responsibility for all the activities of the company is divided on an area basis. The manager for Asia is in charge of producing and selling products in that area.

(ii)   Would the business be structured on a **product-divisional basis**, like this?

In this **product-division structure** the responsibility for buses worldwide, and cars worldwide, are each given to one individual.

(iii)   Or would the business be structured on a **functional basis**, like this?

In this **functional organisation structure**, worldwide control of production is vested in one person, as is the case with sales and marketing.

(iv)   Or would the business be structured on a **matrix basis**, like this?

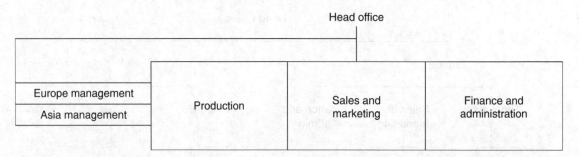

In a **matrix organisation structure**, somebody involved in production in Europe has to report equally to the European manager and to the production manager.

1.7   There are many arguments for and against each structure, and it is not our purpose to go into them here. However, they do have a direct effect on the accounting system, since they determine the following.

- How information is collected, and by whom.
- How information is sent up the management hierarchy.
- How the information is aggregated and summarised.

1.8   In short, the information gives managers a '**view of the world**', and the decisions they take are influenced by the information they receive about the organisation and the wider social environment in which it operates.

Activity 1.1

A report is prepared every month analysing the results of the business. It comes in four sections: a summary for the company as a whole, and then separate reports for Europe, America and the Far East.

(a)   What does this imply about the organisation structure?

(b)   What effect would the imposition of a functional structure have on the work of a junior accounts manager in Europe?

Activity 1.2

Sara Jeeves works for Autobuttle Ltd, a company manufacturing a variety of products of domestic utility. She does work for two individuals. One day, she hears them in furious argument about her job for that day.

'I don't care what you say, I've got to get those figures for Robobutlers to the director of the Automated Domestic Service Division by Thursday. This is a vital need, as she's thinking of killing the product.'

'Give us a break, the UK director's coming on his monthly visit and I've got to put the best possible gloss on our performance.'

What might this tell you about the management structure of Autobuttle Ltd?

2   ACCOUNTING PRACTICES IN DIFFERENT PARTS OF THE ORGANISATION

2.1   An organisation's accounting systems are affected by the **nature of its business transactions** and the **sort of business** it is.

(a)   **Size**. A small business like a greengrocer will have a simple, **cash-based accounting system**, where the main accounting record will probably be the till roll. A large retail business, such as a chain of supermarkets, will have **elaborate accounting systems** using advanced computer technology covering a large number of product ranges and sites.

(b)   **Type of organisation**

(i)   A **service business** might need to record the time employees take on particular jobs, as accounting on a job or client basis is often a feature of service businesses (such as firms of accountants).

(ii)   A **public sector organisation**, such as a government department, may be more concerned with the monitoring of expenditure against performance targets than with recording revenue.

(iii) A **manufacturing company** will account both for unit sales and revenue, but needs to keep track of costs for decision-making purposes and so on.

(c)   **Organisation structure**. Accounting information can influence the **structure** of the organisation, as the way in which accounting information is **aggregated** and **summarised** will reflect the reporting structure of the organisation. For example, in a business managed by area, accounts will be prepared on an area basis.

2.2   We can take the point in paragraph 2.1(c) a bit further to discuss the different **accounting procedures** in different areas of the organisation, on the bases outlined in section 1 of this chapter.

BPP
PUBLISHING

2.3   Remember, of course, that nearly all organisations will have some sort of **functional reporting** (eg revenue and production), but will differ in the extent to which these form the basis for analysing the performance of the organisation at a higher level.

2.4   From this we can deduce that accounting procedures relate to the following.

- Collecting and **recording** accounting data.
- Providing and **reporting** accounting information.

Accounting procedures and geographical structure

2.5   An organisation's **geographical structure** must be taken into account.

(a) It might be **dispersed** over several different countries in the world. (Of course this might be true of a functional organisation as well, but we are focusing on the special problems of accounting in different countries here.)

(b) It might also be very **decentralised** in each country.

2.6   Taking the idea of an **organisation spread over many different countries, and organised on an area basis,** there are a number of ways in which the accounting procedures will be specifically affected by geography.

(a) **Different currencies.** The accounting system must deal with the consequences of foreign exchange.

(i) **Recording information.** A customer might want to pay in, say, French francs, whilst some elements of the product might have been imported from Italy and so have been paid for in a different currency.

(ii) **Reporting information.** If you wanted to compare the performance of a Belgian subsidiary company with that, say, of a subsidiary in Uruguay, you may have firstly to convert the results to a common currency (eg sterling), and then isolate the difference caused by the changes in exchange rates alone.

(b) **Different legal and accounting requirements.** Many countries have completely different **legal standards and requirements** for recording accounting information. In some countries, regulatory authorities issue a chart of accounts, down to minute detail. In the UK, on the other hand, companies can prepare accounts as they wish provided that those which are published for the benefit of shareholders conform to the Companies Act 1985 and accounting standards: in other respects, the auditors assess whether the accounts give a **true and fair view**.

(c) **Different ways of doing business** (for example, the length of credit normally allowed), might mean that the emphasis of the accountant's job differs from country to country. In a country in which payments are made by cash, management of debtors is likely to take up far less time and effort than in a country where extended credit periods are the norm.

(d) There might be a number of factors relating to the **political, economic, social** and **technological factors** which can affect a country's accounting practices.

For example, some economies have had **persistently high rates of inflation** (Bolivia once had an inflation rate of 1000% per year, and some other countries still have inflation rates of over 100% per year). This can have a significant effect on **pricing** and on **measuring performance.**

Accounting procedures and product information

2.7 Information is sometimes reported on a **product basis**.

2.8 This involves both **recording** and **reporting issues**. This is because the functional activities of buying and selling, paying expenses and so forth are still the same, but the resulting information is grouped in a particular way to highlight revenue earned and costs incurred by a particular product.

2.9 **Recording accounting information relating to revenue is usually easy**. An individual product has a selling price, and it is relatively simple to record unit sales.

2.10 **Costs are more problematic**. After all, electricity expenses can be incurred making a number of products. Material might be divided between products. Some companies have **elaborate coding systems** which track individual items of expenditure and allocate them between products. (This is the purpose of **standard costing systems**.)

2.11 The importance of **cost information** is not just a feature of a product-division structured organisation, as this information is necessary for **decision making** in any organisation.

2.12 In a **product-division structure**, administrative functions are carried out by individual product divisions. However, there will still be some areas (eg research and development) which are shared by all divisions, and it might not be easy to allocate these common costs.

Accounting procedures and business functions

2.13 In the rest of this section we will be looking at **typical business functions** and how they are accounted for. The following relates not just to functionally structured organisations, of course, as all organisations will have procedures for sales and marketing, finance and accounting, and each department has different requirements for **recording** and **reporting information**.

2.14 For convenience, we can identify the following functions.

(a) **Sales and marketing**. This includes the following.

- Sales order processing
- Distribution
- Invoicing
- Credit control
- Management of debtors
- Market research
- Advertising
- Public relations

(b) **Production**. This can include the following.

- Purchasing
- Control of raw materials and finished goods
- Stocks
- Costing
- Capital equipment purchasing

(c) **Finance and administration**. This includes the following.

- Accounting function
- Treasury functions
- Credit control
- The management of debtors and creditors
- Personnel management

(d) There are also business activities which cross the divide between various functions.

(i) **Research and development** (R&D) of new products and processes is mostly under the control of the production function. However, the marketing function is also concerned, as it determines what new products and services customers actually desire. In larger companies R&D is a separate function.

(ii) **Personnel** issues might also be the concern of the individual functional departments. For example, the production function will know which staff are needed for particular jobs. In some instances, they will need to assess whether someone is technically competent.

(iii) **Information management**. Some organisations have an **Information Director** on the Board of Directors, to manage issues relating to information technology.

(iv) The functions of the organisation need to be **integrated** in some way, and their activities **planned** and **coordinated**. This might be achieved by the executive board, or there might be a small **corporate planning department** which will **plan the direction** the organisation should take, in consultation with the other functional departments.

Sales and marketing

2.15 The selling and marketing activity ensures that a commercial organisation **'earns its keep'**. Sales and marketing staff have a direct relationship with the customer. Quick and speedy satisfaction of customer orders is therefore a prime requirement for this function.

2.16 The accounting procedures will involve the following.

(a) **Receipt of orders**, perhaps over the phone. These requests from customers must be converted into a form suitable for input to the accounting system.

(b) Accounting information will thus relate to both the order and the customer.

(i) The order must relate to a **real item** of product or service that the organisation provides. Details of availability might be found from stock records.

(ii) Perhaps more effort will go into the accounting procedures relating to **customers**. Credit sales, orders and invoices are only the beginning of what will hopefully be an ongoing **relationship** between the organisation and customer.

(c) Many of the accounting procedures in the selling and marketing function will relate to the **management of debtors**, which has great implications for the sound financial management of an organisation (it must not run out of cash).

(i) **Matching** invoiced amounts to orders, and cash receipts to invoiced amounts, so that the organisation receives money owed. To this end, it is possible that **invoice lists** will be prepared, and also the **sales ledger reviewed**, every month.

(ii)   **Reviewing** unpaid amounts and chasing them. The preparation of a **debtors age analysis** is a regular procedure.

(iii)   **Calculating** discounts and so on is necessary to find the right amount to invoice.

(d)   As well as **recording information** about sales and cash receipts, accounting information in the sales and marketing function might be used by managers in **making decisions,** and in **monitoring the performance** of the business. Consider the following examples.

- Sales of particular products
- Sales in a region or area
- The efficiency of the organisation of the sales function

(e)   Other accounting information in sales and marketing will relate to **advertising expenditure, distribution,** the calculation of **commission** for sales staff and so on. In these cases, accounting information is used for the purposes of **cost control.**

Production

2.17   Accounting procedures in the production function are probably more varied than in the sales function, simply because the variety of activities in developing a product or service is greater than in selling it.

2.18   **Purchasing goods and services.** Accounting procedures relating to purchases include the following.

- Recording the purchase invoice in the appropriate expense and creditor accounts.

- Ensuring that bills are paid when they fall due.

In some respects, the accounting procedures for creditors are similar to those for debtors, in terms of **matching invoices with goods received.** The total level of creditors must be kept under control.

2.19   **Stock control.** Stock control also affects the sales and marketing function in relation to finished goods, but also involves the **timing** of the purchases mentioned above, especially of raw materials. **Enough stock,** neither too much nor too little, must be available for production.

2.20   **Production control** is involved in monitoring the progress of production. Obviously, this is less of a problem with service industries, which do not make complex manufactured products. One of the purposes of production control is to ensure that **materials costs are minimised,** subject to required standards of quality.

2.21   Accounting procedures might involve a **standard costing system,** to keep track of **costs** and **unexpected variances** in prices and usage of the inputs necessary for production. (Recording cost information is the subject of Unit 6 of the AAT Intermediate stage.)

2.22   **Wages and salaries** are an important part of the total costs an organisation incurs on production. However, the payroll is likely to be run by the accounts department. The production function will keep details such as **timesheets** and **job sheets.**

Finance and administration

2.23 The **finance function** runs the accounting systems for all the other functions, so that for example the debtors or sales ledger may well be run by the accounts department.

2.24 The **accounts department** is responsible for receipts and payments, for managing working capital (such as debtors and creditors) and for trying to ensure that there is a sufficient flow of funds at the right times to ensure that bills can be paid.

2.25 The accounts department may also be involved in the **preparation of the payroll** of the business. Certain information is provided by the personnel department, and some by the production function (eg about hours worked), but the accounts department eventually ensures that people get paid.

2.26 The **finance function** is responsible for the management of the organisation's relationship with financial institutions such as banks.

2.27 In short, the accounts department work is comprised of the **regular production of reports and accounting information** (eg every month).

2.28 The accounts department also checks the **integrity of accounting data**. Control accounts help to ensure that errors or inconsistencies in accounting data are identified.

Activity 1.3

'Non profit orientated organisations should not have to prepare accounts.' Briefly state whether or not you agree with this proposition, and why.

Summary

2.29 Accounting activities in an organisation relate to both the **recording** of information and the **reporting** of information.

(a) **Recording transactions data** is necessary so that all revenues, expenses, assets and liabilities are captured by the accounting system to give a representation in numerical form of the activities of the organisation.

(b) **Reporting information** is necessary to make more use of this basic data.

2.30 Accounting recording practices differ in different parts of the organisation, depending on the **type of activities** carried out in that part of the organisation.

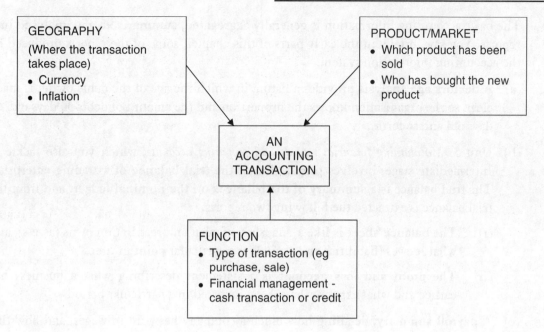

Activity 1.4

(a)   What, briefly, is the purpose of an accounting system?

(b)   Why might an organisation's bankers be interested in the output of a firm's accounting system?

3   INTERNAL AND EXTERNAL REPORTS

3.1   At the Foundation stage, the basic documentation for an accounting system was covered (eg invoices, credit notes and timesheets) in the course of learning about credit transactions, cash transactions and payroll transactions. As we have seen above, this is, by and large, a matter of **recording** information.

3.2   The next question relates to what you do with the information once it has been recorded, in the ledgers and various books of account. In this section, we provide an introduction to the subject of **reporting**.

3.3 The basic accounting information is generally **aggregated**, **summarised**, and **analysed** into reports. You saw, briefly in the early parts of this chapter, some of the reports produced by the accounting information system.

    (a) A **debtors age analysis** provides a listing in which the age of the debts owing is made clear, so the organisation knows the proportion and the amount of debts 30 days old, 60 days old and so forth.

    (b) Unit 5: *Maintaining financial records and preparing accounts*, which you also tackle at Intermediate stage, involves preparation of the **trial balance** of a trading enterprise. The trial balance is a **summary of the balances on the nominal ledger**, and from the trial balance is extracted the following two reports.

        (i) The **balance sheet** is like a 'snapshot' of what an organisation owns (assets), and what it owes (liabilities and capital) at a particular point in time.

        (ii) The **profit and loss account** is a statement describing what a business has earned and what expenses have been incurred in a particular period.

    (c) A **payroll summary**, detailing how much a company has paid in wages, and how this cost is allocated between departments for a particular period, is another type of report produced by an accounting system.

    (d) You can probably think of even more reports, but here are some examples.

- A list of sales revenue by area.
- Analysis of costs over a period.
- Profit by division.
- A list of items in stock and their valuation to give a total value.

3.4 There are a large number of reports which must be submitted to **external agencies**, too.

    (a) There are various returns to be sent to the **Inland Revenue**, in relation to PAYE and deductions for National Insurance.

    (b) Returns have to be sent to **HM Customs & Excise** for Value Added Tax.

    (c) Every year, a limited company must prepare **financial statements for submission to shareholders**. These comprise a balance sheet, a profit and loss account, a statement of total recognised gains and losses and a cash flow statement.

The rules for preparing financial statements for publication to shareholders are quite strict. This is so that management have as little latitude as possible to massage the numbers so as to mis-state the organisation's performance.

Also, financial statements provide necessary information to **debtors** and **creditors** of the business. (Do you remember that a limited liability company is one whereby the owners are not liable for the debts of the business?)

    (d) If a business has borrowings from the bank, especially if they are significant, then the bank will want to see proof that the business is generating enough cash to pay interest on its loans. A bank might wish to see **cash flow statements** on a regular basis.

    (e) Some kinds of organisations are required to file **special returns** on a regular basis to the authorities. This is particularly true of **banks** and **financial services companies**. Banks must report details of assets and liabilities to the Bank of England to assess their solvency. Other companies, for example those which run investment schemes or which give 'financial advice', must report to the appropriate **regulatory organisation**.

3.5 The requirements of these reports can sometimes be quite onerous, especially as the consequences for filling them in wrongly can be severe. (For example, there are heavy penalties for errors in VAT returns.)

3.6 There are advantages, then, in an accounting system in which these external reporting requirements are taken account of in the way that information is collected and treated, and the ease with which it can be manipulated.

3.7 In practice, this means that when the accounting system is designed, a number of the following options might be taken.

(a) **Ledger accounts** can be set up for those assets, liabilities and items of income and expenditure which need to be reported.

(b) **Memorandum accounts** can be established to record this information specifically (for example, the memorandum sales ledger details individual debtor accounts).

(c) An **appropriate coding system** can be devised, especially in a computer system, so that the relevant data can be easily extracted from the accounting records.

3.8 It is possible, however, that these reporting requirements, especially if they are complex, will not be built into the accounting system. Moreover, **information of a non-accounting nature** might also be required to complete the report.

3.9 In many cases, it is possible that the information for the reports will be **separately extracted** from the accounting records and relevant files, and a **model created**. In a computer system, this will mean that data extracted from the records might have to be input manually into a spreadsheet model so that it can be manipulated in the right format.

3.10 The problems of reporting to external agencies can be summarised as follows.

- **Identifying the data** as it falls from the transaction itself into the accounting system
- **Tagging the data** as it flows round the accounting system
- **Pulling this data** out of the accounting system, with other data of the same type
- **Aggregating, analysing** and **rearranging the data** in a format suitable for the report

Despatching completed reports and returns

3.11 Completed reports should only be despatched once **authorisation** has been given by the appropriate person. For example, internal reports such as a payroll summary which might be submitted to cost centre managers once a month should only be despatched when the payroll manager authorises this to be done. The payroll clerk preparing this report should therefore send a covering note or memorandum to the payroll manager which highlights the fact that the report is ready for despatch **subject to his authorisation.**

DEVOLVED ASSESSMENT ALERT

When completing devolved assessment tasks, always make sure that you think about your own organisation and its accounting and reporting systems. Any day-to-day experience that you are able to draw upon will be invaluable when completing assessments.

Activity 1.5

Give one example of a periodic return which has to be made to an outside agency by any organisation with which you are familiar. What is the main purpose of this return?

Key learning points

- The many different kinds of organisation may be classified as follows.

  - By type of activity
  - By size of business
  - Profit orientated or non-profit orientated
  - Legal status and ownership

- Large organisations are headed by a **person** or **committee** who is responsible for the **direction** that an organisation takes. This responsibility might lie with one of the following.

  - Chief Executive
  - Managing Director
  - Board of directors
  - Executive committee

- Organisations may be structured **geographically,** on a **product-divisional basis**, on a **functional basis,** or on a **matrix basis**.

- An organisation's accounting systems are affected by the following factors.

  - The size of the business
  - The type of organisation
  - The organisation structure

- The accounting procedures of an organisation will be specifically affected by geography in the following ways.

  - Different currencies
  - Different legal and accounting requirements
  - Different ways of doing business
  - Political, economic, social and technological factors

- The following main business functions may be identified within an organisation.

  - Sales and marketing
  - Production
  - Finance and administration

- Accounting activities in an organisation relate to both the **recording** of information and the **reporting** of information.

- Reports may be **internal** or **external**.

Quick quiz

1   How are sole traders, partnerships and limited companies distinguished from each other?

2   List eight functions of the sales and marketing department.

3   List four reports which are produced by an organisation's accounting information system.

4   What are the main returns submitted to the following external agencies in relation to?

    (a) Inland Revenue
    (b) HM Customs & Excise
    (c) Shareholders

5   What report might a bank wish to see on a regular basis if a business has borrowed a significant amount of money from the bank? Why?

6   What are the main problems associated with reporting to external agencies?

Answers to quick quiz

1   In the eyes of the law: the business affairs of sole traders are not distinguished from their personal affairs; partners in a partnership are personally liable for the debts of a business; and a limited company is a separate legal personality.

2   • Sales order processing
     • Distribution
     • Invoicing
     • Credit control
     • Debtor management
     • Market research
     • Advertising
     • Public relations

3   • Debtors age analysis
     • Balance sheet
     • Profit and loss account
     • Payroll summary

4   (a) PAYE/NI deductions
     (b) Value Added Tax
     (c) Financial statements (annual)

5   Cash flow statements - in order to see proof that the business is generating enough cash to repay the interest on its loan.

6   • Identifying the data in the first place
     • Tagging the data as it flows round the accounting system
     • Pulling the data out of the accounting system
     • Aggregating, analysing and rearranging the data in a format suitable for the report

Answers to activities

Answer 1.1

(a) The implication is that the business is organised primarily on a geographical basis.

(b) The junior manager might report, not to an area boss responsible for all the business's activities in an area, but directly to a regional or central finance department.

Answer 1.2

It sounds as if Autobuttle Ltd employs a matrix management structure. In this, authority is divided. The example highlights one of the disadvantages (dual authority) of matrix structures but there are advantages in flexibility, too.

Answer 1.3

Non-profit orientated organisations, like clubs or charities, need to prepare accounts to keep a record of the sums received from supporters and paid to beneficiaries. Also, if such an organisation pays out more than it receives it will eventually cease to function. Reports are used to assess performance, and to communicate information. Moreover, non profit making organisations still have assets and liabilities. Charities need to send returns to the Charities Commission.

Answer 1.4

(a) Accounting systems are used to record and manipulate data, and to report information.

(b)   An organisation's bank will obviously know about the organisation's cash transactions. However the bank will also wish to know about the organisation's trading activity generally. This information gives a general indication as to the security of any loans or overdrafts.

Answer 1.5

The example given might be, for example, a return made to a trade association or a return to a government agency, such as Census of Production returns required by the Office for National Statistics.
See paragraph 3.4.

Chapter 2 Business and accounting information

Chapter topic list

1   Business information
2   Accountants as information providers
3   Management information systems
4   The qualities of accounting information

Learning objectives

On completion of this chapter you will be able to:

	Performance criteria	Range statement
• prepare reports in the appropriate form and present them to management within required timescales	7.1.6	7.1.1-4
• identify, collate and present relevant information in accordance with the conventions and definitions used by outside agencies	7.2.1	7.2.1-2
• present reports and returns in accordance with outside agencies' requirements and deadlines	7.2.4	7.2.1-2
• *describe the main types of external organisations requiring reports and returns: regulatory; grant-awarding; information collecting*	n/a	n/a

Italicised objectives are areas of knowledge and understanding underlying the elements of competence for Unit 7.

BPP PUBLISHING

1   BUSINESS INFORMATION

Identifying the information you need

1.1   Whether you are preparing reports internally for your organisation or externally for outside agencies, you need to **identify the information which is relevant** to what you are doing. Various questions may arise.

- What is meant by information?
- What is the purpose of information?
- What is **good** information?

1.2   The process of assessment for which you are preparing may be based on the following.

(a)   **Receiving** a certain amount of information from the assessors.

(b)   **Selecting** essential and relevant items from that information.

(c)   **Manipulating** those items to formulate a communication of your own which is *sent* - supposedly - to other people in the given situation, and - in fact - to the assessor.

(d)   If you are assessed directly on your performance in your workplace, then the process is essentially similar, except that the communication which you prepare and on which you are assessed is sent to the people for whom it is actually intended

1.3   This Interactive Text works on the same basis. You may **receive** all the information that this text offers you, but it will be of little practical value to you, unless you **understand, select, record, remember** and **use** that information to develop useable skills. You must make it your own, ie 're-process' it for your own purposes.

1.4   The ways in which information is **presented** and the ways people **select** information can have important implications for which pieces of information they use. Some readers of this Interactive Text will probably begin their study of Unit 6 by going to the start of Chapter 1 on page 3. If they do, they will have missed all of the points in the Introduction. Other readers will review the introductory pages before starting Chapter 1 and will therefore be aware of the introductory points covered there.

The purpose of the information

1.5   You need to be sure of the **purpose** to which the information will be put. Your manager or supervisor may be required to make **reports and returns of various kinds**. Some reports and returns may be required by parts of the organisation for which your manager works.

(a)   A branch expected to make returns to its head office.

(b)   A company in a group which is required to make reports and returns to the 'parent' company or 'holding' company which owns it.

The chief purpose of these internal reports and returns is **to help in making business decisions**.

1.6   Other reports and returns are required by **external agencies** or **organisations**. VAT returns are an example which we have already mentioned. **Grant application forms** are another example. Someone applying for a government grant will need to get together data of various kinds, perhaps including forecast data about how a business is expected to progress in the future, to support its application for a grant. A **trade association** to which a business chooses to belong might expect regular returns to be made by members so that it can be sure that the member business is continuing to meet its conditions of membership.

1.7 From the point of view of you and your manager or supervisor, the purpose of **collecting** together and **presenting** the information needed by the external organisations is mainly to **comply with the requirements of that organisation, with regulations or with the law**.

Defining 'information' and 'data'

> **KEY TERM**
>
> **Information** means 'telling' it also means 'what is told' - items of knowledge, news or whatever.

1.8 You will probably have heard the word **data** (plural of the Latin word '*datum*') used in scientific or business contexts (as in 'data processing'), and it is correct to refer to data in the plural. Common usage tends to refer to data in the singular. Don't worry - either is acceptable.

> **KEY TERM**
>
> **Data** are the raw materials (facts, figures etc) which become **information**, when they are processed so as to have meaning for the person who receives them, leading to action or decision of some kind.

1.9 The processing of data may involve **classifying, selecting, sorting, analysing, calculating** and various means of **communicating**.

1.10 For example, train departure times are **data**: a schedule which groups those times according to destination and lists them in order of departure is **information** for a potential passenger on one of the trains.

(Files are used to provide data for processing and to store data/information after processing)

What is good information?

1.11 There are some general principles as to what makes good information. Good information will have the following characteristics.

(a) It will be **relevant to a user's needs**.

    (i) **Identifying the user**. Information must be suited and sent to the **right person**, ie one who needs it to do a job, or to make a decision.

    (ii) **Getting the purpose right**. Information is effective only when it **helps a user to act or make a decision**. If you ask someone the way to the nearest train station, you do not expect or need to be told that the weather is fine, or even that there is a very interesting train station in another town some miles away.

(iii) **Getting the volume right**. Information must be **complete for its purpose**, ie not omitting any necessary item: it should also be no more in volume that the user will find helpful or be able to take in.

Consider information as the answer to a particular enquiry or problem, anything else being strictly 'icing on the cake', and you will not fall into the trap of irrelevance.

(b) **Be accurate within the user's needs**. Downright falsehood and error are fatal to effective communication of any sort. It may, however, be impossible - or at least time-consuming and expensive - to gather, process and assimilate information that is minutely detailed. An approximation or an average figure is often sufficient to our needs. If you asked: 'Is it hot in Brighton in August?' because you were planning a holiday, you would be happy to hear that it 'averaged 78°F': you would waste time and effort poring over a sheet of daily temperature readings for the last five years.

(c) **Inspire the user's confidence**. Information should not give the user reason to mistrust, disbelieve or ignore it, eg because it is out-of-date, badly presented or from an unreliable source. It should be **verifiable** by reference, or by application (which risks finding out the hard way, if the information is incorrect).

(d) **Be timely**. Information must be **readily available** within the time period which makes it useful: ie it must be in the **right place** at the **right time**. A beautifully researched and presented report will be of no value if it arrives on a manager's desk too late to influence his decision on the matter in hand. A report or return to an outside agency which misses the specified date for submission may be valueless, or may incur sanctions or penalties.

(e) **Be appropriately communicated**. Information will lose its value if it is not clearly communicated to the user in a **suitable format** and through a **suitable medium**. For example, your words and symbols should be familiar or explained to the user; the layout of text, tables and graphics should be easy to read; a telephone call may not be appropriate for complex or confidential matters, or those requiring written records (eg legal documents).

(f) **Be cost-effective**. Good information should **not cost more than it is worth**. Gathering, storing, retrieving and communicating an item of information may require expense of time, energy and resources. If the expense is greater than the potential value of the item, re-consider whether the information is necessary to such a degree of accuracy, completeness and so on, or even necessary at all.

1.12 Information is the life blood of an organisation, flowing through it and prompting actions and decisions: without information, no-one in an organisation could take a single effective action. As a simple example, giving an order to a subordinate is a flow of information: the manager or supervisor gathers data about a problem, 'processes' it to decide what needs to be done and then communicates a decision as an order to a subordinate.

Activity 2.1

Identify the characteristics of good information.

Business information

> **KEY TERM**
>
> **Business information** is any information which relates to the organisation and activities of one or more businesses.

1.13 The above definition includes the following.

- Information about 'business' in general.
- Information generated by and about each organisation.

Demand for information

1.14 There is a **constant demand** for information within the organisation, and also from outside. **Internal demand** comes from every member of the organisation. Management, for example, demand the following.

(a) Records of **past** and **current transactions** to be stored for confirmation, later analysis and so on.

(b) **Routine information** on which to base current operations and decisions (for example, the information on a customer order dictates how many items, and of what sort, must be supplied from stock, delivery and payment arrangements and so on).

(c) Information about **past trends** and **current operations** on which to base planning and decision making. For example, the past rate at which raw materials were consumed by a production process would dictate the frequency and amount of stock orders in the future; trends in the market, ie customer demand for a product or service, would indicate the area, level and pricing of an organisation's activity.

(d) Information about **performance** to compare with plans, budgets, and forecasts for the purposes of **control**, ie checking for and correcting errors and shortcomings.

The main types of information required in preparing **periodic performance reports** for management are information about past trends and current operations and information about performance.

1.15 The **quantity** and **quality** of financial information provided to managers depend on their level in the organisation's structure.

(a) **Strategic information** is needed by **senior managers** who are involved in setting objectives for the organisation as a whole. In an organisation with various branches or subsidiaries, senior managers will need information on the efficiency and profitability of each of them if it is considering, for example, how to reduce or expand the organisation's operations.

(b) **Tactical information** will be needed by **middle managers** who are looking to ensure that the organisation's existing resources and structure are used efficiently and effectively. Middle managers will require financial information in order to decide how to improve performance in all parts of the organisation, for example by introducing new control measures.

(c) **Operational information**. **'Front-line'** managers such as works supervisors and foremen require information on the day-to-day operations of the organisation.

Financial information will be required on direct and indirect costs, idle time and overtime costs.

1.16 We have also seen that there is **external demand** for information from various sources. The main types of external organisation requiring reports and returns are as follows.

- Information-collecting agencies
- Regulatory bodies
- Grant awarding agencies

Sources of business information

Internal sources

1.17 (a) A lot of data is gathered by an organisation in the course of its business. It will appear on the various documents used by the firm such as the following.

- Invoices
- Orders
- Delivery notes
- Job cards

This gathering of data involves **formal systems** for collecting or measuring data - measuring output, sales, costs, cash receipts and payments, purchases, stock turnover and so on. In other words, there must be established procedures for the following. What data is collected, how frequently, by whom, by what methods, and how it is processed, filed and/or communicated as information.

(b) An organisation will also take advantage of and indeed rely on **informal communication** between managers and staff (by word-of-mouth, at meetings, by telephone).

External sources

1.18 Obtaining information from outside the organisation might be **formally** delegated to particular individuals. These might include the following.

- The tax or legal expert
- The Market Research manager
- The secretary who has to make travel arrangements

It might also be **informal.**

1.19 Informal gathering of information from outside sources goes on all the time, consciously or unconsciously, because the employees of an organisation learn what is going on in the world around them - from **newspapers, television, experience** or **other people**.

1.20 Alternatively, an organisation can 'tap into' data banks compiled by other organisations for example the Office for National Statistics or the DTI. Various publications - specific **trade journals** or more **general magazines** such as *Management Today* - can be helpful in judging trends and setting standards. A business can employ a **research organisation** such as MORI or Gallup to carry out an investigation into market trends or other matters of interest. The **Internet** is now a very useful source of information as well. We will look in detail at other sources of statistical information in Chapter 3.

Activity 2.2

(a) Information of various kinds is required from within an organisation, and also from outside.

Task

Make a list of as many outside agencies requiring reports or returns from a typical limited company as you can.

(b) *Task*

In the case of a particular organisation, for example one which you work for or have worked for, identify any special kinds of reports and returns which it is required to present to outside agencies.

(c) In sections (a) and (b) of this activity, we have considered the external demand for information from organisations.

Task

Now make a list of some of the 'external' information demands in the form of reports, forms and returns on you as an individual or your household. A list of five will be long enough.

2 ACCOUNTANTS AS INFORMATION PROVIDERS

2.1 **Financial accounting** consists of a mixture of 'line operations', **keeping data records** and **providing information**. The functions of the financial accountant include **communicating information**. Although financial accounting is also concerned with operational matters, such as receiving and paying cash, borrowing and repaying loans, granting credit to customers and chasing late payers in the debt collection process.

KEY TERMS

- **Financial accounting** is largely a process of keeping data records and providing information.

- **Cost and management accounting** is concerned entirely with providing information in the form of periodic performance reports or special 'one-off' reports.

2.2 Examples of cost and management accounting information are as follows.

- Information about product costs and profitability
- Information about departmental costs and profitability
- Cost information to help with pricing decisions
- Budgets and standard costs
- Actual performance (in accounting terms), and variances between actual and budget
- Information to help with the evaluation of one-off decisions

2.3 With whom do accountants communicate? Management accountants communicate mainly with **other managers**. Financial accountants provide information about the organisation to the **'outside world'**. Users of accounting information who are outside the organisation's management are as follows.

- Equity investors (ie shareholders)
- Loan creditors (such as debenture holders, banks)
- Employees

- Financial analysts and advisers
- Business contacts - notably customers and trade creditors and suppliers
- Government
- The general public

3 MANAGEMENT INFORMATION SYSTEMS

Users of accounting information

3.1 Among the users of information are other managers, who need **tactical information** to help them plan and control the resources of the organisation in the most **effective** and **efficient** way, so as to enable the organisation to achieve its **objectives**.

Information systems in an organisation

> **KEY TERM**
>
> A **management information system (MIS)** is 'A collective term for the hardware and software used to drive a database system with the outputs, both to screen and print, being designed to provide easily assimilated information for management'.
>
> CIMA *Computing Terminology*

3.2 The accountant provides information to others, in **reports** and **statements**, and **communication**, of course, is the process of providing information to others. It has been suggested that there are several large and fairly distinct management information systems within an organisation (although they do overlap and are interrelated). These are as follows.

(a) The **financial information system**, with which we are mainly concerned in this Interactive Text

(b) The **logistics information system** (concerned with the physical flow of goods through production and to the customer, or the physical provision of services to the customer)

(c) The **personnel information system** (concerned with employees and employee records)

3.3 There might also be a distinct **research and development information system**, and a **marketing information system** and so on. However, the financial information system is essential to help managers to plan and control the activities of their organisation, because of the following reasons.

(a) The objectives of the organisation will be **financial ones** (perhaps to maximise profits or return on investment)

(b) The objectives of the organisation will be **subject to financial constraints** (for example a hospital service aims to provide patient care, subject to the restrictions of what it can afford within its budget allowance)

3.4 As you should appreciate, accounting information is used by managers throughout an organisation, and accountants are important providers of management information. It has been suggested that **an organisation's accounting systems are at the core of its MIS**.

In what form might accounting information be communicated?

3.5 Information can be communicated in the following ways.

- Visually
- Verbally
- Electronically (by computer system)

3.6 It may be helpful to think of a **formal accounting information system** as taking the form of a series of **reports** and **accounting statements**. In cost and management accounting, these would include the following (some of which are used in later examples provided in this Interactive Text).

- Cost statements
- Product profit statements
- Budgets
- Standard cost statements
- Operating statements, comparing actual results against budget
- Forecast profit and cost statements
- Breakeven statements and contribution statements
- Investment appraisal and payback forecasts for capital expenditure decision making
- Job cost estimates

3.7 Financial accounting information is extracted from the financial accounting records, and results (for companies) in the **annual report and accounts**, which is produced for shareholders. In the case of large companies, a copy of the report and accounts must be filed with the **Registrar of Companies**, and so the financial accounting information is made available to a wider public.

3.8 Some **external information** user groups, such as the **Inland Revenue** and banks as lenders, have access to more detailed information about business organisations than that provided in the annual report and accounts prepared by the financial accountant.

3.9 Some companies provide reports for the benefit of employees. These **employee reports** are often a simplified version of the **annual report and accounts**, expressed in terms that non-management as well as management employees can understand. They are designed to show employees how the organisation has been performing, and to indicate what consequences the good or bad performance has for employees and employment prospects. The major significance of employee reports is that companies which produce them recognise their moral obligation to provide financial information to their employees, and that employees, not just shareholders, have an interest in the well-being of their organisation.

Activity 2.3

Outline as many different types of accounting report produced by your department (or any department with which you are familiar) as you can. To what extent do they display the qualities of good information, as identified in Activity 2.1?

Activity 2.4

An organisation has started to collect monthly information regarding employment and labour costs from its various departments. At the moment it only records average rates of pay in each department. Suggest three other items of management information that you believe should be collected relating to employment.

4   THE QUALITIES OF ACCOUNTING INFORMATION

The purpose of information

4.1   As we have already seen, information needs to have a **purpose**.

(a)   **Financial accounting information** helps external users to assess management performance and the prospects of the organisation. (Management must give account of itself to the organisation's owners, hence the principal need for the annual report and accounts).

(b)   **Management accounting information** must also have a purpose, and accounting reports should be produced with this end in view.

4.2   **Communication** has the general purpose of stimulating change, or enabling inter-group activities to take place. If you think about it, any communication that does not do one of these two things would be **useless** and **purposeless**.

4.3   Communication that **stimulates change** involves giving someone an item of information that makes him or her **take a decision**, for example a planning decision or a control decision, a decision about what to do next or how to deal with someone.

4.4   Communication that **enables inter-group activities to take place** involves work that is done by two or more people in conjunction. One must let the other know what he or she is doing or wants to be done. At a simple level, for example, the marketing department might set itself a target of selling 10,000 units of product X: to achieve this target, it must let the production department know what it wants to sell, to ensure that 10,000 units will be made available from the production line.

The quality of information

4.5   For accounting reports to have value, **they must act as a spur to management**. Managers should take planning or control decisions to earn favourable reports (or avoid bad ones), and when significant adverse reports occur, managers must investigate them with a view to **taking control action**.

Reports will not provide an impetus for management action unless the information contained in them possesses **certain qualities**. We discussed qualities of information in general earlier in this chapter. These qualities or attributes are explained with particular reference to accounting information in the following paragraphs.

4.6   The quality of communication is important because of the following reasons.

(a)   People need to know **what is expected of them** - ie they need a goal or target, such as a budget target or a performance standard to reach.

(b)   People also need to know **how they are doing** - ie how their actual performance is measuring up to their target.

Good quality information about targets and plans, and reliable feedback of actual results, are essential for this planning and control cycle to work properly.

4.7 *The Corporate Report*, a publication which argued that companies do not provide enough information about themselves, listed the desirable characteristics of accounting reports. Such reports must have the following qualities.

- Relevant
- Understandable
- Reliable
- Complete
- Objective
- Timely
- Comparable

These qualities are appropriate both to **internal** and **external information**.

4.8 **Objectivity**. Accounting reports ought as far as possible to be **objective**. Any subjective opinions that are formulated should be made by the information users, not the information providers. For example, a variance statement will indicate differences between actual costs and budgeted costs, and any variances that exceed a certain amount (eg 10% of budget). However, managers responsible for planning or control decisions must decide whether these reported variances are too high or not.

4.9 **Comparability**. Accounting information, especially information about return on investment, costs and profits, should enable users to make **suitable comparisons**. Here are some examples of such comparisons.

(a) Comparing actual costs against budget

(b) Comparing actual return on capital employed (ROCE) against target, or last year's ROCE

(c) Comparing the forecast return from an investment against the target or cut-off rate

(d) Comparing one company's profits, dividends and earnings per share against another's

For information to provide comparability, it ought to be prepared on a consistent basis. (This is one of the reasons for having Accounting Standards). Return on capital employed (ROCE) is a performance measure to which we shall return to in a later chapter.

DEVOLVED ASSESSMENT ALERT

In an assessment, be prepared to compare the results of one organisation with those of another organisation in the same industry. Alternatively, you may be asked to extract accounting information (such as gross profit, net profit, current assets, current liabilities and so on) and use it to complete an **interfirm comparison form**. Such a form may include information relating to the industry best or industry average - all that you need to do is insert the relevant information into the appropriate space.

Possible conflicts

4.10 An accounting report is not a goal in itself, it is simply a means towards the goal of **effective management action**. Unfortunately, many of the desirable attributes listed above can be in conflict with each other.

(a) Information should be **accurate**, but it should also be provided **in time** for managers to make decisions. A report which is produced in haste to meet a deadline might be so inaccurate that it ceases to be sufficiently reliable.

(b) Reports should be **clear** and **comprehensible** to their users, but they must also be **comprehensive**. If the information in a report covers complex topics it would be inadvisable to 'keep it simple'. Managers should be educated to understand the information they receive, and information should not necessarily be downgraded to the assumed level of comprehension of its users.

(c) **Accuracy, comprehensiveness, timeliness** (eg using computers) are desirable attributes of information which involve costs. The need to control costs, and ensure that benefits exceed costs incurred, conflicts with all these aspects.

4.11 The attitude of non-accounting managers to accounting reports is often hostile. Accountants might be regarded as interfering busybodies, or even as a group whose purpose is to create more work and find fault with others.

(a) **Budget preparation** might be regarded as a pointless, time-consuming exercise that the accountants and senior managers impose on other managers.

(b) **Budgetary control reports** and other performance reports can show how badly a manager is doing, and so be a weapon which senior managers use in getting their subordinates to try harder.

4.12 The response of people to the information they are given depends on the following.

- How the information is communicated to them
- How good the information is

(a) It is much better to **communicate directly** with the person who will use the information. For example, regular information about the labour productivity in Section X should be sent direct to the supervisor of Section X: the supervisor might resent receiving the information through his boss or his boss's boss.

(b) **Regular reports** will enable any control action to be taken before the situation gets out of hand, but reports that are too frequent can be irritating as well as unnecessary. Information to help with planning decisions obviously needs to be received in time for the decisions to be taken.

(c) Information should contain **all the necessary qualities** referred to earlier. Accountants should be wary in particular of making information unclear or misleading.

(d) Information should be given **without the suggestion of a threat**. This is important in the case of control reports. Reports on actual performance compared with target will provoke **defensive** and **hostile** reactions from the managers receiving them if they believe that poor results will be automatically blamed on them. Getting blamed is all too easily associated with loss of promotion prospects or loss of bonuses.

Activity 2.5

(a) Identify four stages in the processing of information.

(b) Demand for information within an organisation usually originates from two main sources, these being categorised as internal and external.

Specify three examples from each category.

Key learning points

- The demand for business information comes from **within the organisation,** from **external organisations** and from **individuals** on a personal level.

- In a business environment, reports and returns may need to be presented to other parts of the organisation or to external organisations. We need to **identify, collate** and **present** the information in a way which best fits the purpose of the report or return.

    ° Often, an internal report or return will be needed to help in **making business decisions**.

    ° In reports or returns to external organisations, compliance with **laws, regulations** or **requirements** is often what is most important.

- When preparing both internal and external reports, you must identify the **relevant information.**

- **Information** means 'telling' or 'what is told'.

- **Data** are the raw materials which become information when they are processed.

- Good information has the following qualities.

    ° Relevant
    ° Accurate
    ° Inspires the user's confidence
    ° Timely
    ° Appropriately communicated
    ° Cost-effective

- Business information sources may be **internal** or **external**.

- **Financial accounting** is largely a process of keeping data records and providing information. **Cost and management accounting** is concerned entirely with providing information in the form of periodic performance reports or special 'one-off' reports.

- A **management information system (MIS)** is a collective term for the hardware and software used to drive a database system with the outputs, both to screen and print, being designed to provide easily assimilated information for management.

- The purpose of **financial accounting information** is to help external users to assess management performance and the prospects of the organisation.

- Internal and external reports must be as follows.

    ° Relevant
    ° Understandable
    ° Reliable
    ° Complete
    ° Objective
    ° Timely
    ° Comparable

Quick quiz

1   What might the processing of data involve?

2   What is business information?

3   What are the main types of financial information provided to managers?

4   What are the main external sources of information for an organisation?

5   Who are the main users of accounting information who are outside the organisation's management?

6   What are the main distinct management information systems within an organisation?

7   How might information be communicated?

8   For whom is the annual report and accounts of an organisation produced for?

BPP
PUBLISHING

9   One of the desirable characteristics of accounting reports is that they must be comparable. Give four examples of suitable comparisons.

Answers to quick quiz

1   Classifying, selecting, sorting, analysing and communicating.

2   Any information which relates to the organisation and activities of one or more businesses.

3   • Strategic
        • Tactical
        • Operational

4   • Tax/legal expert
        • Market research manager
        • Media (newspaper/television/radio)
        • Databanks such as the Office for National Statistics/DTI
        • Publications (trade journals)
        • Research organisations (MORI/Gallup)
        • Internet

5   • Shareholders
        • Loan creditors
        • Employees
        • Customers
        • Government
        • General public

6   Financial, logistics and personnel information systems.

7   Visually, verbally or electronically.

8   Shareholders of the company.

9   • Actual cost against budget
        • Actual return on capital employed (ROCE) against target, (or last year's ROCE)
        • Forecast return from an investment against the target
        • Profits of one company against the profits of another

Answers to activities

Answer 2.1

Your answer should cover the points set out below.

Good information is:

(a)   relevant to the needs of the user;
(b)   relevant to the purpose of the user;
(c)   complete for its purpose, and not including irrelevant matter;
(d)   accurate within the requirements of the user;
(e)   reliable, and capable of verification;
(f)   timely, given its purpose;
(g)   communicated in an appropriate manner;
(h)   cost-effective.

Answer 2.2

(a)   There is no 'definitive' list, but your answer probably included most of the following outside agencies.

        (i)   Inland Revenue.
        (ii)   Customs and Excise.
        (iii)   Department of Trade and Industry (Companies House).
        (iv)   The organisation's bankers.
        (v)   Local government agencies (eg planning departments; grant-awarding agencies).

(vi)   Shareholders.

(b)   Your answer will of course depend upon the organisation which you chose. For example, if you work for a health authority, you should know that the authority must make returns to the Department of Health. If you worked for a bank, you would probably know that the bank must make certain returns to the Bank of England, while a building society must report to the Building Societies Commission. In some industries, trade associations require members to submit regular returns to confirm that they continue to meet the requirements of membership.

(c)   Your answer probably included some of the following examples.

(i)   If you are a taxpayer, the Inland Revenue may require you to complete an annual tax return.

(ii)   The law requires householders in Britain to complete forms listing residents for the purposes of the electoral register.

(iii) Every ten years, householders are required (again, by law) to complete census return forms. The last Census was in 1991.

(iv)   If you need to make an insurance claim, your insurer will require you to complete a form, with a detailed report on the accident, damage or loss which has occurred.

(v)   The Association of Accounting Technicians expects you to maintain Student Record Sheets and an Accounting Portfolio.

Answer 2.3

Obviously your answer will depend upon the type of department you work in, and its particular procedures.

Bear in mind that many management reports include a lot of numbers, with perhaps very little commentary. A common fault with internal reports is to include too much detail, with numbers shown with too many digits.

Answer 2.4

Your answer could include three items from the following list, although other items might also be given.

(a)   Numbers employed.
(b)   Numbers of starters and leavers.
(c)   Hours worked.
(d)   Vacancies.
(e)   Numbers of absentees.

Answer 2.5

(a)   The processing of information (or data) consists of four main stages.

(i)   *Receipt or gathering of the data* - ie 'input' to the system. There are various sources of information, and relevant data will have to be obtained, selected and put into a format that will be useful for further processing. In the preparation of an employee's wage payment slip, for example, time sheets or machine logs will be consulted to see how much work the employee has put in: relevant details (hours worked, units produced) will be selected. Information will be gathered from payroll records as to the appropriate wage system and scale for the employee.

(ii)   *Recording and manipulation of the data.* Whether done manually, or by a computer, this will involve 'inputting' data into 'hard' form, and then analysing or handing it in various ways: selection, sorting and arrangement, calculation, reproduction etc. In our example, of the pay advice slip, hours worked will be recorded alongside pay rate per hour, together with deductions for tax and national insurance, bonuses and allowances etc. Calculations will then be made as to total taxable pay, amount of tax payable on it, and so the net amount which the employee will 'take home'. The information will be copied so that both the employer and the employee have it.

(iii) *Storage of information.* Basically, this means 'filing' although again a computer can do it without requiring paper output and storage. Storage also implies 'retrieval', since information should only be kept for a reason - ie that it will be needed for further processing one day. Our employee's wage slip will go into the organisation's files (or computer) and will be retrieved when the organisation is preparing P60 forms at the end of the tax year, and/or putting together a report on the growth of its total wage bill over 5 years etc. (It will also go into the employee's home 'files', so that he can check the details against his P60 certificate, plan his own budget for the coming months based on past take-home pay etc).

(iv) *Communication of information.* Relevant interested parties are finally supplied with the information. The employee gets his pay advice slip with his pay packet.

These four stages can be portrayed in a diagram as below.

(b) *Internal demand*

[Three of :]

(i) Records of transactions for confirmation, later analysis etc.

(ii) Information for planning and decision making. For example, the volume of last month's sales may influence the level of this month's stock holding.

(iii) Routine information for operating decisions. For example, a customer placing an order, where the information about quantities, prices, delivery dates/addresses etc initiates action; or the information about hours worked or units produced which goes into payroll calculations.

(iv) Information about performance to be compared with plans, budgets and forecasts for the purposes of control and correction.

Each of these *types* of demand will offer many different specific examples.

External demand

[Three of :]

(i) Customers, who require delivery information, invoices and/or statements requesting payment, information about the product in order to decide whether to buy it etc.

(ii) Suppliers and sub-contractors, who require instructions, purchase orders, confirmation etc.

(iii) Parties interested in the financial performance of the organisation - eg the shareholders, investors etc.

(iv) Outside agencies requiring information for surveys, or for their own activities - eg the Inland Revenue (tax), HM Customs and Excise (VAT), DSS (National Insurance contributions), Health and Safety Executive.

Chapter 3   *Statistical information*

Chapter topic list

1   Using statistics

2   Populations and types of data

3   Sources of statistical data

Learning objectives

On completion of this chapter you will be able to:

	Performance criteria	Range statement
• prepare reports in the appropriate form and present them to management within the required timescales	7.1.6	7.1.1
• *understand the main sources of government statistics*	n/a	n/a

Italicised objectives are areas of knowledge and understanding underlying the elements of competence for Unit 7.

BPP PUBLISHING

1 USING STATISTICS

The meaning of 'statistics'

> ### KEY TERM
>
> **Statistics** or quantitative data is the name given to data in the form of figures.

1.1 In a business environment, all sorts of quantitative data may be available to a manager or supervisor, for example on production levels, costs or sales. On their own, the numbers are unlikely to mean very much. How can a manager make sense of the numbers? This depends partly on the purpose for which the information is needed.

1.2 Note that the word 'statistics' has three meanings.

(a) Firstly, it is used to describe a **group of figures**. For example, figures relating to a country's imports and exports are often referred to as 'trade statistics' and the figures kept by cricket commentators on past matches are called 'statistics'.

(b) Secondly, it is used as **an abbreviation for 'statistical method'**, which means the methods by which data (that is, **numbers** obtained as a result of counting or measuring something) are presented. The importance of 'statistical method' is that it enables a large mass of meaningless data to be condensed into a more readily **understandable** form.

(c) Thirdly, it has come to mean **the way in which the data are interpreted**, once they have been presented in a satisfactory form.

1.3 'Statistics' therefore covers the following.

- Collecting data
- Presenting the data in a useful form
- Interpreting the data

Knowledge of statistical techniques is important to you not just because you can use these techniques to **present** information in reports and returns. It is also important because you will often need to **interpret** information which uses statistical techniques.

The use and abuse of statistics

1.4 Statistics should be compiled only if they have a **purpose**. If they are not going to be used for anything, then there is no point in having them.

- The **purpose** of having particular statistics ought to be established.
- A **statistical measure** should be selected which achieves this purpose.

1.5 The following dangers should be noted.

(a) Statistical data will be collected and analysed in a confusing and unclear way.

(b) The statistical measures that are selected will not be suitable for the purpose for which they are being used.

(c) Statistics will be interpreted incorrectly, and used to draw incorrect conclusions.

The incorrect use and interpretation of statistics is an **abuse of statistics,** which you should learn to recognise and to avoid.

1.6 EXAMPLE: USING STATISTICS

Study the following statements, and set out the errors in them.

(a) 30% of students taking accountancy examinations pass. 60% of law students pass solicitors' examinations. Clearly, there are more qualified solicitors than qualified accountants.

(b) 30,000 French citizens can speak Russian, and 60,000 Russians can speak French. Clearly, French is more widely spoken in Russia than Russian in France.

1.7 SOLUTION

Statement (a) shows how percentages without actual total figures can be misleading. If 10,000 accountancy students take examinations each year and just 2,000 law students take solicitors' examinations, the actual numbers becoming qualified each year would be 3,000 accountants and 1,200 lawyers: more accountants than lawyers, not the other way round.

Statement (b) shows how total figures without averages or percentages can be misleading. If the 30,000 French citizens speaking Russian come from a population of 50,000,000, whereas the 60,000 Russians speaking French come from a population of 200,000,000 we could argue that since a **larger proportion** of French citizens speak Russian than Russians speak French, Russian is more widely spoken in France than French in Russia.

Activity 3.1

Comment on the following statements.

(a) Sales of footwear are up on last year, but not as much as clothing.
(b) Turnover of company X has increased by 150% in the past two years.

2 POPULATIONS AND TYPES OF DATA

Defining the population

> **KEY TERM**
>
> A **statistical survey** is a survey which involves collecting statistics to help answer a question.

2.1 Consider a cat food manufacturer who wants to find out what proportion of cat owners use his particular brand. You might think that the first step to take in conducting such a survey is to **collect data,** that is, to ask people what they feed their cats. In fact there are quite a few things to think about first, otherwise a survey can go wrong from the start. If a survey does start off on the wrong track, the data subsequently collected and the conclusions subsequently drawn will be **useless**.

2.2 A famous example of this occurred years ago in the United States, when an organisation was asked to conduct an **opinion poll** (which is a form of statistical survey) on whether the next president was likely to be Democrat or Republican. The survey was carried out, but in the wrong way. The surveyors *telephoned* people, and far more Republicans than Democrats had telephones. The survey was useless, because it **had not been planned properly**.

2.3 The reason why the opinion poll turned out so badly, was that the **population** for the survey had not been defined properly. The opinion poll should have used the population 'all Americans of voting age', whereas it actually used the population 'all Americans with a telephone'. In the cat food example, the population is 'all people who look after cats', not 'all people who feed their cats tinned food'. (This population will be too small, as some cats are fed fresh or dried food.)

> ### KEY TERM
>
> In statistics, the word **population** refers to the entire collection of items being considered.

Attributes and variables

2.4 The data gathered for a particular purpose may be of several types. The first major distinction is between **attributes** and **variables**.

> ### KEY TERMS
>
> - An **attribute** is something an object has either got or not got. It cannot be measured.
> - A **variable** is something which can be measured.

For example, an individual is either male or female. There is no measure of *how* male or *how* female somebody is: the sex of a person is an attribute. The height of a person can be measured according to some scale (such as centimetres), the height of a person is therefore a variable.

2.5 Variables can be further classified as **discrete** or **continuous**.

> ### KEY TERMS
>
> - **Discrete variables** are variables which can only take specific values. The range of possible values is split into a series of steps. For example, the number of goals scored by a football team may be 0, 1, 2 or 3 but it cannot be 1.2 or 2.1. Although the average number of children per family in a population might be 2.4, each family can only have a discrete (whole) number of children.
>
> - **Continuous variables** are variables which may take on any value. They are measured rather than counted. For example, it may be considered sufficient to measure the heights of a number of people to the nearest cm but there is no reason why the measurements should not be made to the nearest 0.001 cm. Two people who are found to have the same height to the nearest cm could almost certainly be distinguished if more precise measurements were taken.

Activity 3.2

Look through the following list of surveys and decide whether each is collecting data on attributes, discrete variables or continuous variables.

(a) A survey of statistics text books, to determine how many diagrams they contain.

(b) A survey of cans on a supermarket shelf, to determine whether or not each has a price sticker on it.

(c) A survey of athletes, to find out how long they take to run a mile.

(d) A survey of the results of an examination, to determine what percentage marks the students obtained.

(e) A survey of the heights of telegraph poles in England, to find out if there is any variation across the country.

Primary data and secondary data

2.6 The data used in a statistical survey, whether variables or attributes, can be either **primary data** or **secondary data**.

KEY TERMS

- **Primary data** are data collected especially for the purpose of whatever survey is being conducted. **Raw data** are primary data which have not been processed at all, but are still just (for example) a list of numbers.

- **Secondary data** are data which have already been collected elsewhere, for some other purpose, but which can be used or adapted for the survey being conducted.

2.7 An advantage of using primary data is that the investigator knows where the data came from, the circumstances under which they were collected, and any limitations or inadequacies in the data.

2.8 In contrast, inadequacies of secondary data include the following.

(a) Limitations in the data might not be known to the investigator, because he or she did not collect them

(b) The data might not be entirely suitable for the purpose they are being used for

2.9 Secondary data are sometimes used despite their inadequacies, simply because they are **available cheaply**, whereas the extra cost of collecting primary data would far outweigh their extra value.

DEVOLVED ASSESSMENT ALERT

Accuracy is more important than speed. Make sure that you do not rush through the tasks to be completed in your assessment - take time to read through the instructions and the situation carefully before you make a start on the tasks. You will then have a better chance of completing your assessment as accurately as possible.

3 SOURCES OF STATISTICAL DATA

Primary data

3.1 Primary data have to be gathered from a **source**. Methods of collecting primary data include the following.

- Personal investigation
- Teams of investigators
- Questionnaires

Personal investigation

3.2 **Personal investigation** involves the investigator collecting all the data himself, for example by interviewing people, or by looking through historical records.

3.3 This method of collecting data has the following **disadvantages**.

- It is time consuming
- It is expensive
- It is limited to the amount of data a single person can collect.

Personal investigation has the **advantage** that the data collected are likely to be **accurate** and **complete,** because the investigator knows exactly what he wants and how to get it. He is not relying on other people to do the survey work.

Teams of investigators

3.4 A survey could be carried out by a **team of investigators** who collect data separately and then pool their results.

3.5 A team of investigators can cover a larger field than a single investigator but will still be **expensive**. The members of the team must be carefully briefed to ensure that the data they collect are **satisfactory**. This method is sometimes called **delegated personal investigation**.

Questionnaires

3.6 With a **questionnaire,** the questions which need to be answered for the survey are listed and are either sent to a number of people (so that they can fill in their answers and send the questionnaires back) or used by investigators to interview people (perhaps by approaching people in the street and asking them the questions).

3.7 Questionnaires can provide a **quick** and **cheap** method of conducting a survey, but suffer from several defects which may lead to **biased results**.

(a) The people completing the forms (the respondents) may place **different interpretations** on the questions. This problem will be aggravated if the questions are badly phrased.

(b) Large numbers of forms **may not be returned** or may only be returned **partly completed**. This may well lead to biased results as the people replying are likely to be those most interested in the survey.

(c) Respondents may give **false** or **misleading information** if, for example, they have forgotten material facts or want to give a favourable impression.

3.8 In addition, if the questionnaire is being used by an interviewer (on the telephone or in the street), then the following problems could arise.

(a) The interviewer may not really understand the questions.

(b) The interviewer may not understand the replies, or may note down replies wrongly because of personal bias.

Secondary data

> **KEY TERM**
>
> **Secondary data** are data that were originally collected as primary data for one purpose, or for general use, but are now being used for another purpose.

3.9 For example, the government collects data to help with making decisions about running the country, and makes these data available to the public.

3.10 Examples of secondary data are as follows.

(a) **Published statistics**. For example, the UK Government publishes statistics through the Office for National Statistics (ONS). The European Union and the United Nations also publish statistics. So do various newspapers and accountancy bodies.

(b) **Historical records**. The type of historical record used for a survey obviously depends on what survey is being carried out. An accountant producing an estimate of future company sales might use historical records of past sales.

Sources of published statistics

3.11 The range of published economic, business and accounting data is very wide, and a comprehensive knowledge of sources is impracticable. However, the main sources of relevant government statistics form a part of the knowledge and understanding which you are expected to have for Unit 7.

3.12 All published statistics are a source of **secondary data**. Great care must be taken in using them, since the data may not be obtained or classified in precisely the same way as primary data collected **specifically** for the purpose of the current statistical analysis would be.

3.13 Despite the general shortcomings of secondary data, there are many circumstances in which published statistics can be of great value. Many government statistics are compiled at least partly for the purpose of being used in **further analysis** and explanatory notes are given so that the user of the data knows to what extent they are relevant to his needs and what level of confidence he can have in the results of his analysis.

The Office for National Statistics and other bodies

3.14 In April 1996 the Office for National Statistics was set up, as the **independent government agency** responsible for compiling, analysing and disseminating many of the UK's economic, social and demographic statistics. It is responsible to the Chancellor of the Exchequer and publishes the following.

- The *Monthly Digest of Statistics* (which gives data for the recent past)
- The *Annual Abstract of Statistics* (which gives data over a longer periods)
- *Economic Trends* (published monthly)
- *Financial Statistics* (published monthly)

3.15 The **European Union** (formerly the European Community) has a Statistical Office which gathers statistics from each of the member countries. This produces several statistical publications, including *Basic Statistics of the Community*.

3.16 The **United Nations** also publishes some statistics on the world economy (for example the *Statistical Yearbook*), and a *Yearbook of Labour Statistics* is published by the International Labour Organisation.

3.17 In the remainder of this section, we shall concentrate on **government statistical publications in the UK**. You need to be aware of what publications are available and the general nature of the information they contain.

The Employment Gazette

3.18 The Department of Education and Employment publishes statistics monthly about **employment** and **unemployment**, and about **retail prices**. The statistics, published monthly in the *Employment Gazette* by the ONS include, for example, statistics on the following.

- Retail prices
- Employment
- Unemployment
- Unfilled job vacancies
- Wage rates
- Overtime and short time working
- Stoppages at work

3.19 Retail prices are very important to a wide variety of users.

(a) For the **government**, the Retail Prices Index (RPI) indicates the degree of success there has been in fighting inflation.

(b) For **employees**, the RPI may give an indication of how much wages need to rise to keep pace with inflation.

(c) For **consumers**, the RPI indicates the increases to be expected in the prices of goods in shops.

(d) For **businesses**, the RPI may give a broad indication of how much costs should have been expected to rise over recent years and months.

The Bank of England Quarterly Bulletin

3.20 The Bank of England issues a **quarterly bulletin** which includes data on banks in the UK, the money supply and government borrowing and financial transactions.

Population data

3.21 Data on the **UK population**, such as population numbers in total and by region, births, deaths and marriages, are produced monthly by the ONS in a quarterly publication entitled

Population Trends. It also produces an **annual statistical review**. Every ten years, there is a full **census** of the whole population, and results of the census are published. The last census was in 1991.

The Blue Book and the Pink Book

3.22 *The Blue Book on National Income and Expenditure* is published annually by the ONS, giving details of the following.

(a) **Gross national product** (analysed into sections of the economy such as transport and communication, insurance, banking and finance, public administration and defence)

(b) **Gross national income** (analysed into income from self-employment, income from employment, profits of companies, income from abroad and so on)

(c) **Gross national expenditure** (analysed into expenditure on capital goods, expenditure by consumers and by public authorities, imports and so on)

3.23 This information is augmented by more detailed statistics, also provided in the Blue Book. There is also an annual *Pink Book* on *the UK Balance of Payments* which analyses the following.

- The UK's external trade
- External capital transactions (inflows and outflows of private capital)
- Official financing

The Annual Abstract of Statistics

3.24 Most government statistics of economic and business data are brought together into a **main reference book**, the *Annual Abstract of Statistics*, which is published by the ONS. Notes about the data and definitions of the data provided are contained in the book. If you can, take the opportunity to browse through this publication at your college or public library.

The Monthly Digest of Statistics

3.25 The ONS's *Monthly Digest of Statistics* is an **abbreviated version** of the *Annual Abstract*, updated and published **monthly**. The information included in the *Monthly Digest* covers a wide area, such as the following items.

- Industrial output
- Production costs
- Prices and wages
- Social services
- Law enforcement
- National income
- External trade
- Retailing
- Transport
- Construction
- Agriculture
- Food

Financial Statistics

3.26 The ONS publishes a **monthly compilation of financial data** in *Financial Statistics*. This gives statistics on a variety of financial topics, such as the following.

(a) Government income, expenditure and borrowing

(b) Assets and liabilities of banks and statistics on other financial institutions, such as building societies, unit trusts, investment trusts, insurance companies and pension funds

(c) Companies (profits, sources and uses of capital funds, acquisitions and mergers, share trading and so on)

(d) Personal sector finance (loans for home buying, consumer credit, personal income expenditure and saving and so on)

(e) The overseas sector

(f) The money supply

(g) Issues of capital and Stock Exchange transactions

(h) Exchange rates, interest rates and share prices

Economic Trends

3.27 Like the *Monthly Digest of Statistics* and *Financial Statistics*, *Economic Trends* is a monthly publication of the ONS. As its name implies, its main purpose is to **indicate trends**, and the publication includes **graphs** as well as **numerical statistics**.

Activity 3.3

Identify which of the following are secondary data sources.

(a) *Economic Trends* (published by the Office for National Statistics).

(b) The *Monthly Digest of Statistics* (published by the Office for National Statistics).

(c) Data collected for an attitude survey by means of personal interviews, using a non-random sampling method.

(d) Historical records of sales revenues to be used to prepare current forecasts.

Activity 3.4

Name five important sources of statistical data published by the government in the UK and state briefly what each one contains.

Activity 3.5

The *Annual Abstract of Statistics* includes long-term analyses of statistics for which more detailed analyses are available elsewhere.

In which publications would you find detailed short-term statistics covering the following? Identify the publisher in each case, and the frequency of publication.

(a) The level of unemployment.
(b) Trends in road transport.
(c) UK imports and exports.
(d) Geographical distribution of the resident population.
(e) The Retail Prices Index.

Activity 3.6

A manufacturing company has a copy of the *Employment Gazette* which contains statistics relating to:

(a) employment and unemployment;
(b) earnings.

State for what practical purposes both (a) and (b) could be used by the company.

Activity 3.7

An accountant is studying the *Employment Gazette* and is particularly interested in the Retail Price Index.

(a) How could the company use this information in practice?
(b) Explain whether this information is primary or secondary data.

Key learning points

- **Statistics** is the name given to data in the form of figures, and covers the following.

  ° Collecting data
  ° Presenting data in a useful form
  ° Interpreting the data

- The incorrect use and interpretation of statistics in an **abuse** of statistics.

- A **statistical survey** is a survey which involves collecting statistics in order to answer a question.

- In statistics, the word **population** refers to the entire collection of items being considered.

- An **attribute** is something an object has either got or not got - it cannot be measured. A **variable** is something which can be measured, and may be either **discrete** (ie it can only take a specific value) or **continuous** (ie it may take on any value).

- Data may be either **primary** (collected specifically for the purpose) or **secondary** (collected elsewhere for some other purpose).

- Primary data may be collected as follows.

  ° Personal investigation
  ° Teams of investigators
  ° Questionnaires

- All **published statistics** are a source of secondary data. Examples include: *The Monthly Digest of Statistics; The Annual Abstract of Statistics; Economic trends; Financial Statistics; Employment Gazette*; and the *Bank of England Quarterly Bulletin*.

Quick quiz

1   What does statistics cover?

2   What are the three main dangers of using statistics?

3   Are the following discrete or continuous variables?

    (a) The number of cars in a family
    (b) The height of pupils in a class
    (c) The temperature on Easter day last year
    (d) The number of pupils in a class

4   What is the main advantage of using primary data?

5   Why are secondary data sometimes used instead of collecting primary data?

6   Who are the main publishers of secondary data?

BPP
PUBLISHING

7   Where might you find information about wage rates in Britain?

Answer to quick quiz

1   **Collecting** data, **presenting** them in a useful form and **interpreting** them.

2   • Statistical data will be collected and analysed in a confusing and unclear way
      • Unsuitable statistical measures will be selected
      • Statistics will be interpreted incorrectly and used to draw incorrect conclusions

3   (a)   Discrete
      (b)   Continuous
      (c)   Continuous
      (d)   Discrete

4   The collector knows where the data came from, the circumstances under which they were collected and any limitations or inadequacies in the data.

5   Because they are available cheaply.

6   • The UK Government (Office for National Statistics)
      • The European Union
      • The United Nations
      • The Department of Education and Employment
      • The Bank of England

7   The Employment Gazette (published by the Office for National Statistics).

Answers to activities

Answer 3.1

(a)   The statement does not make clear whether the increase in sales is an increase in sales volume or sales value (or both). Were more pairs of footwear sold, or was the total sales revenue higher? Of course, the statement would also convey more information if a figure were put on the increase.

      The words 'not as much as clothing' are ambiguous. Does this mean that sales of footwear are increasing at a slower percentage rate than sales of clothing? Or perhaps it means that the cash increase in footwear sales is lower than the cash increase in clothing sales.

(b)   Turnover may have shown a spectacular rise because two years ago sales were particularly low. It should also be indicated whether the percentage rise is in cash terms, after adjustment for general inflation, or after adjustment for changes in prices in the company's industry.

Answer 3.2

(a)   The number of diagrams in a textbook is a *discrete variable*, because it can only be counted in whole number steps. You cannot, for example, have 26½ diagrams or 47.32 diagrams in a book.

(b)   Whether or not a can possesses a sticker is an *attribute*. It is not something which can be measured. A can either possesses the attribute or it does not.

(c)   How long an athlete takes to run a mile is a *continuous variable*, because the time recorded can in theory take any value, for example 4 minutes 2.0643 seconds.

(d)   The percentage obtained in an examination is a *discrete variable*, taking whole number values between 0% and 100%. The discrete values might include half percent steps, if the examination is the sort where you could be awarded ½%. But it would not be possible to score, say, 62.32%, so the variable is not continuous.

(e)   The height of a telegraph pole is a *continuous variable*.

Answer 3.3

(a), (b) and (d).

Economic Trends and the *Monthly Digest of Statistics* are both sources of secondary data provided by the government. Historic sales data were not collected specifically for the preparation of forecasts, therefore they are also secondary data. Data collected through personal interview for a particular project are primary data.

Answer 3.4

(a)   *The Annual Abstract of Statistics*

Most government statistics of economic and business data are brought together into a main reference book, the *Annual Abstract of Statistics* published by the Office for National Statistics (ONS). The information is provided by a number of government departments. Notes and definitions of the statistical data provided are contained in the publication.

(b)   *The Monthly Digest of Statistics*

This is an abbreviated version of the *Annual Abstract* and is published monthly.

(c)   *Financial Statistics*

This is published monthly by the ONS. It gives a range of useful financial and monetary statistics for the UK including:

(i)   financial statistics of central government and local authority borrowings;
(ii)   banking statistics;
(iii)   income and profits of companies and capital issues;
(iv)   interest rates;
(v)   gold and foreign currency reserves;
(vi)   the balance of payments.

(d)   *Economic Trends*

This is also published monthly by the ONS. It contains figures and graphs on topics which include production, labour, external trade, investment, prices, wages and earnings.

(e)   *The Employment Gazette*

This is published monthly by the ONS. It provides figures on labour and on prices including:

(i)   retail prices;
(ii)   employment;
(iii)   unemployment;
(iv)   unfilled job vacancies;
(v)   wage rates;
(vi)   overtime and short time working;
(vii)   stoppages at work.

Answer 3.5

(a)   *Employment Gazette*, published monthly by the ONS.

(b)   The *Monthly Digest of Statistics*, published monthly by the ONS.

(c)   The *Balance of Payments* ('the pink book') published annually by the ONS.

(d)   *Population Trends*, published quarterly by the ONS.

(e)   Employment Gazette (see (a)).

Answer 3.6

(a)   Regional employment statistics could help the company in deciding where to locate a new factory.

(b)   Earnings data will show the company's management how the company employees' wages compare with the national or regional averages.

Answer 3.7 _____

(a)   The RPI indicates the general level of price inflation for consumers, and therefore provides a yardstick by which the prices faced by the company can be assessed, including input prices such as materials and labour as well as selling prices.

(b)   The RPI is secondary data because it has been compiled by the government from price survey information and not for the company's own purposes.

Chapter 4   Presenting information: graphs

Chapter topic list

1   Drawing and using graphs

2   Straight line graphs

3   Scattergraphs

4   Ogives

Learning objectives

On completion of this chapter you will be able to:

	Performance criteria	Range statement
• prepare reports in the appropriate form and present them to management within required timescales	7.1.6	7.1.3
• *use diagrammatic methods to present information*	n/a	n/a

Italicised objectives are areas of knowledge and understanding underlying the elements of competence for Unit 7.

1   DRAWING AND USING GRAPHS

KEY TERM

A **graph** is a form of **visual display**. A graph shows, by means of either a straight line or a curve, the relationship between two variables.

1.1   In particular, graphs show how the value of one variable changes given changes in the value of the other variable.

1.2   For example, a graph might be used to show how:

(a)   sales turnover changes over time;

(b)   a country's population changes over time;

(c)   total costs of production vary with the number of units produced.

1.3   The variable whose value is influenced by the value of the other variable is referred to as the **dependent variable**. In the examples above, sales turnover, population and total costs would be the dependent variables in (a), (b) and (c) respectively.

The variable whose value affects the value of the dependent variable is known as the **independent variable**. In the examples above, these are time in (a) and (b) and number of units produced in (c).

1.4   The relationship between variables can often be presented more clearly in graph form than in a table of figures, and this is why graphs are so commonly used.

Using graphs well

1.5   A graph has a **horizontal axis**, the x axis, and a **vertical axis**, the y axis. The x axis is used to represent the **independent variable** and the y axis is used to represent the **dependent variable**. Their intersection is known as the **origin** and should be labelled 0.

1.6   If time is one variable, it is always treated as the independent variable. When time is represented by the x axis on a graph, we have a **time series**. The analysis of time series is covered in Chapter 7 of this Interactive Text.

1.7   (a)   **All axes should be labelled,** with the variable which they represent (say, sales) and the scale in which they are measured (say, £'000).

(b)   If the data to be plotted are derived from calculations, rather than given in the task set, make sure that there is a **neat table** in your working papers.

(c)   The scales on each axis should be selected so as to use as much of the available space as possible. **Do not cramp a graph into one corner.**

(d) In some cases it is best not to start a scale at zero so as to avoid having a large area of wasted paper. This is perfectly acceptable as long as the scale adopted is clearly shown on the axis. One way of avoiding confusion is to **break the axis** concerned, as follows.

(e) **The scales on the x axis and the y axis should be marked.** For example, if the y axis relates to amounts of money, the axis should be marked at every £1, or £100 or £1,000 interval or at whatever other interval is appropriate. The axes must be marked with values to give the reader an idea of how big the values on the graph are.

(f) **A graph should not be overcrowded with too many lines**. Graphs should always give a clear, neat impression. Avoid lines crossing each other unless their intersection is meaningful.

(g) **A graph must always be given a title**, and where appropriate, a reference should be made to the source of data.

(h) **Graph paper is particularly necessary when total accuracy is required**, for example, when you wish to find the exact point where two lines intersect. All graphs should be prepared on ruled or square paper at least.

DEVOLVED ASSESSMENT ALERT

Make sure that you always follow the guidelines that we have listed in paragraphs 1.5 - 1.7 for drawing graphs well when completing tasks in your devolved assessments.

2 STRAIGHT LINE GRAPHS

KEY TERM

A **straight line graph** is one which can be expressed by a formula $y = a + bx$ where a and b are fixed, constant values and x and y are the variables.

2.1 Here are some examples of straight line graphs.

$y = 100 + 3x$
$y = 1,000 + 0.2x$
$y = -60 + 12x$

There are no x^2, x^3, x^4, $\sqrt{x}$ or $1/x$ terms. If there were, the corresponding graphs would not be straight lines.

2.2 To draw a straight line graph, we need only plot two points and join them up with a straight line.

2.3 EXAMPLE: STRAIGHT LINE GRAPH (1)

To draw y = 50 + 2x we can take any two points, for example these two.

When x = 0,   y = 50
When x = 10,   y = 50 + 20 = 70

These can be plotted on graph paper, or input into a modern spreadsheet package, and the points joined up and the line extended as follows.

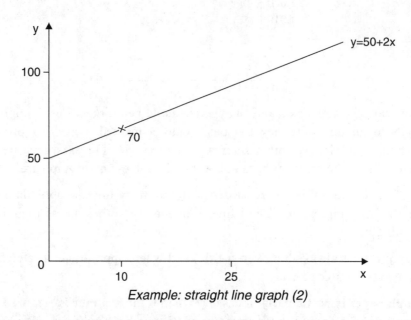

Example: straight line graph (2)

2.4 EXAMPLE: STRAIGHT LINE GRAPH (2)

An accounting technician who is about to retire intends to use his savings and retirement gratuity totalling £52,000 to set up a retail business. He plans to employ three assistants whose weekly salaries will be £120, £96, and £80 respectively, together with a commission of 3% on their individual sales. The shop expenses apart from the assistants' remuneration are expected to amount to £240 a week, and the goods to be sold will be bought at 25% less than the prices at which he sells them. You can assume that stock levels will remain constant.

Tasks

(a) Draw a graph to show total weekly expenses for sales ranging from £1,000 to £5,000 a week.

(b) Draw a graph from which can be read the weekly sales necessary to yield weekly profits from nil to £500.

2.5 SOLUTION

(a) The costs of the business are partly fixed and partly variable. Fixed costs are costs that are a given amount each week, and these are as follows.

	£
Salaries (120 + 96 + 80)	296
Expenses	240
	536

The variable costs are costs that vary with sales. These are as follows.

Commission	3% of sales
Purchase costs	75% of sales
	78% of sales

(b) Total weekly costs are C = 536 + 0.78 S, where S = weekly sales.

This can be drawn as a straight line on a graph. To draw a straight line, we need only plot two points. Any points can be chosen, but x = 0 is always an easy one to use. Here x = 0 and x = 5,000 have been selected.

Sales £		*Costs* £
0	(536 + 0)	536
5,000	(536 + 0.78 × 5,000)	4,436

Weekly sales are shown on the x axis and costs on the y axis, because the graph is intended to show how costs vary with sales, or how costs depend on sales volume. The y axis is used to represent the dependent variable, the x axis to represent the independent variable.

2.6 The sales necessary to achieve a profit of a given amount can also be shown as a straight line on a graph, with profit on the x axis and sales on the y axis, because the graph will show what sales must be to achieve a given profit figure. Sales are being treated as the dependent variable.

We need to establish two points on the line to construct a graph.

$$\text{Profit}\quad P = S - 0.78S - 536$$

where S   is the weekly sales
       0.78S   is the variable cost of sales
       536   is the weekly fixed expenditure

       P   = 0.22S − 536

(a) When profit is 0:

       0   = 0.22S − 536
       0.22S   = 536
       S   = 2,436.4

(b) When profit is 500:

       500   = 0.22S − 536
       0.22S   = 500 + 536 = 1,036
       S   = 4,709.1

BPP PUBLISHING

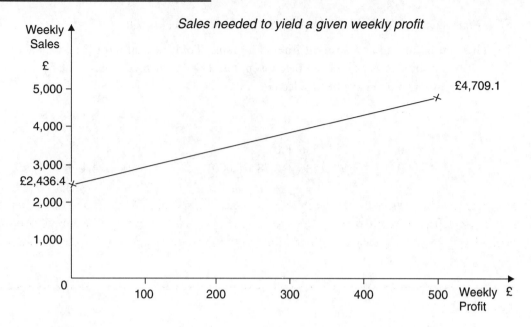

Interpreting graphs

2.7 **Graphs can be misleading if they are not read properly**, and when you need to interpret the meaning of data in a graph you should:

(a) **study what the x axis and y axis represent**. The variable on the x axis will be the independent variable and the variable on the y axis will be the dependent variable. Hence in the graph in Paragraph 2.6 weekly sales are treated as the dependent variable since we are trying to determine how much sales need to be in order to earn a given profit - sales are dependent on profit for the purposes of the graph;

(b) **look at the scales on the x axis and y axis**. Both of the graphs below show $y = 100 + 10x$, but with different scales on the x axis.

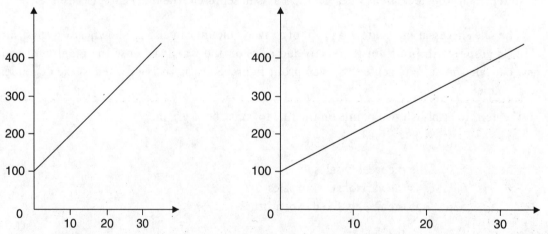

The steeper slope of the left hand graph can be deceptive. This important point has been made before, and you should be ready to comment on it;

(c) **consider whether the most suitable dependent variable has been selected for presenting the data**. For example, if a graph is presented showing sales over a period of time, it might take units sold as the dependent variable.

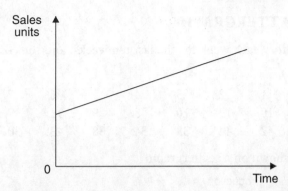

However, if selling **prices** have fallen, the increase in units sold might be explained by the lower prices, and total **turnover** might even have fallen. Turnover might be a more suitable dependent variable for the y axis, depending on the purposes for which the graph is to be used.

Activity 4.1

The figure below shows the profits of four divisions within a firm during the period from 20X0 to 20X5.

Task

Criticise the graph by outlining a series of rules for correct graphical presentation.

3   SCATTERGRAPHS

> ### KEY TERM
>
> **Scattergraphs** are graphs which are used to exhibit data, rather than equations which produce simple lines or curves, in order to compare the way in which two variables vary with each other.

3.1   The x axis of a scattergraph is used to represent the independent variable and the y axis represents the dependent variable.

3.2   To construct a scattergraph or scatter diagram, we must have several pairs of data, with each pair showing the value of one variable and the corresponding value of the other variable. Each pair is plotted on a graph. The resulting graph will show a number of pairs, scattered over the graph. The scattered points might or might not appear to follow a trend.

3.3   EXAMPLE: SCATTERGRAPH

The output at a factory each week for the last ten weeks, and the cost of that output, were as follows.

Week	1	2	3	4	5	6	7	8	9	10
Output (units)	10	12	10	8	9	11	7	12	9	14
Cost (£)	42	44	38	34	38	43	30	47	37	50

The data could be shown on a scattergraph.

(a)   The cost depends on the volume of output: volume is the independent variable and is shown on the x axis.

(b)   You will notice from the graph that the plotted data, although scattered, lie approximately on a rising trend line, with higher total costs at higher output volumes. (The lower part of the y axis has been omitted, so as not to waste space. The break in the y axis is indicated by the jagged line.)

Curve fitting

3.4   For the most part, scattergraphs are used to try to identify **trend lines**.

3.5   If a trend can be seen in a scattergraph, the next step is to try to draw a trend line. Fitting a line to scattergraph data is called **curve fitting**.

3.6   The reason for wanting to do this is to make predictions.

(a)   In the previous example, we have drawn a trend line from the scattergraph of output units and production cost. This trend line might turn out to be, say, y = 10 + 3x. We could then use this trend line to establish what we think costs ought to be, approximately, if output were, say, 10 units or 15 units in any week. (These 'expected' costs could subsequently be compared with the actual costs, so that managers could judge whether actual costs were higher or lower than they ought to be.)

(b)   If a scattergraph is used to record sales over time, we could draw a trend line, and use this to forecast sales for next year.

3.7   The trend line could be a straight line, or a curved line. The simplest technique for drawing a trend line is to make a visual judgement about what the closest-fitting trend line seems to be.

3.8   Here is another example of a scattergraph with a trend line added.

The line passes through the point x = 0, y = 20, so if its equation is y = a + bx, we have a = 20. The line also passes through x = 89, y = 100, so:

100   = 20 + (b × 89)

b   = $\frac{(100 - 20)}{89}$

= 0.9.

The line is y = 20 + 0.9x.

BPP
PUBLISHING

Activity 4.2

The quantities of widgets produced by WDG Ltd during the year ended 31 October 20X1 and the related costs were as follows.

Month	Production Thousands	Factory cost £'000
20X0		
November	7	45
December	10	59
20X1		
January	13	75
February	14	80
March	11	65
April	7	46
May	5	35
June	4	30
July	3	25
August	2	20
September	1	15
October	5	35

You may assume that the value of money remained stable throughout the year.

Tasks

(a) Draw a scatter diagram related to the data provided above, and plot on it the line of best fit.

(b) Now answer the following questions.

    (i) What would you expect the factory cost to have been if 12,000 widgets had been produced in a particular month?

    (ii) What is your estimate of WDG's monthly fixed cost?

Activity 4.3

A wholesaling business incurs three types of cost per product line carried in stock. Two of these costs, for product P only, are as follows.

Cost type	Annual cost (£)
I	$2.5x$
II	$\dfrac{225{,}000}{x}$

where x units represents the maximum stock carried.

Tasks

(a) For values of x equal to 50, 100, 200, 250, 300, 350, 400, 500 and 600, calculate and tabulate the values of both costs, I and II, and the total costs I and II.

(b) Using one sheet of graph paper, plot cost I, cost II and the total of costs I and II, each against the values of x. Comment upon the features displayed in the three plots of your graph, and advise the business of the best value for x.

(c) (i) If cost type III is a constant £600 regardless of the size of x, superimpose a plot of this cost on your graph in (b).

    (ii) If you were to plot the total of all three costs, I, II and III, describe and comment upon the form it would take. (Do not present this plot.)

4   OGIVES

4.1   EXAMPLE: OGIVES (1)

Consider the following frequency distribution.

Number of faulty units rejected on inspection	Frequency f	Cumulative frequency
up to 1	5	5
up to 2	5	10
up to 3	3	13
up to 4	1	14
	14	

An ogive would be drawn as follows.

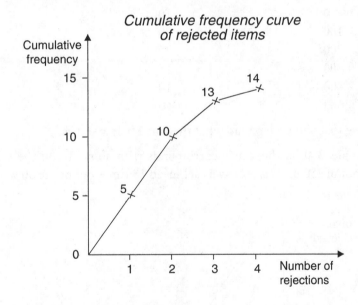

4.2   The ogive is drawn by plotting the cumulative frequencies on the graph, and joining them with straight lines. Although many ogives are more accurately curved lines, you can use straight lines in drawing an ogive in work for an assessment.

4.3   For grouped frequency distributions, where we work up through values of the variable, the cumulative frequencies are plotted against the **upper** limits of the classes. For example:

(a)   for the class 'over 200, up to and including 250', the cumulative frequency should be plotted against 250;

(b)   for the class 'from 100 up to but not including 150' the cumulative frequency for a continuous variable should be plotted against 150. For a discrete variable, it would be plotted against the highest value less than 150, probably 149.

4.4   We can also draw ogives to show the cumulative number of items with values greater than or equal to some given value.

4.5   EXAMPLE: OGIVES (2)

(a)   Output at a factory over a period of 80 weeks is shown by the following frequency distribution.

Output per week Units	Number of weeks output achieved
> 0 ≤ 100	10
> 100 ≤ 200	20
> 200 ≤ 300	25
> 300 ≤ 400	15
> 400 ≤ 500	10
	80

(b)   If we wished to draw an ogive to show the number of weeks in which output exceeded a certain value, the cumulative total would begin at 80 and drop to 0.

In drawing an ogive when we work down through values of the variable, the descending cumulative frequency should be plotted against the lower limit of each class interval.

Lower limit of interval	Frequency f	Cumulative ('more than') frequency
0	10	80
100	20	70
200	25	50
300	15	25
400	10	10
500	0	0

Make sure that you understand what the curve below shows.

For example, 350 on the x axis corresponds with about 18 on the y axis. This means that output of 350 units *or more* was achieved 18 times out of the 80 weeks.

What information does an ogive provide?

4.6 An ogive represents a **cumulative frequency distribution** and it can be used to show what range of values contain given proportions of the total population. For example, it can be used to find the following:

- The range of values of the first 50% of the population
- Within what range of values the middle 50% of the population falls

4.7 These particular pieces of information can be obtained by finding the following from the ogive.

(a) The value of the **middle item in the range**, corresponding to a cumulative frequency of 50% of the **total**. For example, if there are 11 data items, the middle item would be the sixth. If there are ten data items, we would take the fifth item.

The **middle item of n data items** is the $[(n + 1)/2]$th where n is an odd number and the $(n/2)$th where n is an even number (it is not usually worth worrying about the fact that when n is even, there are two items which are equally 'in the middle').

The value of the middle item is called the **median** value;

(b) The value of the item which is **a quarter (25%) of the way through the cumulative frequencies** (running from low values up to high values). For example, if there are 11 data items, this would be the third item. If there are ten data items, it would be taken as the mid-way point between the second and third items: the '2½th' item. However, one might decide to approximate and take the third item.

This quarter-way-through item is called the **lower quartile** or the **first quartile**;

(c) the value of the item which is **three quarters (75%) of the way through the cumulative frequencies**. For example, if there are 11 data items, this would be the value of the ninth item.

This three-quarters-way-through value is called the **upper quartile** or the **third quartile**. (The second quartile is the median.)

4.8 EXAMPLE: OGIVES (3)

The production of each manufacturing department of your company is monitored weekly to establish productivity bonuses to be paid to the members of that department.

250 items have to be produced each week before a bonus will be paid. The production in one department over a 40 week period is shown below.

382	367	364	365	371	370	372	364	355	347
354	359	359	360	357	362	364	365	371	365
361	380	382	394	396	398	402	406	437	456
469	466	459	454	460	457	452	451	445	446

Tasks

(a) Form a frequency distribution of five groups for the number of items produced each week.

(b) Construct the ogive for the frequency distribution established in (a).

(c) Establish the value of the median from the ogive.

(d) Establish the values of the upper and lower quartiles.

(e) Interpret the results that you obtain in (c) and (d).

4.9   SOLUTION

(a) The first step is to decide on the **size of class intervals for a grouped frequency distribution**, given that the requirement here is for five classes.

Highest value amongst the data	469
Less lowest value amongst the data	347
Range of values	122

This gives a minimum average class interval of $\dfrac{122}{5}$ = 24.4, say 25.

However, it is not obvious what the lowest and highest values of each class would be, and it might be easier to make the class intervals 30. This would give a range of values of $30 \times 5 = 150$, which is 28 more than the range of 122 that we need. By sharing the 'excess' between the low and high ends of the range and also looking for suitable lower and upper limits to each class, we arrive at classes from 341 - 370 to 461 - 490.

Class	Frequency f	Cumulative frequency
341 - 370	17	17
371 - 400	9	26
401 - 430	2	28
431 - 460	10	38
461 - 490	2	40
	40	

(b) The ogive is now constructed by marking units along the x axis and cumulative frequency along the y axis. The first class interval is 341 - 370, and so the x axis starts at 340.

Ogive of weekly production

(c)   The median is the ½ × 40 = 20th value. Reading off from the ogive, this value is 382 units per week.

(d)   The upper quartile is the ¾ × 40 = 30th value. The lower quartile is the ¼ × 40 = 10th value. Reading off from the ogive, these values are 441 units and 359 units respectively.

(e)   These values show that in half of the weeks production was in the range 359 to 441 units, with the middle-of-the-range value (the median) being 382, which is closer to the lower quartile than to the upper quartile.

Activity 4.4

Annual profit data from 50 similar construction companies in 20X8 are as follows.

Annual profit £million	Number of companies	Cu. fr
−10 to under −5	2	2
−5 to under 0	0	2
0 to under 5	2	4
5 to under 10	3	7
10 to under 15	6	13
15 to under 20	11	24
20 to under 25	13	37
25 to under 30	9	46
30 to under 35	4	50

Tasks

(a)   Construct a cumulative frequency distribution and draw the ogive (cumulative frequency curve) on graph paper.

(b)   Use your ogive to estimate the three quartiles and explain their meaning.

(c)   Deduce from your ogive the profit exceeded by the top 10% of companies.

(d)   Deduce from your ogive the number of companies, out of 500 similar companies to those above, whose annual profit in 20X8 was between £8,000,000 and £18,000,000.

Key learning points

- **Graphs** are a form of visual display. They show the relationship between two variables.

- A **dependent variable** is one whose value is influenced by the value of another variable. An **independent variable** is one whose value affects the value of the dependent variable.

- A graph has a **horizontal axis** (x axis) and a **vertical axis** (y axis). These axes intersect at the **origin.**

- If time is one variable, and is represented by the x axis, we have a **time series.**

- An axis break can be used to indicate a non-zero starting point.

- A straight line graph may be drawn by plotting only two points and joining them up with a straight line.

- **Scattergraphs** exhibit data rather than equations. They are drawn to compare the way in which two variables may vary with each other. They are generally used to identify trend lines.

- An **ogive** is a curve which shows the cumulative number of items with a value less than or equal to, or greater than or equal to a certain amount. Ogives can be used to show what range of values contain given proportions of the total population. An ogive can also be used to find the **median**, **lower quartile** (first quartile) and **upper quartile** (third quartile).

Quick quiz

1   What is a dependent variable?

2   What is the formula for a straight line graph?

3   On a scattergraph, which axis represents the independent variable?

4   What does an ogive show?

5   How would you calculate the middle item of n data items?

Answers to quick quiz

1   A variable whose value is influenced by the value of another variable.

2   y = a + bx, where a and b are fixed constant values and x and y are the variables.

3   The x axis.

4   The cumulative number of items with a value less than or equal to or greater than or equal to a certain amount.

5   - For an odd number of data items, the middle item $= \dfrac{(n+1)}{2}$

    - For an even number of data items, the middle item $= \dfrac{n}{2}$

Answers to activities

Answer 4.1

The graph is extremely unclear and could be improved in the following ways.

(a)   The axes are not labelled. The horizontal axis (the x axis) should represent the independent variable, being time in this case. So it should be labelled 20X0, 20X1, ... 20X5. Similarly the vertical axis (the y axis) should represent the dependent variable, being profits in this case.

(b)   An indication should be given of whether the profits have been adjusted in any way. In particular, it would be useful to have profit figures adjusted for inflation, so that the changes in profits shown by the graph are all changes in real terms.

(c)   The graph has no heading. Every graph should have a title explaining what variables are being displayed against each other. In the given case the heading could be 'Profits of divisions W, X, Y and Z during the period 20X0 to 20X5'.

(d)   Crosses should be marked on the graph to indicate the points plotted. The given graph merely has smooth curves which presumably pass through where the crosses should be. Marking the actual points will help the reader of the graph to judge how much estimation has been carried out in trying to draw the best curves through the points.

(e)   A graph should not be overcrowded with too many lines. Graphs should always give a clear, neat impression. The given graph has too many lines on it for a clear impression to be given.

(f)   If the data to be plotted are derived from calculations, there should be a neat table showing the actual figures accompanying the graph, stating the source of the figures. No such information is given here.

Answer 4.2

Tutorial note. Your answers to parts (b) and (c) may have been slightly different from those given here, but they should not have been very different, because the data points lay very nearly along a straight line.

(a)   *WDG Ltd - Scatter diagram of production and factory costs, November 20X0-October 20X1*

(b)   (i)   The estimated factory cost for a production of 12,000 widgets is £70,000.

        (ii)   The monthly fixed costs are indicated by the point where the line of best fit meets the vertical axis (costs at zero production). The fixed costs are estimated as £10,000 a month.

Answer 4.3

Tutorial note. You may have found cost curve II and the curve for total costs difficult to draw neatly. In such cases you may find it best to join the dots with straight lines and add a note that ideally a smooth curve should be drawn.

(a)

Maximum stock	Cost I	Cost II 225,000	Total cost
x	2.5x	x	I + II
	£	£	£
50	125	4,500	4,625
100	250	2,250	2,500
200	500	1,125	1,625
250	625	900	1,525
300	750	750	1,500
350	875	642.9	1,517.9
400	1,000	562.5	1,562.5
500	1,250	450	1,700
600	1,500	375	1,875

(b) In the graph, the straight line for cost I shows that this cost rises linearly with x. The curve for cost II shows that this cost falls as x rises, though the rate of fall gradually diminishes. The total cost curve falls then rises. The optimum value of x is where total costs are minimised, at x = 300.

(c) See graph. A curve for the total costs would have exactly the same shape as the curve for costs I and II, but would be £600 higher for all values of x.

Graph of cost against maximum stock

Answer 4.4

Tutorial note. Part (c) illustrates the fact that figures other than quartiles can be obtained from an ogive. The value exceeded by any required proportion of the population can be found.

(a)

Profit £m Under	No. companies (frequency)	'Less than' cumulative frequency
– 5	2	2
0	0	2
5	2	4
10	3	7
15	6	13
20	11	24
25	13	37
30	9	46
35	4	50
	50	

See the graph below.

(b)   First quartile: 25% of companies have a profit less than this. Q_1 is £14,600,000.

Second quartile
or median: 50% of companies have a profit less than this. Q_2 is £20,400,000.

Third quartile: 75% of companies have a profit less than this. Q_3 is £25,700,000.

(c)   The top 10% of companies by profit are the top five companies.

The 90th percentile profit is £29,400,000.

(d)   5.8 companies achieved a profit of less than £8,000,000.

19.6 companies achieved a profit of less than £18,000,000.

19.6 – 5.8 = 13.8 companies achieved a profit between £8,000,000 and £18,000,000.
Thus, 10 × 13.8 = 138 companies out of 500 are estimated to have had an annual profit between
£8,000,000 and £18,000,000 in 19X8.

Ogive of annual profits of construction companies

Chapter 5 Presenting information: tables and charts

Chapter topic list

1 Tables

2 Frequency distributions

3 Charts

Learning objectives

On completion of this chapter you will be able to:

	Performance criteria	Range statement
• prepare reports in the appropriate form and present them to management within required timescales	7.1.6	7.1.3
• *present information using the following methods: written reports; diagrammatic; tabular*	n/a	n/a
• *tabulate accounting and other quantitative information*	n/a	n/a

Italicised objectives are areas of knowledge and understanding underlying the elements of competence for Unit 7.

1 TABLES

1.1 **Raw data** (for example, the list of results from a survey, or a list of accounting balances) need to be summarised and analysed, to give them meaning. This chapter is concerned with different ways of presenting data using tables and charts. We will start with one of the most basic ways, the preparation of a table.

KEY TERM

Tabulation means putting data into tables. A table is a matrix of data in rows and columns, with the rows and the columns having titles.

1.2 Since a table is **two-dimensional**, it can only show two variables. For example, the resources required to produce items in a factory could be tabulated, with one dimension (rows or columns) representing the items produced and the other dimension representing the resources.

Resources for production

	Product items				
	Alpha	*Beta*	*Gamma*	*Delta*	*Total*
	£	£	£	£	£
Resources					
Direct material Alpha	X	X	X	X	X
Direct material Beta	X	X	X	X	X
Direct labour grade skilled	X	X	X	X	X
Direct labour grade semi-skilled	X	X	X	X	X
Supervision	X	X	X	X	X
Machine time	X	X	X	X	X
Total	X	X	X	X	X

1.3 To tabulate data, you need to recognise what the two dimensions should represent, prepare rows and columns accordingly with suitable titles, and then insert the data into the appropriate places in the table.

Guidelines for tabulation

1.4 The table in paragraph 1.2 illustrates certain guidelines which you should apply when presenting data in tabular form. These are as follows.

(a) The table should be given a **clear title**.

(b) All columns should be **clearly labelled**.

(c) Where appropriate, there should be **clear sub-totals**.

(d) A **total column** may be presented; this would usually be the right-hand column.

(e) A **total figure** is often advisable at the bottom of each column of figures.

(f) Tables should not be packed with too much data so that the information presented is difficult to read.

1.5 EXAMPLE: TABLES

The total number of employees in a certain trading company is 1,000. They are employed in three departments: production, administration and sales. 600 people are employed in the production department and 300 in administration. There are 110 males under 21 in employment, 110 females under 21, and 290 females aged 21 years and over. The remaining employees are males aged 21 and over.

In the production department there are 350 males aged 21 and over, 150 females aged 21 and over and 50 males under 21, whilst in the administration department there are 100 males aged 21 and over, 110 females aged 21 and over and 50 males aged under 21.

Draw up a table to show all the details of employment in the company and its departments and provide suitable secondary statistics to describe the distribution of people in departments.

1.6   SOLUTION

(a)   The basic table required has as its two dimensions:

    (i)   departments;
    (ii)   age/sex analysis.

(b)   Secondary statistics (not the same thing as secondary data) are supporting figures that are supplementary to the main items of data, and which clarify or amplify the main data. A major example of secondary statistics is percentages. In this example, we could show either:

    (i)   the percentage of the total work force in each department belonging to each age/sex group, or

    (ii)   the percentage of the total of each age/sex group employed in each department.

In this example, (i) has been selected but you might consider that (ii) would be more suitable. Either could be suitable, depending of course on what purposes the data are being collected and presented for.

(c)   *Analysis of employees*

	Production No	Production %	Administration No	Administration %	Sales No		Sales %	Total No		Total %
Males 21 yrs +	350	58.4	100	33.3	40	**	40.0	490	*	49.0
Females 21 yrs +	150	25.0	110	36.7	30	**	30.0	290		29.0
Subtotals 21 yrs +	500	83.4	210	70.0	70		70.0	780		78.0
Males under 21	50	8.3	50	16.7	10	**	10.0	110		11.0
Females under 21	50 *	8.3	40	* 13.3	20	**	20.0	110		11.0
Subtotals under 21	100	16.6	90	30.0	30		30.0	220		22.0
Total	600	100.0	300	100.0	100		100.0	1,000		100.0

*   Balancing figure to make up the column total
** Balancing figure then needed to make up the row total

Significant digits and decimal places

1.7   Before we go any further we should say something about significant digits and decimal places.

1.8   Sometimes a decimal number has too many digits in it for practical use. This problem can be overcome by rounding the decimal number to a **specific number of significant digits** using the following rule.

If the first digit to be discarded is greater than or equal to five, then add one to the previous digit. Otherwise the previous digit is unchanged.

1.9   EXAMPLE: SIGNIFICANT DIGITS

(a)   187.392 correct to five significant digits is 187.39.

Discarding a 2 causes nothing to be added to the 9.

(b)   187.392 correct to four significant digits is 187.4.

Discarding the 9 causes one to be added to the 3.

(c)   187.392 correct to three significant digits is 187.

Discarding a 3 causes nothing to be added to the 7.

1.10   You may be asked to make calculations correct to a certain number of **decimal places** and this is also done by applying the rule above.

1.11   EXAMPLE: DECIMAL PLACES

(a)   49.28723 correct to four decimal places is 49.2872.

Discarding a 3 causes nothing to be added to the 2.

(b)   49.28723 correct to three decimal places is 49.287.

Discarding a 2 causes nothing to be added to the 7.

(c)   49.28723 correct to two decimal places is 49.29.

Discarding the 7 causes one to be added to the 8.

(d)   49.28723 correct to one decimal place is 49.3.

Discarding the 8 causes one to be added to the 2.

(e)   49.28723 correct to two significant digits is 49.

Discarding a 2 causes nothing to be added to the 9.

DEVOLVED ASSESSMENT ALERT

When presenting data in tabular form, you must follow the guidelines as stated in Paragraph 1.4 of this chapter. If you follow these guidelines you are likely to earn extra credit in your assessment.

Activity 5.1

Set out the main guidelines which should be followed when data is presented in tabular form.

Rounding errors

1.12   **Rounding errors** may become apparent when, for example, a percentage column does not add up to 100%. When figures in a table are rounded and then added up, the effect of rounding will depend on the method of rounding used.

To avoid bias, any rounding should be to the nearest unit and the potential size of errors should be kept to a tolerable level by rounding to a small enough unit (for example to the nearest £10, rather than to the nearest £1,000).

Tally marks

1.13 **Tally marks** are another simple way of presenting data. If we measured the number of jobs completed by each employee during one week, the data could be collected and presented as follows.

Employee	Jobs completed	
Lynn	₦₦ ////	= 9
Alison	₦₦ ₦₦ ////	= 14
Stuart	₦₦ //	= 7
Emma	///	= 3

Extraction and interpretation of key information from tabulated data

1.14 In an assessment you may be asked to extract and interpret key information from tabulated data. Look back at the table in paragraph 1.6, and study the following comments which could be made about the information presented.

(a) 49% of the total workforce is made up of males who are 21 years old or more, and 29% of the total workforce is made up of females who are 21 years old or more. The workforce is therefore made up primarily of workers who are 21 years old or more.

(b) The percentage of the workforce who are under 21 years old is 22. (Males and females in this age group both make up 11% of the total workforce.) We may conclude that most of the employees making up the workforce are 21 years old or more.

(c) The production department is made up of 58.4% of males who are 21 years old or more, and 25% of females who are 21 years old or more. There are therefore significantly more males than females employed in the production department (just over twice as many in fact).

Males and females employed in the production department who are under 21 years of age form only 16.6% of the total employees in this department. Males and females employed in this age group both make up 8.3%.

(d) 70% of the employees of both the administration and the sales departments are aged 21 years or more. This is slightly less than the corresponding figure of 83.4% in the production department. The production department therefore employs a higher number of employees who are 21 years old or more than both the administration and sales departments. The administration department employs more females than males who are aged under 21 years old.

(e) The sales department employs slightly more males than females who are 21 years old or more, in contrast the administration department employs slightly more females than males in this age group. The sales department employs twice as many females than males who are under 21 years old.

1.15 Make sure that you can present data in a tabulated form, and then extract and interpret the key information.

Information for Activities 5.2 and 5.3

The number of telephones installed in a country in 1960 was 5,246,000. Ten years later in 1970 the number was 6,830,000, and by 1980 the total installed in that year was 12,654,000. Another ten years later the number for 1990 was 10,194,000. In 1960 B Co Ltd saw 2,114,000 of its telephones installed, more than any other kind; A Co Ltd was second with 1,810,000; C Co Ltd third with 448,000; and the 'all others' group accounted for 874,000. In 1970 A Co Ltd was in first position with 3,248,000; C Co Ltd was second with 1,618,000; B Co Ltd third with 1,288,000; and the 'all others' group installed fewer telephones than ten years earlier: 676,000. In 1980 A Co Ltd installations alone, 5,742,000, exceeded total installations of just 20 years earlier. B Co Ltd was in second position with 3,038,000; C Co Ltd third with 2,228,000; and the 'all others' group installed just 1,646,000. 1990 data indicated that relative positions remained the same since 1980 with A Co Ltd at 4,932,000, B Co Ltd at 3,138,000, C Co Ltd at 1,506,000 and 'all others' at 618,000.

Activity 5.2

Convert the information given above into tabular form.

Activity 5.3

(a) Interpret the same data by calculating and further tabulating appropriate percentages to show comparisons of the telephone installations by the producers in the four years given.

(b) Comment on the percentage trends in (a).

Activity 5.4

By 1999, Healthy Healthfoods Ltd had been in business for ten years. It now employs 20,770 people, of whom the largest group (36%) were sales staff, the next largest group (21%) were buyers and the third largest group (18%) were administrative staff. Other groups of employees made up the rest of the staff.

Things had been very different when the company first began operations in 1990. Then, it had just 4,200 employees, of whom the 1,260 buyers were the biggest group; there were 1,176 sales staff and just 840 administrative staff.

By 1993, the company had nearly doubled in size, employing 7,650 people, of whom 2,448 were buyers, 2,372 were sales staff and 1,607 were administrators.

By 1996, the company employed 12,740 people, and the growth in numbers had been most noticeable amongst sales staff, of whom there were 4,840. There were 3,185 buyers. Administrative staff had increased substantially in number to 2,550.

The company's managing director has been very pleased with the growth in business over the past nine years, but has tried to limit the growth in the numbers of staff who are not sales staff, buyers or administrative staff.

Tasks

Present the given data in tabular form.

Are there any comments you would make about what the information in the table should tell the managing director of the company?

2   FREQUENCY DISTRIBUTIONS

2.1   If a large number of measurements of a particular variable is taken (for example the number of units produced per employee per week) some values may occur more than once. A **frequency distribution** is obtained by recording the number of times each value occurs.

2.2   EXAMPLE: FREQUENCY DISTRIBUTION

(a) The output in units of 20 employees during one week was as follows.

65	71	68	70
69	70	69	68
70	69	67	67
72	74	73	69

71	70	71	70

(b) If the number of occurrences is placed against each output quantity, a frequency distribution is produced.

Output of employees in one week in units

Output Units	Number of employees (frequency)
65	1
66	0
67	2
68	2
69	4
70	5
71	3
72	1
73	1
74	1
	20

(c) The number of employees corresponding to a particular volume of output is called a **frequency**. When the data are arranged in this way it is immediately obvious that 69 and 70 units are the most common volumes of output per employee per week.

Grouped frequency distributions

2.3 It is often convenient to group frequencies together into bands or classes. For example, suppose that the output produced by each of 20 employees during one week was as follows, in units.

1,087	850	1,084	792
924	1,226	1,012	1,205
1,265	1,028	1,230	1,182
1,086	1,130	989	1,155
1,134	1,166	1,129	1,160

2.4 An ungrouped frequency distribution would not be a helpful way of presenting the data, because each employee has produced a different number of units in the week.

2.5 The range of output from the lowest to the highest producer is 792 to 1,265, a range of 473 units. This range could be divided into classes of say, 100 units (the **class width** or **class interval**), and the number of employees producing output within each class could then be grouped into a single frequency, as follows.

Output Units	Number of employees (frequency)
700 - 799	1
800 - 899	1
900 - 999	2
1,000 - 1,099	5
1,100 - 1,199	7
1,200 - 1,299	4
	20

 BPP PUBLISHING

Grouped frequency distributions of continuous variables

2.6 **Grouped frequency distributions** can be used to present data for continuous variables. To prepare a grouped frequency distribution, a decision must be made about how wide each class should be.

(a) The size of each class should be appropriate to the nature of the data being recorded, and the most appropriate class interval varies according to circumstances.

(b) The upper and lower limits of each class interval should be suitable 'round' numbers, for class intervals which are in multiples of 5, 10, 100, 1,000 and so on. For example, if the class interval is 10, and data items range in value from 23 to 62 (discrete values) the class intervals should be 20-29, 30-39, 40-49, 50-59 and 60-69, rather than 23-32, 33-42, 43-52 and 53-62.

(c) With continuous variables, either:

(i) the upper limit of a class should be 'up to and including ...' and the lower limit of the next class should be 'over ...'; or

(ii) the upper limit of a class should be 'less than ...', and the lower limit of the next class should be 'at least ...'.

Cumulative frequency distributions

2.7 A cumulative frequency distribution can be used to show the total number of times that a value above or below a certain amount occurs (see the example below).

2.8 **EXAMPLE: GROUPED CUMULATIVE FREQUENCY DISTRIBUTION**

(a) The volume of output produced in one day by each of 20 employees is as follows, in units.

18	29	22	17
30	12	27	24
26	32	24	29
28	46	31	27
19	18	32	25

(b) We could present a grouped frequency distribution as follows.

Output (Units)	Number of employees (frequency)
Under 15	1
15 or more, under 20	4
20 or more, under 25	3
25 or more, under 30	7
30 or more, under 35	4
35 or more	1
	20

(c) The two possible cumulative frequency distributions for the same data are as follows.

	Cumulative frequency		Cumulative frequency
≥ 0	20	< 15	1
≥ 15	19	< 20	5
≥ 20	15	< 25	8
≥ 25	12	< 30	15
≥ 30	5	< 35	19
≥ 35	1	< 47	20

Notes

(i)   The symbol > means 'greater than' and ≥ means 'greater than, or equal to'. The symbol < means 'less than' and ≤ means 'less than or equal to'.

These symbols provide a convenient method of stating classes.

(ii)   The first cumulative frequency distribution shows that of the total of 20 employees:

(1)   19 produced 15 units or more;
(2)   15 produced 20 units or more;
(3)   12 produced 25 units or more;

and so on.

(iii)   The second cumulative frequency distribution shows that of the total of 20 employees:

(1)   one produced less than 15 units;
(2)   five produced less than 20 units;
(3)   eight produced less than 25 units;

and so on.

Activity 5.5

Records of the patients suffering from either minor or major ailments seen by doctors at a local clinic over the last few years show the following.

In 1990, a total of 2,550 patients were seen: of these 650 were adult men, 800 were adult women, and the remainder were children. Of the men, 234 were suffering from a minor ailment; of the women and children, 360 and 616, respectively, were suffering from minor ailments.

In 1995, a total of 2,900 patients were seen by the doctors, 750 being men, 1,060 women, and the remainder children. Of the men, 320 were suffering a minor ailment, whereas 550 women and 720 children had this type of ailment.

Tasks

(a)   What is the purpose of representing this type of data in tabular form?

(b)   Draw up a table showing all the data by class of patient, ailment type and year. Insert in your table both actual numbers and percentages, calculating the latter on a base of the total number of patients seen in each year, correct to one decimal place.

(c)   Give three appropriate interpretations of the information your table provides.

Activity 5.6

The commission earnings for January 20X0 of the salesmen in a mobile phone company were as follows (in pounds).

60	35	53	47	25	44	55	58	47	71
63	67	57	44	61	48	50	56	61	42
43	38	41	39	61	51	27	56	57	50
55	68	55	50	25	48	44	43	49	73
53	35	36	41	45	71	56	40	69	52
36	47	66	52	32	46	44	32	52	58
49	41	45	45	48	36	46	42	52	33
31	36	40	66	53	58	60	52	66	51
51	44	59	53	51	57	35	45	46	54
46	54	51	39	64	43	54	47	60	45

Task

Prepare a grouped frequency distribution classifying the commission earnings into categories of £5 commencing with '£25 and less than £30'.

3   CHARTS

3.1   Instead of presenting data in a table, it might be preferable to provide a visual display in the form of a **chart**.

3.2   **The purpose of a chart is to convey the data in a way that will demonstrate its meaning or significance more clearly than a table of data would.** Charts are not always more appropriate than tables, and the most suitable way of presenting data will depend on the following.

(a)   **What the data are intended to show.** Visual displays usually make one or two points quite forcefully, whereas tables usually give more detailed information.

(b)   **Who is going to use the data.** Some individuals might understand visual displays more readily than tabulated data.

3.3   Types of chart that might be used to present data include the following.

- Pie charts
- Bar charts

Pie charts

KEY TERM

A **pie chart** is a chart which is used to show pictorially the relative size of component elements of a total.

3.4   It is called a pie chart because it is **circular**, and so has the **shape of a pie** in a round pie dish and because the 'pie' is then cut into slices. Each slice represents a part of the total.

3.5   Pie charts have sectors of varying sizes, and you need to be able to draw sectors fairly accurately. To do this, you need a protractor. Working out sector sizes involves converting parts of the total into equivalent degrees of a circle. A complete 'pie' = 360°: the number of degrees in a circle = 100% of whatever you are showing. An element which is 50% of your total will therefore occupy a segment of 180°, and so on.

Alternatively, you could use a computer with either graphics software or a spreadsheet with graphing capability (such as ChartWizard in Microsoft Excel).

Two pie charts are shown as follows.

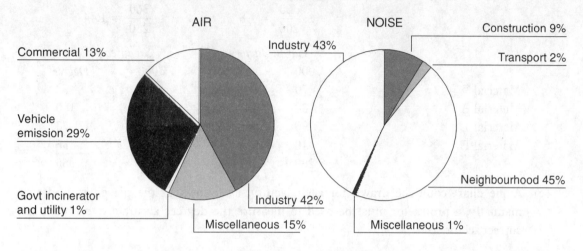

Breakdown of air and noise pollution complaints, 20X0

3.6   You can see that we have used **shading** to distinguish the segments from each other. **Colour** can be used in the same way. Where you have, say, two pie charts showing two populations made up of the same components but in different proportions, the use of shading, and colour make the information much more user-friendly, as we shall see below.

3.7   EXAMPLE: PIE CHARTS

The costs of materials at the Cardiff Factory and the Swansea Factory during January 20X0 were as follows.

	Cardiff factory		Swansea factory	
	£'000	%	£'000	%
Material W	70	35	50	20
Material A	30	15	125	50
Material L	90	45	50	20
Material E	10	5	25	10
	200	100	250	100

Show the costs for the factories in pie charts.

3.8   SOLUTION

To convert the components into degrees of a circle, we can use either the percentage figures or the actual cost figures.

(a)   Using the percentage figures, the total percentage is 100%, and the total number of degrees in a circle is 360°. To convert from one to the other, we multiply each percentage value by 360°/100% = 3.6.

	Cardiff factory		Swansea factory	
	%	Degrees	%	Degrees
Material W	35	126	20	72
Material A	15	54	50	180

Material L	45	162	20	72
Material E	5	18	10	36
	100	360	100	360

(b) Using the actual cost figures, we would multiply each cost by

$$\frac{\text{Number of degrees}}{\text{Total cost}}$$

Cardiff factory	*Swansea factory*
$\dfrac{360}{200} = 1.8$	$\dfrac{360}{250} = 1.44$

	Cardiff factory		*Swansea factory*	
	£'000	*Degrees*	*£'000*	*Degrees*
Material W	70	126	50	72
Material A	30	54	125	180
Material L	90	162	50	72
Material E	10	18	25	36
	200	360	250	360

(c) A pie chart could be drawn for each factory, as follows. If the pie chart is drawn manually, a protractor must be used to measure the degrees accurately to obtain the correct sector sizes.

3.9 Using a computer makes the process much simpler, especially using a spreadsheet. You just draw up the data in a spreadsheet and click on the chart button to create a visual representation of what you want. Note that you can only use colour effectively if you have a colour printer!

3.10 The **advantages of pie charts** are as follows.

(a) They give a simple pictorial display of the relative sizes of elements of a total.

(b) They show clearly when one element is much bigger than others.

(c) They can sometimes clearly show differences in the elements of two different totals. In the example above, the pie charts for the Cardiff and Swansea factories show how the Cardiff factory's costs mostly consist of material L and material W, whereas at the Swansea factory, material A is the largest cost element.

3.11 The **disadvantages of pie charts** are as follows.

(a) They show only the relative sizes of elements. In the example of the two factories, for instance, the pie charts do not show that costs at the Swansea factory were £50,000 higher in total than at the Cardiff factory.

(b) They involve calculating degrees of a circle and drawing sectors accurately, and this can be time consuming unless computer software is used.

(c) It is often difficult to compare sector sizes easily. For example, suppose that the following two pie charts are used to show the elements of a company's sales.

Without the percentage figures, it would not be easy to see how the distribution of sales had changed between 1999 and 2000.

DEVOLVED ASSESSMENT ALERT

In order to draw pie charts accurately in an assessment remember that you will need to use a protractor. You will also need to be able to calculate the number of degrees which will occupy each different sector of the pie by multiplying the percentage value by 360°/100%.

Activity 5.7

The European division of Scent to You Ltd, a flower delivery service has just published its accounts of the year ended 30 June 20X0. The sales director made the following comments.

'Our total sales for the year were £1,751,000, of which £787,000 were made in the United Kingdom, £219,000 in Italy, £285,000 in France and £92,000 in Germany. Sales in Spain and Holland amounted to £189,000 and £34,000 respectively, whilst the rest of Europe collectively had sales of £145,000 in the twelve months to 30 June 20X0.'

Task

Present the above information in the form of a pie chart. Show all of your workings.

Bar charts

3.12 The bar chart is one of the most common methods of presenting data in a visual form.

KEY TERM

A **bar chart** is a chart in which quantities are shown in the form of bars.

3.13 There are a number of types of bar chart.

(a) Simple bar charts
(b) Component bar charts, including percentage component bar charts
(c) Multiple (or compound) bar charts
(d) Histograms, which are a special type of bar chart

Simple bar charts

KEY TERM

A **simple bar chart** is a chart consisting of one or more bars, in which the length of each bar indicates the magnitude of the corresponding data item.

3.14 EXAMPLE: SIMPLE BAR CHART

A company's total sales for the years from 20X1 to 20X6 are as follows.

Year	£'000
20X1	800
20X2	1,200
20X3	1,100
20X4	1,400
20X5	1,600
20X6	1,700

The data could be shown on a simple bar chart as follows.

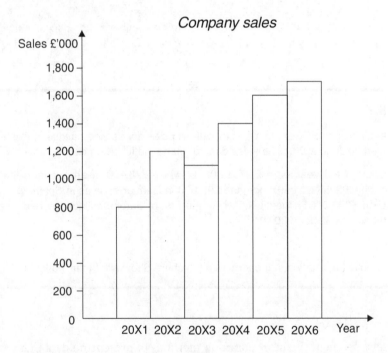

3.15 Each axis of the chart must be clearly labelled, and there must be a scale to indicate the magnitude of the data. Here, the y axis includes a scale for the amount of sales, and so readers of the bar chart can see not only that sales have been rising year by year (with 20X3 being an exception) but also what the actual sales have been each year.

3.16 Simple bar charts serve two purposes.

(a) They show the actual magnitude of each item.

(b) They enable you to compare magnitudes, by comparing the lengths of bars on the chart.

Component bar charts

> ### KEY TERM
>
> A **component (or multiple or compound) bar chart** is a bar chart that gives a breakdown of each total into its components.

3.17 EXAMPLE: COMPONENT BAR CHART

Charbart plc's sales for the years from 20X7 to 20X9 are as follows.

	20X7	*20X8*	*20X9*
	£'000	£'000	£'000
Product A	1,000	1,200	1,700
Product B	900	1,000	1,000
Product C	500	600	700
Total	2,400	2,800	3,400

3.18 A component bar chart would show the following.

- How total sales have changed from year to year
- The components of each year's total

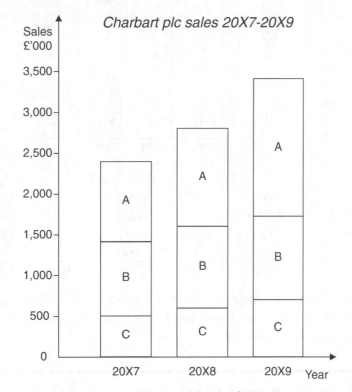

3.19 The bars in a component bar chart can be drawn in the following ways.

- Side by side
- With no gap between them
- With gaps between them, as in the diagram here

3.20 In this diagram the growth in sales is illustrated and the significance of growth in product A sales as the reason for the total sales growth is also fairly clear. The growth in product A sales would have been even clearer if product A had been drawn as the bottom element in each bar instead of the top one.

Percentage component bar charts

3.21 The difference between a component bar chart and a percentage component bar chart is that with a component bar chart, **the total length of each bar** (and the length of each component in it) **indicates magnitude**. A bigger amount is shown by a longer bar. With a percentage component bar chart, total magnitudes are not shown. If two or more bars are drawn on the chart, the total length of each bar is the same. The only varying lengths in a percentage component bar chart are the lengths of the sections of a bar, which vary according to the relative sizes of the components. So it is a bit like a pie chart with the sections drawn in a row instead of in a circle.

3.22 EXAMPLE: PERCENTAGE COMPONENT BAR CHART

(a) In a percentage component bar chart, **all the bars are of the same height**. The information in the earlier example of sales of Charbart plc (paragraph 3.17) could have been shown in a percentage component bar chart as follows.

Workings	20X7		20X8		20X9	
	£'000	%	£'000	%	£'000	%
Product A	1,000	42	1,200	43	1,700	50
Product B	900	37	1,000	36	1,000	29
Product C	500	21	600	21	700	21
Total	2,400	100	2,800	100	3,400	100

(b) This chart shows that sales of C have remained a steady proportion of total sales, but the proportion of A in total sales has gone up quite considerably, while the proportion of B has fallen correspondingly.

Information for Activities 5.8 and 5.9

TAA is a trading company. The sales of its four products P, Q, R and S over the period 20X0-20X2 were as follows.

		Units sold		
	P	*Q*	*R*	*S*
20X0	560	330	810	400
20X1	620	300	760	520
20X2	650	270	710	670

Activity 5.8

You have been asked to carry out the following tasks.

(a) Represent the data given above in the form of a percentage component bar chart.

(b) Comment on the trends in sales of the products.

Activity 5.9

Given that selling prices were £3.50, £5.00, £3.00 and £6.50 for products P, Q, R and S respectively throughout 20X0-20X2, calculate the percentage change in TAA's total sales revenue between 20X0 and 20X2, and comment upon your result.

Multiple bar charts (compound bar charts)

> **KEY TERM**
>
> A **multiple bar chart (or compound bar chart)** is a bar chart in which two or more separate bars are used to present sub-divisions of data.

3.23 EXAMPLE: MULTIPLE BAR CHART

(a) The output of Rodd Ltd in the years from 20X6 to 20X8 is as follows.

	20X6 *'000 units*	*20X7* *'000 units*	*20X8* *'000 units*
Product X	180	130	50
Product Y	90	110	170
Product Z	180	180	125
Total	450	420	345

(b) The data could be shown in a multiple bar chart as follows.

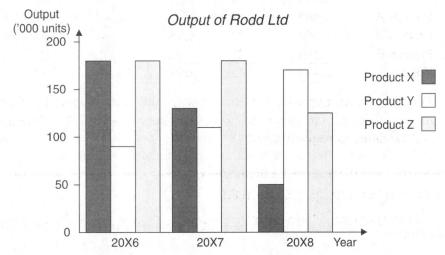

3.24 A multiple bar chart uses **several bars for each total.** In the above example, the sales in each year are shown as **three separate bars,** one for each product, X, Y and Z. Multiple bar charts are sometimes drawn with the bars **horizontal** (extending from the y axis) instead of vertical.

3.25 Multiple bar charts present similar information to component bar charts, except that:

(a) **multiple bar charts do not show the grand total** (in the above example, the total output each year) whereas component bar charts do;

(b) **multiple bar charts illustrate the comparative magnitudes** of the components more clearly than component bar charts.

DEVOLVED ASSESSMENT ALERT

In an assessment, you will probably be told the type of chart that you are required to draw. If not, then you need to think carefully about the information that you are trying to communicate in your graph. For example, if you wish information about grand totals to be communicated, you will probably want to draw a **component bar chart** since this type of chart conveys such information. If however, it is more important to communicate the comparative magnitudes, then you will probably want to draw a **multiple bar chart**.

Histograms

KEY TERM

A **histogram** is a form of bar chart but with important differences. It is used when **grouped data of a continuous variable** are presented. It can also be used for discrete data, by treating the data as continuous so there are no gaps between class intervals: for example with an athlete's times in the 100 metres, using $\geq 9.75 < 10.0, \geq 10.00 < 10.25, \geq 10.25, < 10.5$ etc.

3.26 The number of observations in a class is represented by **the area covered by the bar**, rather than by its height.

3.27 EXAMPLE: HISTOGRAMS

(a) The weekly wages of employees of Salt Lake Ltd are as follows.

Wages per employee	Number of employees
> £ 40 ≤ £ 60	4
> £ 60 ≤ £ 80	6
> £ 80 ≤ £ 90	6
> £ 90 ≤ £120	6
> £120 ≤ £150	3

The class intervals for wages per employee are not all the same, and range from £10 to £30. This is because basic wages are supplemented by overtime payments for certain employees of some grades and not others.

(b) A histogram is drawn as follows.

Step 1. The **width** of each bar on the chart is proportionate to the corresponding class interval. In other words, the bar representing wages of > £40 ≤ £60, a range of £20, will be twice as wide as the bar representing wages of > £80 ≤ £90, a range of only £10.

Step 2. For the purpose of calculating the height of the bar, a **standard width of bar** is selected. This should be the size of class interval which occurs most frequently. In our example, class intervals of £20 and £30 each occur twice. An interval of £20 will be selected as the standard width.

Step 3. Each frequency is then:

- divided by the actual class interval;
- multiplied by the standard class interval;

to obtain the **height** of the bar in the histogram.

Class interval	Size of interval	Frequency	Adjustment	Height of bar
> £ 40 ≤ £ 60	£20	4	× 20/20	4
> £ 60 ≤ £ 80	£20	6	× 20/20	6
> £ 80 ≤ £ 90	£10	6	× 20/10	12
> £ 90 ≤ £120	£30	6	× 20/30	4
> £120 ≤ £150	£30	3	× 20/30	2

(c) Note the following points.

   (i) The bars are drawn with their width as the **actual class interval**, and the height as calculated.

   (ii) Because the class intervals of the first two bars are the same as the standard interval (20), the heights of the bars are the same as the class frequencies.

   (iii) The third bar will be twice as high as the class frequency (6) would suggest, to compensate for the fact that the class interval, £10, is only half the standard size.

   (iv) The fourth and fifth bars will be two thirds as high as the class frequencies (6 and 3) would suggest, to compensate for the fact that the class interval, £30, is 150% of the standard size.

Histogram of weekly earnings: Salt Lake Ltd

The advantages and disadvantages of histograms

3.28 Histograms are frequently used to display **grouped frequency distributions graphically**.

   (a) They display clearly the **comparative frequency of occurrence** of data items within classes.

   (b) They indicate whether the range of values is **wide** or **narrow**, and whether most values occur in the **middle** of the range or whether the frequencies are more **evenly spread**.

3.29   Consider these two histograms.

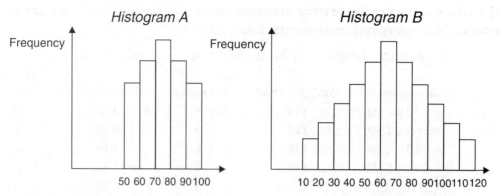

In (A) there is a narrower range of values than in (B). Both have the most frequently occurring value somewhere in the middle of the range (70-80 with A and 60-70 with B).

Now compare these two histograms.

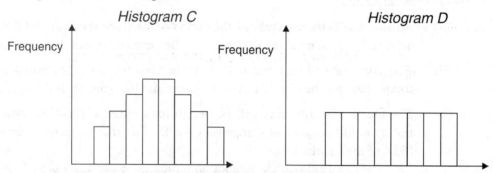

The most frequently occurring values in histogram C are towards the **middle** of the range, whereas in histogram D, values occur with **equal frequency** across the entire range.

3.30   The main disadvantages of histograms are as follows.

(a)   If a histogram represents sample data, the measurements in the histogram might give a **false sense of accuracy**. The sample data will not be an **exact** representation of the population as a whole. This is true, however, of all forms of graphical representation.

(b)   If the histogram is showing data about a **continuous** variable, the sharp steps of the histogram bars would be a little **misleading**.

Frequency polygons

3.31   A histogram can be converted into a **frequency polygon**, which is drawn on the assumption that **within each class interval**, the frequency of occurrence of data items is **not evenly spread**. There will be more values at the end of each class interval nearer the histogram's peak (if any), and so the **flat top on a histogram bar should be converted into a rising or falling line**.

3.32   A frequency polygon is drawn from a histogram as follows.

•   Marking the mid-point of the top of each bar in the histogram
•   Joining up all these points with straight lines

3.33   The ends of the diagram (the mid-points of the two end bars) should be joined to the base line at the mid-points of the next class intervals outside the range of observed data. These intervals should be taken to be of the same size as the last class intervals for observed data.

3.34 EXAMPLE: FREQUENCY POLYGON

The following grouped frequency distribution represents the values on a printing machine's console which is read at the end of every day.

Reading	Number of occasions
> 800 ≤ 1,000	4
> 1,000 ≤ 1,200	10
> 1,200 ≤ 1,400	12
> 1,400 ≤ 1,600	10
> 1,600 ≤ 1,800	4
	40

Prepare a frequency polygon.

3.35 SOLUTION

A histogram is first drawn, in the way described earlier. All classes are of the same width.

Histogram of printing machine readings

The mid-points of the class intervals outside the range of observed data are 700 and 1,900.

Activity 5.10

Your company is preparing its published accounts and the chairman has requested that the assets of the company be compared in a component bar chart for the last five years. The data are contained in the following table.

Asset	20X3	20X4	20X5	20X6	20X7
	£'000	£'000	£'000	£'000	£'000
Property	59	59	65	70	74
Plant and machinery	176	179	195	210	200
Stock and work in progress	409	409	448	516	479
Debtors	330	313	384	374	479
Cash	7	60	29	74	74

Tasks

(a) Construct the necessary component bar chart.
(b) Comment on the movements in the assets over the five year period.

Extraction and interpretation of key information from charts

3.36 The barchart in example 3.14 may be interpreted as follows.

(a) Company sales have risen steadily between 20X1 and 20X6 (from £800,000 to £1,700,000).

(b) Company sales were at their maximum in 20X6 (£1,7000,000).

(c) Company sales have increased each year except for 20X3, when sales dropped from £1,200,000 to £1,100,000 resulting in a fall of £100,000.

(d) The greatest increase in company sales was seen between 20X1 and 20X2 when sales increased by £400,000 (£800,000 to £1,200,000).

(e) The smallest increase in company sales was seen between 20X5 and 20X6 when sales increased by only £100,000 (£1,600,000 to £1,700,000).

Activity 5.11

Luke Skywalker Ltd is preparing its published accounts and the finance director has requested that the turnover of the company be compared in the form of a bar chart for the last five years. The data are contained in the following table.

	1995 £'000	1996 £'000	1997 £'000	1998 £'000	1999 £'000
Turnover	981	1,020	1,121	1,244	1,306

Tasks

(a) Construct a simple bar chart which represents the given data relating to turnover.
(b) Comment on the turnover for Luke Skywalker Ltd over the five year period.

Key learning points

- **Tabulation** means putting data into tables. A **table** is a matrix of data in rows and columns.

- **Charts** often convey the meaning or significance of data more clearly than would a table.

- A **piechart** is used to show in picture form the relative sizes of component elements of a total.

- A **barchart** is a way of presenting data where quantities are shown in the form of bars on a chart. The different types of bar chart are as follows.

  o Simple
  o Component
  o Multiple
  o Histogram

- **Frequency distributions** are used if values of particular variables occur more than once.

Quick quiz

1 What are the main guidelines for tabulation?

2 What are the disadvantages of piecharts?

3 What are the main purposes of simple bar charts?

4 How would you select a standard width of bar when calculating the height of the bars in a histogram?

Answers to quick quiz

1. • The table should have a clear title.
   • All columns should be clearly labelled.
   • Clear sub-totals should be included.
   • Columns should be totalled showing a total figure.
   • Tables should be spaced out, so that the information presented may be read easily.

2. • They show relative sizes of elements, and not actual values.
   • Time consuming calculations which involve calculating degrees of a circle need to be carried out.

3. • To show the actual magnitude of each item.
   • To enable you to compare magnitudes by comparing the lengths of bars on the chart.

4. Select the size of the class interval which occurs most frequently.

Answers to activities

Answer 5.1

The main rules of good tabular presentation are as follows.

(a) The table should be given a clear title.

(b) Each column should be clearly labelled, with a description as well as the units in which the items are being measured.

(c) There must not be too many columns, or else the reader of the table will become confused. A maximum of ten columns could be a guideline to follow.

(d) Where appropriate there should be clear sub-totals.

(e) A total column may be presented. This would normally be the extreme right hand column.

(f) A total figure at the bottom of each column of figures is often advisable.

(g) Figures should not be given to too many significant figures. An element of rounding will often make the table easier to follow, with significant information being highlighted.

(h) The source of the data should be stated, so that the reader could refer to that source if he wished to take his analysis further.

Answer 5.2

New telephone installations (by company)

Company	Installations (thousands)			
	1960	1970	1980	1990
A Co Ltd	1,810	3,248	5,742	4,932
B Co Ltd	2,114	1,288	3,038	3,138
C Co Ltd	448	1,618	2,228	1,506
Others	874	676	1,646	618
Total	5,246	6,830	12,654	10,194

Answer 5.3

(a)

Company	Installations (percentages)			
	1960	1970	1980	1990
A Co Ltd	34.5	47.6	45.4	48.4
B Co Ltd	40.3	18.8	24.0	30.8
C Co Ltd	8.5	23.7	17.6	14.8
Others	16.7	9.9	13.0	6.0
Total	100.0	100.0	100.0	100.0

(b) A Co Ltd was the second largest installer in 1960, but was the market leader in 1970, 1980 and 1990, with an apparently secure grip on nearly half the market.

B Co Ltd's share of the market dropped sharply between 1960 and 1970, but the company has since been steadily recovering market share.

C Co Ltd did very well between 1960 and 1970, but has not been able to sustain its growth rate, and has lost market share since 1970.

Other companies have maintained a small and variable market share. There is no sign of a serious challenge to the three main companies.

Answer 5.4

The two dimensions of the table should be:

(a)   years;
(b)   each group of employees, including a category for 'others'.

It would also be possible to include percentage growth over the years.

The entries in the 'cells' of the table could be actual numbers of employees, percentages of the total work force or both.

Analysis of employee groups at Healthy Healthfoods Ltd

	1990		1993			1996			1999		
	Number empl'd	% of total	Number empl'd	% of total	% growth in total	Number empl'd	% of total	% growth in total	Number empl'd	% of total	% growth in total
Sales staff	1,176	28	2,372	31	102	4,840	38	104	7,477	36	54
Buyers	1,260	30	2,448	32	94	3,185	25	30	4,362	21	37
Administrative staff	840	20	1,607	21	91	2,550	20	59	3,739	18	47
Other groups	924	22	1,223	16	32	2,165	17	77	5,192	25	140
Total	4,200	100	7,650	100	82	12,740	100	67	20,770	100	63

The table shows that there has been a substantial increase in the number of sales staff over the years, with the percentage of employees who are sales staff rising from under 30% in 1990 to 36% in 1999. There has been a decrease in the proportion of employees who are buyers, and a small decrease in the proportion who are administrative staff. The managing director's concern about the rapid growth in other groups of employees might be justified. The percentage increase in their numbers between 1996 and 1999 suggests that efforts to control their numbers have not yet had much success.

Answer 5.5

(a)   The purpose of tabulating data is to make information easier to read and interpret. It is possible to include much information in a relatively compact table, and tables are particularly suitable for numerical data. Organising data into a table with appropriate columns and row headings allows the reader to make comparisons between categories easily.

(b)   *Patients seen by doctors 1990 and 1995*

	1990						1995					
	Minor ailment		Major ailment		Total		Minor ailment		Major ailment		Total	
	No	%	No	%	No	%	No	%	No	%	No	%
Men	234	9.2	416	16.3	650	25.5	320	11.0	430	14.8	750	25.8
Women	360	14.1	440	17.3	800	31.4	550	19.0	510	17.6	1,060	36.6
Children	616	24.2	484	18.9	1,100	43.1	720	24.8	370	12.8	1,090	37.6
Total	1,210	47.5	1,340	52.5	2,550	100.0	1,590	54.8	1,310	45.2	2,900	100.0

(c)   (i)   In 1995, a lower percentage of all patients had major ailments but a higher percentage had minor ailments than in 1990.

(ii)   In 1995, a lower percentage of children but a higher percentage of women were seen by doctors than in 1990.

(iii)   In 1995, a lower percentage of children patients had major ailments (33.9% as against 44.0%) and a higher percentage of women patients had minor ailments (51.9% as against 45.0%) than in 1990.

Answer 5.6

We are told what classes to use, so the first step is to identify the lowest and highest values in the data. The lowest value is £25 (in the first row) and the highest value is £73 (in the fourth row). This means that the class intervals must go up to '£70 and under £75'.

We can now set out the classes in a column, and then count the number of items in each class using tally marks.

Class interval	Tally marks	Total
£25 and less than £30	///	3
£30 and less than £35	////	4
£35 and less than £40	## ##	10
£40 and less than £45	## ## ##	15
£45 and less than £50	## ## ## ///	18
£50 and less than £55	## ## ## ##	20
£55 and less than £60	## ## ///	13
£60 and less than £65	## ///	8
£65 and less than £70	## /	6
£70 and less than £75	///	3
Total		100

You should be able to *interpret* tabulated data, and express an interpretation in writing. In this activity, an interpretation of the data is fairly straightforward.

(a) Commission per assistant for August 20X0 ranged between £25 and £75.

(b) Most commissions were in the middle of this range, with few people earning commissions in the lower and upper ends of the range.

Answer 5.7

Workings	Sales £'000		Degrees
United Kingdom	787	(787/1,751 × 360)	162
Italy	219		45
France	285		58
Germany	92		19
Spain	189		39
Rest of Europe	145		30
Holland	34		7
	1,751		360

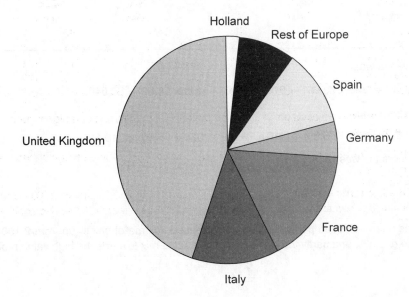

Scent to you Ltd
Sales for the year ended 30 June 20X0

BPP PUBLISHING

Answer 5.8

Tutorial note. In a percentage component bar chart, all the bars are the same height. Only proportions are indicated, not absolute magnitudes.

(a)   The percentages required for the bar chart are as follows.

Year	Percentage of total units sold			
	P	Q	R	S
20X0	26.7	15.7	38.6	19.0
20X1	28.2	13.6	34.6	23.6
20X2	28.3	11.7	30.9	29.1

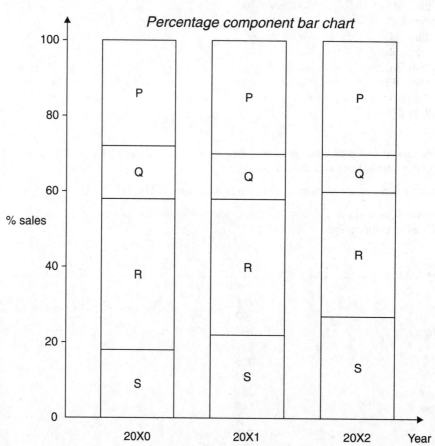

(b)   Product S is clearly becoming increasingly important in relative terms and product R is becoming correspondingly less important. Product Q's sales are also falling in percentage terms, and product P's sales are growing slightly in percentage terms. All these trends are also apparent in the figures for units sold.

Answer 5.9

In 20X0, total revenue was

(560 × £3.50) + (330 × £5.00) + (810 × £3.00) + (400 × £6.50) = £8,640.

In 20X2, total revenue was

(650 × £3.50) + (270 × £5.00) + (710 × £3.00) + (670 × £6.50) = £10,110.

The percentage increase was

$$\frac{10,110-8,640}{8,640} \times 100\% = 17\%$$

This increase has been achieved partly through an increased volume of sales (up from 2,100 units to 2,300 units, an increase of 9.5%) and partly through a shift in the sales mix towards the high value product S.

Answer 5.10

(a) Acceptable bar charts could be drawn vertically or horizontally.

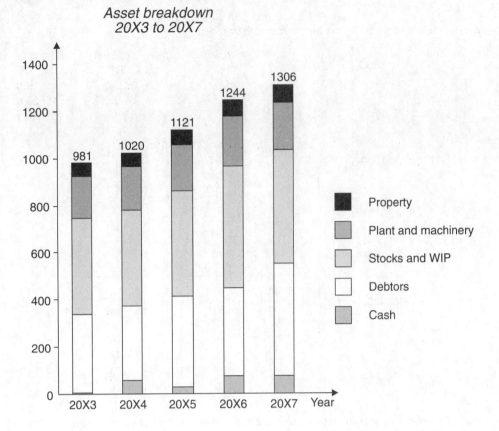

*Asset breakdown
20X3 to 20X7*

(b) The bar chart clearly shows that total assets have risen steadily over the five year period. Property remained static from 20X3 to 20X4, and showed only small increases from then on. Plant and machinery and stocks and work in progress both rose slowly from 20X3 to 20X4 and more steeply from 20X4 to 20X6, and then declined from 20X6 to 20X7. Debtors have behaved unevenly but with an increasing trend: total assets rose from 20X6 to 20X7 only because of the large increase in debtors over this period. Cash balances have also behaved unevenly but they exhibit an increasing trend over the five year period.

BPP PUBLISHING

Answer 5.11

(a)

Luke Skywalker Ltd
Turnover 1995 - 1999

(b) The bar chart clearly shows that turnover has increased steadily between 1995 and 1999. Turnover increased by the greatest amounts between 1997 and 1998 (£123,000 (£1,244,000 – £1,121,000)) and by the smallest amount between 1995 and 1996 (£39,000 (£1,020,000 – £981,000).

Chapter 6   Averages and time series

Chapter topic list

1   Averages

2   The analysis of time series

Learning objectives

On completion of this chapter you will be able to:

	Performance criteria	Range statement
• prepare reports in the appropriate form and present them to management within the required timescales	7.1.6	7.1.3
• *analyse time series*	n/a	n/a

Italicised objectives are areas of knowledge and understanding underlying the elements of competence for Unit 7.

BPP PUBLISHING

1 AVERAGES

1.1 The standards of competence for Unit 6 require you to know and understand **time series analysis**, which involves statistics recorded over a period of time. Before looking at time series analysis in detail in the next section of this chapter, we need to be clear about the concept of an **average**.

KEY TERM

An **average** is a representative figure that is used to give some impression of the size of all the items in a population.

1.2 The three main types of average used are as follows.

- The arithmetic mean
- The mode
- The median

1.3 An average, whether it is a mean, a mode or a median, is a **measure of central tendency**. By this we mean that while a population may range in values, these values will be distributed around a **central point**. This central point, or average, is therefore in some way **representative** of the population as a whole.

The arithmetic mean

1.4 This is the best known type of average. For ungrouped data, it is calculated by the formula shown below.

KEY TERM

$$\text{Arithmetic mean} = \frac{\text{Sum of values of items}}{\text{Number of items}}$$

1.5 EXAMPLE: ARITHMETIC MEAN

The demand for a product on each of 20 days was as follows (in units).

    3 12 7 17 3 14 9 6 11 10 1 4 19 7 15 6 9 12 12 8

The **arithmetic mean** of daily demand is calculated as follows.

$$\frac{\text{Sum of daily demand}}{\text{Number of days}} = \frac{185}{20} = 9.25 \text{ units}$$

The arithmetic mean of a variable x is shown as $\bar{x}$ ('**x bar**').

Thus in the above example $\bar{x}$ = 9.25 units.

1.6 In the above example, demand on any one day is never actually 9.25 units. The arithmetic mean is merely an **average representation** of demand on each of the 20 days.

The arithmetic mean of data in a frequency distribution

1.7 The concept of the frequency distribution was explained earlier. In our previous example, the frequency distribution would be shown as follows.

Daily demand *x*	*Frequency* *f*	*Demand × frequency* *fx*
1	1	1
3	2	6
4	1	4
6	2	12
7	2	14
8	1	8
9	2	18
10	1	10
11	1	11
12	3	36
14	1	14
15	1	15
17	1	17
19	1	19
	20	185

$$\bar{x} = \frac{185}{20} = 9.25$$

Sigma, Σ

1.8 The statistical notation for the arithmetic mean of a set of data uses the symbol Σ (sigma).

KEY TERM

Σ **(sigma)** means 'the sum of' and is used as shorthand to mean the sum of a set of values.

Thus, in the previous example:

(a) Σ f would mean the sum of all the frequencies, which is 20.

(b) Σ fx would mean the sum of all the values of 'frequency multiplied by daily demand', that is, all 14 values of fx, so Σ fx = 185.

The symbolic formula for the arithmetic mean

1.9 Using the Σ sign, the formula for the arithmetic mean of a frequency distribution is given as follows.

KEY TERM

Arithmetic mean of a frequency distribution, $\bar{x} = \dfrac{\Sigma fx}{n}$ or $\dfrac{\Sigma fx}{\Sigma f}$

where n is the number of values recorded, or the number of items measured.

The arithmetic mean of grouped data in class intervals

1.10 Another common problem is to calculate (or at least approximate) the arithmetic mean of a frequency distribution, where the frequencies are shown in **class intervals**.

1.11 EXAMPLE: ARITHMETIC MEAN OF GROUPED DATA

Using the example in Paragraph 1.5, the frequency distribution might have been shown as follows.

Daily demand	Frequency
> 0 ≤ 5	4
> 5 ≤ 10	8
> 10 ≤ 15	6
> 15 ≤ 20	2
	20

An arithmetic mean is calculated by taking **the mid point of each class interval**, on the assumption that the frequencies occur evenly over the class interval range. Note that the variable is **discrete**, so the first class includes 1, 2, 3, 4 and 5, giving a mid point of 3. With a **continuous variable** (such as quantities of fuel consumed in litres), the mid points would have been 2.5, 7.5 and so on.

Daily demand	Mid point	Frequency	
	x	f	fx
> 0 ≤ 5	3	4	12
> 5 ≤ 10	8	8	64
> 10 ≤ 15	13	6	78
> 15 ≤ 20	18	2	36
		Σf = 20	Σfx = 190

Arithmetic mean $\bar{x} = \dfrac{\Sigma fx}{\Sigma f} = \dfrac{190}{20} = 9.5$ units

Because the assumption that frequencies occurred evenly within each class interval is not quite correct in this example, giving a Σfx total of 190 not 185, our mean of 9.5 is not exactly correct, and is in error by 0.25. This is known as an **approximating error**. As the frequencies become larger, its size becomes smaller. Usually frequency distributions are a great deal larger than this so there is no need to be concerned if you produce an approximating error in your calculations.

Activity 6.1

For the week ended 29 May, the wages earned by the 69 operators employed in the machine shop of Mechaids Ltd were as follows.

Wages	Number of operatives
under £ 60	3
£60 and under £ 70	11
£70 and under £ 80	16
£80 and under £ 90	15
£90 and under £100	10
£100 and under £110	8
£110 and under £120	6
	69

Task

Calculate the arithmetic mean wage of the machine operators of Mechaids Ltd for the week ended 29 May.

The mode

> **KEY TERM**
>
> The **mode** is an average which means 'the most frequently occurring value'.

1.12 EXAMPLE: THE MODE

The daily demand for stock in a ten day period is as follows.

Demand Units	Number of days
6	3
7	6
8	1
	10

The mode is 7 units, because it is the value which occurs **most frequently**.

The mode in grouped frequency distributions

1.13 In a grouped frequency distribution, the mode can only be **estimated approximately**.

1.14 The method of making this estimate is as follows.

Step 1. Establish which is the class with the highest frequency (the modal class).

Step 2. The mode is taken as

$$L + \frac{(F_1 - F_0) \times c}{2F_1 - F_0 - F_2}$$

where   L   =   the lower limit of the modal class
        F_0 =   the frequency of the next class below the modal class
        F_1 =   the frequency of the modal class
        F_2 =   the frequency of the next class above the modal class
        c   =   the width of the modal class (class interval)

1.15 This formula only works if the modal class, the next class below it and the next class above it all have the same class interval.

1.16 EXAMPLE: THE MODE IN GROUPED FREQUENCY DISTRIBUTIONS

Calculate the mode of the following frequency distribution.

Value		Frequency
At least	*Less than*	
10	25	6
25	40	19
40	55	12
55	70	7
70	85	3

1.17 SOLUTION

The modal class is the class with the **highest frequency**, that is, the class between 25 and 40, so L is 25. The class interval (c) is 15. F_1 is 19, the frequency of the modal class. F_0 is the frequency of the class below the model class, that is the class 10-25, which is 6. F_2 is the frequency of the class 40-55, which is 12.

The estimated mode is:

$$25 + \frac{(19 - 6) \times 15}{(2 \times 19) - 6 - 12}$$

$$= \quad 25 + \frac{(13 \times 15)}{(38 - 18)}$$

$$= \quad 25 + 9.75$$

$$= \quad 34.75$$

The median

1.18 The third type of average is the **median**.

> **KEY TERM**
>
> The **median** is the value of the middle member of a distribution.

1.19 The median of a set of ungrouped data is found by arranging the items in ascending or descending order of value, and **selecting the item in the middle of the range**. A list of items in order of value is called an **array**.

1.20 EXAMPLE: THE MEDIAN

The median of the following nine values:

| 8 | 6 | 9 | 12 | 15 | 6 | 3 | 20 | 11 |

is found by taking the middle item (the fifth one) in the array:

| 3 | 6 | 6 | 8 | 9 | 11 | 12 | 15 | 20 |

The median is 9.

The median of the following ten values

| 8 | 6 | 7 | 2 | 1 | 11 | 3 | 2 | 5 | 2 |

would be the fifth item in the array, that is 3.

| 1 | 2 | 2 | 2 | 3 | 5 | 6 | 7 | 8 | 11 |

With an even number of items, we could take the arithmetic mean of the two middle ones (in this example, $(3 + 5)/2 = 4$, but when there are many items it is not worth doing this.

The median of an ungrouped frequency distribution

1.21 The median of an ungrouped frequency distribution is found in a similar way but we have to keep a running total of how many times things have occurred - **a cumulative frequency**. Thus the median of the following distribution is as follows.

Value x	Frequency f	Cumulative frequency
8	3	3
12	7	10 (3 + 7)
16	12	22 (10 + 12)
17	8	30 (22 + 8)
19	5	35 (30 + 5)
	35	

would be the $(35 + 1)/2 = $ 18th item. The 18th item has a value of 16, as we can see from the cumulative frequencies in the right hand column of the above table.

The median of a grouped frequency distribution

1.22 The median of a grouped frequency distribution, like the arithmetic mean and the mode, can only be **estimated approximately**.

1.23 The method of making this estimate is as follows.

Step 1. First, we must find the class to which the middle item belongs (the median class).

Step 2. We then use the following formula.

$$\text{Median} = L + \left(\frac{R}{f} \times c\right)$$

where L is the lower limit of the median class

c is the size of the class interval of the class

f is the frequency of the class

R is the difference between the middle item ($(n + 1)/2$ for odd n, $n/2$ for even n) and the cumulative total of frequencies up to the end of the preceding class.

1.24 EXAMPLE: MEDIAN OF A GROUPED FREQUENCY DISTRIBUTION

The average monthly earnings of 135 employees of Comedian Ltd have been analysed as a grouped frequency distribution as follows.

Average monthly earnings More than £	Not more than £	No of employees	Cumulative frequency
120	140	12	12
140	160	49	61
160	180	25	86
180	200	18	104
200	220	17	121
220	240	14	135
		135	

What are the median monthly earnings of employees of Comedian Ltd?

1.25 SOLUTION

The middle item is the (135 + 1)/2 = 68th item. This occurs in the class £160 – £180.

$$\text{Median} = £160 + (\frac{(68 - 61)}{25} \times £20) = £165.60$$

Activity 6.2

The following grouped frequency distribution gives the annual wages of 200 employees in an engineering firm.

Wages £	Number of employees
5,000 and less than 5,500	4
5,500 and less than 6,000	26
6,000 and less than 6,500	133
6,500 and less than 7,000	35
7,000 and less than 7,500	2

Task

Calculate the mean, the median and the mode of annual wages.

Comparing different types of average

1.26 Above, we have looked at three types of average. Below is a summary of their **advantages** and **disadvantages**. You will get a better understanding of these if you consider them in the light of how they apply to examples of averages given in newspapers and news broadcasts (eg 'the average family contains 2.4 children').

1.27 The **advantages** of the **arithmetic mean** are as follows.

- It is widely understood.
- The value of every item is included in the computation of the mean.
- It is well suited to further statistical analysis.

The **disadvantages** of the **arithmetic mean** are as follows.

(a) **Its value may not correspond to any actual value**. For example, the 'average' family might have 2.4 children, but no family has exactly 2.4 children.

(b) **An arithmetic mean might be distorted by extremely high or low values**. For example, the mean of 3, 4, 4 and 6 is 4.25, but the mean of 3, 4, 4, 6 and 15 is 6.4. The high value, 15, distorts the average and in some circumstances the mean would be a misleading and inappropriate figure.

1.28 The **mode** will be a more appropriate average to use than the mean in situations where it is useful to know the **most common value**. For example, if a manufacturer wishes to start production in a new industry, it might be helpful to know what sort of product made by the industry is most in demand with customers.

1.29 The **advantages** of the mode are as follows.

- It is easy to find
- It is uninfluenced by a few extreme values

1.30 The main **disadvantages** of the mode are as follows.

- It ignores dispersion around the modal value
- Unlike the mean, does not take every value into account
- It is unsuitable for further statistical analysis

1.31 The **median** is only of interest where there is a **range of values** and the middle item is of some significance. Perhaps the most suitable application of the median is in **comparing changes** in a 'middle of the road' value over time.

The median (like the mode) is **unaffected by extremely high or low values**. On the other, its disadvantages are as follows.

- It fails to reflect the full range of values
- Is unsuitable for further statistical analysis

What is a weighted average?

1.32 (a) Suppose you went shopping and spent £36.40 as follows.

Item	Cost
	£
CD	13.00
Cassette	9.00
Book	6.00
Battery	3.40
Lunch	5.00
	36.40

What would you say was the average cost of the items you bought that afternoon?

The total cost was £36.40, and five items were purchased, so the average unit cost was

$$\frac{£36.40}{5} = £7.28$$

(b) But now suppose that instead of just £36.40, you went out and spent a total of £135 as follows.

Item	Number purchased	Cost per item	Total cost
		£	£
CDs	3	13.00	39
Cassettes	5	9.00	45
Books	2	6.00	12
Batteries	10	3.40	34
Lunch	1	5.00	5
	21		135

Now what is the average unit cost of your purchases that afternoon?

The total cost was £135, and 21 items were purchased, so the average unit cost was

$$\frac{£135}{21} = £6.43$$

(c) What has happened here? In the first example, average cost was £7.28 but in the second example - even though the same sort of items were being purchased - average cost dropped to £6.43. Why should that be?

(d) The answer is that in the first example, only one of each item was purchased. So the CD, cassette, book, battery and lunch were all given equal **weight** when it came to working out the average cost.

1.33 In the second example, different numbers of each item were purchased, so they were given **different weights** when the average cost was calculated. For instance, twice as many batteries were bought as cassettes, so the 'weight' for battery cost was twice that for cassette cost. Now you can see why the average cost came down in the second example - more 'weight' was being given to the items which cost less.

Multiplying by the weight

1.34 If somebody had asked us to work out the simple average cost of a book, CD, cassette, battery and lunch, we would have quickly calculated £7.28 as in paragraph 1.32 (a).

1.35 If somebody had asked us to work out the average of two books, three CDs, five cassettes, ten batteries and a lunch, we would first have to multiply the cost of each item by a weight. In this example, the appropriate weight is simply the number of items bought (ie 2, 3, 5, 10 and 1). The result of our calculations is therefore called a **weighted average**.

1.36 The weighted average in the above example happens to be the same as the arithmetic mean of an ungrouped frequency distribution, because all we are doing is multiplying values by their frequency and dividing by the total frequency. In other words, we are working out $\frac{\Sigma fx}{\Sigma f}$, which is the formula for the **arithmetic mean of an ungrouped distribution**. So for this example, it is not too difficult to see what the weighted average is, and what weights to use. But sometimes it is not so obvious to see what the weight should be.

1.37 EXAMPLE: SIMPLE AND WEIGHTED AVERAGE

Sarah, Lisa and Nicole all invest in a business. Sarah invests £10,000 on 1 January 20X8, Lisa invests £18,000 on 1 May 20X8 and Nicole invests £8,000 on 1 October 20X8. What was their average investment for 20X8:

(a) ignoring the dates when they made their investments; and
(b) having regard to the dates when they made their investments?

1.38 SOLUTION

If no account is taken of the investment dates, the average investment is simply £12,000.

$$\text{Average investment} = \frac{£(10,000 + 18,000 + 8,000)}{3}$$

$$= \frac{£36,000}{3}$$

$$= £12,000$$

This is a **simple average** of the three investments.

1.39 The simple average is clearly not a very sensible average, because investments made at the start of the year are in the business longer than those investments made at the end of the year. What we have to do is work out a **weighted average**, and in this example the amounts invested are **weighted** by the number of months they have been invested.

	Investment £	No of months invested	No of months × investment
Sarah	10,000	12	120,000
Lisa	18,000	8	144,000
Nicole	8,000	3	24,000
		23	288,000

So the weighted average investment is $\dfrac{£288,000}{23} = £12,521.74$

DEVOLVED ASSESSMENT ALERT

When completing an assessment, do make sure that you have a reliable calculator with you in order to calculate averages and time series quickly and accurately. Make sure also that you have a spare set of batteries or a spare calculator - and beware of the dangers of using a solar powered calculator!

When is a weighted average used?

1.40   A weighted average will be used whenever a simple average fails to give an accurate reflection of the **relative importance of the items being averaged**.

1.41   We have already seen one use of a weighted average in the accounting field - that of **determining the usefulness of investments** to a business during a year, when those investments were made at different times. Other uses of the weighted average include **calculating the average cost of a product** which is made up from different amounts of components which have different prices. This sort of problem is also dealt with by the use of **index numbers**, which we will look at in the next chapter.

Moving averages

1.42   **Moving averages** are a special type of average used in connection with time series analysis, which we look at in the next section of this chapter.

Information for activities 6.3 and 6.4

The cost accountant of Ware Howser Ltd has calculated standard costs for handling items of stock in a warehouse. The costs are based on the labour time required to deal with stock movements, and are as follows.

Time required for job of handling stock Minutes		Standard cost £
Less than	10	9
≥ 10 and up to	20	11
≥ 20 and up to	40	13
≥ 40 and up to	60	15
≥ 60 and up to	90	23
≥ 90 and up to	120	29
≥ 120 and up to	180	38

The warehouse operates a working day of seven hours per man, and a five-day week. There are 12 men employed. Only one man works on each stock movement.

An examination of the time sheets for a typical week showed that the following costs had been incurred.

Standard cost	Frequency
£	
9	240
11	340
13	150
15	120
23	20
29	20
38	10

Activity 6.3

Using the information above, estimate the mean handling time for a stock movement.

Activity 6.4

(a) Using the information above, estimate the total number of hours in the week spent actively moving items of stock.

(b) What is the percentage capacity utilisation of the labour force in the warehouse?

2 THE ANALYSIS OF TIME SERIES

KEY TERM

A **time series** is a series of figures or values recorded over time.

2.1 Examples of time series are as follows.

- Output at a factory each day for the last month
- Monthly sales over the last two years
- Total annual costs for the last ten years
- The Retail Prices Index each month for the last ten years
- The number of people employed by a company each year for the last 20 years

KEY TERM

A **historigram** is a graph of a time series. (Note the 'r' and the second 'i'; this is not the same as a histogram.)

2.2 For example, consider the following time series.

Year	Sales
	£'000
20X0	20
20X1	21
20X2	24
20X3	23
20X4	27
20X5	30
20X6	28

The historigram is as follows.

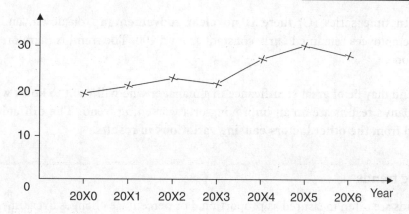

2.3   Note the following points.

- The horizontal axis is always chosen to represent time
- The vertical axis represents the values of the data recorded

2.4   There are several features of a time series which it may be necessary to identify. These are as follows.

- A trend
- Seasonal variations or fluctuations
- Cycles, or cyclical variations
- Non-recurring, random variations

The trend

> **KEY TERM**
>
> The **trend** or 'underlying trend' is the underlying long-term movement over time in the values of the data recorded.

2.5   The following examples of time series show three types of trend.

	Output per labour hour (units)	Cost per unit £	Number of employees
20X4	30	1.00	100
20X5	24	1.08	103
20X6	26	1.20	96
20X7	22	1.15	102
20X8	21	1.18	103
20X9	17	1.25	98
	(A)	(B)	(C)

(a)   In time series (A) there is a **downward** trend in the output per labour hour. Output per labour hour did not fall every year, because it went up between 20X5 and 20X6, but **the long-term movement is clearly a downward one**.

(b)   In time series (B) there is an **upward** trend in the cost per unit. Although unit costs went down in 20X7 from a higher level in 20X6, **the basic movement over time is one of rising costs**.

(c)   In time series (C) there is **no clear movement up or down,** and the number of employees remained fairly constant around 100. The trend is therefore a **static,** or level one.

2.6   A trend may be of great significance to a manager who will want to know whether his or her company's results are on an improving or a worsening trend. **The difficulty is to isolate a trend from the other factors causing variations in results.**

Measuring trends

2.7   Trends are often measured as proportional or percentage changes over time.

For example, if a company's sales are £1,000,000 in 20X8 and £1,200,000 in 20X9, the increase in sales in 20X9 compared with 20X8 is

$$\frac{£200,000}{£1,000,000} \times 100\% = 20\%$$

2.8   EXAMPLE: MEASURING TRENDS

You must always interpret trends carefully. Study the following statements carefully to see if you can spot weaknesses in them.

(a)   Sales of hods went up by 50% this year, whereas sales of zods went up by only 10%. Hods are a much more successful product than zods.

(b)   Accidents at work went up by 200% last year. This is a serious situation and immediate extra safety measures should be taken.

(c)   The workforce has consisted of 1,000 full-time employees over the past four years. Absentee days from work have been as follows.

	Employee days	*Rate of increase*
		%
20X1	3,000	20
20X2	3,600	20
20X3	4,284	19
20X4	5,055	18

The rate of increase in absenteeism is falling, and so the situation is being brought under control.

2.9   SOLUTION

(a)   Statement (a) might be true, but it might not be. It all depends on the actual volume or value of sales of each product. Suppose the actual figures are as follows.

	Sales this year	*Sales last year*	*Growth in sales*
	£	£	%
Hods	3,000	2,000	50
Zods	110,000	100,000	10

Which would *you* regard as the more successful product here, hods with 50% sales growth to £3,000 or zods with 10% sales growth to £110,000?

(b)   Statement (b) might also be true, but again it might be untrue. It all depends on how many accidents there were last year and this year. Is the actual number a significant amount? Were last year's accident figures abnormally low? If the number of accidents rose from just 1 last year to 3 this year, we might conclude that safety at work is still very good, particularly if the workforce is very large.

(c) Statement (c) is highly misleading. The rate of increase in absenteeism has gone down from 20% to 19% to 18% per annum, but absenteeism is still rising, by 600 in 20X2, 684 in 20X3 and 771 in 20X4. The actual annual increase in days lost through absenteeism is rising each year, a sign that the situation is far from being brought under control.

Finding the trend

2.10 There are three principal methods of finding a trend from time series data.

(a) **Inspection**. The trend line can be drawn by eye on a graph in such a way that it appears to lie evenly between the recorded points.

(b) **Regression analysis by the least squares method**. This is a statistical technique to calculate the '**line of best fit**'. This method, which we do not need to discuss in detail here, makes the assumption that the trend line, whether up or down, is a **straight line**. Periods of time (such as quarters for which sales figures are given) are numbered, commonly from 0, and the regression line of the data on those period numbers is found. That line is then taken to be the trend.

(c) **Moving averages**. This method attempts to **remove seasonal (or cyclical) variations** by a process of averaging.

Moving averages

> **KEY TERM**
>
> A **moving average** is an average of the results of a fixed number of periods.

2.11 Since a moving average is an average of several time periods, it is related to the mid-point of the overall period.

2.12 Moving averages could, for example, cover the sales of a shop over periods of seven days (Monday to the next Sunday, Tuesday to the next Monday, Wednesday to the next Tuesday, and so on), or a business's costs over periods of four quarters, or whatever else was appropriate to the circumstances.

2.13 EXAMPLE: MOVING AVERAGES

Year	Sales (units)
20X0	390
20X1	380
20X2	460
20X3	450
20X4	470
20X5	440
20X6	500

Task

Take a moving average of the annual sales over a period of three years.

2.14 SOLUTION

(a) Average sales in the three year period 20X0 - 20X2 were

$$\frac{390 + 380 + 460}{3} = \frac{1,230}{3} = 410.$$

This average relates to the middle year of the period, 20X1.

(b) Similarly, average sales in the three year period 20X1 - 20X3 were

$$\frac{380 + 460 + 450}{3} = \frac{1,290}{3} = 430.$$

This average relates to the middle year of the period, 20X2.

(c) The average sales can also be found for the periods 20X2 - 20X4, 20X3 - 20X5 and 20X4 - 20X6, to give the following.

Year	Sales	Moving total of 3 years sales	Moving average of 3 years sales (÷ 3)
20X0	390		
20X1	380	1,230	410
20X2	460	1,290	430
20X3	450	1,380	460
20X4	470	1,360	453.3
20X5	440	1,410	470
20X6	500		

Note the following points.

(a) The moving average series has five figures relating to the years from 20X1 to 20X5. The original series had seven figures for the years from 20X0 to 20X6.

(b) There is an **upward trend** in sales, which is more noticeable from the series of moving averages than from the original series of **actual** sales each year.

2.15 The above example averaged over a three year period. Over what period should a moving average be taken? The answer to this question is that **the moving average which is most appropriate will depend on the circumstances and the nature of the time series.**

2.16 Note the following points.

(a) A moving average which takes an average of the results in many time periods will **represent results over a longer term** than a moving average of two or three periods.

(b) On the other hand, with a moving average of results in many time periods, **the last figure in the series will be out of date by several periods.** In our example, the most recent average related to 20X5. With a moving average of five years results, the final figure in the series would relate to 20X4.

(c) When there is a known cycle over which seasonal variations occur, such as all the days in the week or all the seasons in the year, the most suitable moving average would be one which covers **one full cycle.**

Activity 6.5

What is a moving average? For what purpose are such averages used?

Activity 6.6

Sales in pounds of a particular product for the last five years have been: 100, 110, 108, 112, 106.

Calculate a 3-year moving average to the nearest pound.

Activity 6.7

What is meant by the 'underlying trend' in a time series?

Seasonal variations

> **KEY TERM**
>
> **Seasonal variations** are short-term fluctuations in recorded values, due to different circumstances which affect results at different times of the year, on different days of the week, at different times of day, or whatever.

2.17 Here are some examples.

(a) Sales of ice cream will be higher in summer than in winter, and sales of overcoats will be higher in autumn than in spring.

(b) Shops might expect higher sales shortly before Christmas, or in their winter and summer sales.

(c) Sales might be higher on Friday and Saturday than on Monday.

(d) The telephone network may be heavily used at certain times of the day (such as mid-morning and mid-afternoon) and much less used at other times (such as in the middle of the night).

2.18 'Seasonal' is a term which may appear to refer to the seasons of the year, but its meaning in time series analysis is somewhat broader, as the examples given above show.

2.19 EXAMPLE: SEASONAL VARIATIONS

The number of customers served by a company of travel agents over the past four years is shown in the following historigram.

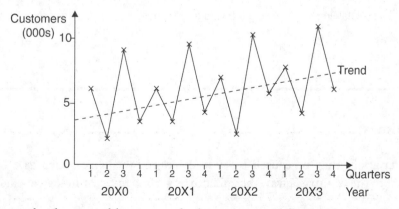

In this example, there would appear to be **large seasonal fluctuations** in demand, but there is also a **basic upward trend**.

Cyclical variations

2.20 In business, cyclical variations are commonly associated with **economic cycles**, successive booms and recessions in the economy. **In a boom,** the rate of increase in economic activity (economic growth) is **higher than normal,** while in a **recession**, the level of economic activity (the output of goods and services) is **falling**.

2.21 Economic cycles may last a few years. Cyclical variations are **longer-term than seasonal variations**.

Activity 6.8

The following figures relate to the sales (in tens of thousands) of widgets during the period 1985 to 2000.

Year	Sales
1985	55
1986	52
1987	45
1988	48
1989	65
1990	70
1991	62
1992	55
1993	58
1994	75
1995	80
1996	77
1997	55
1998	73
1999	85
2000	90

Task

Draw a graph showing the sales year by year for the period and superimpose on it the five year moving average line.

Activity 6.9

Write brief notes explaining the following terms to a colleague.

(a) The mean
(b) The median
(c) Time series.

Random variations

2.22 Random variations may be caused by unforeseen circumstances, such as a change in the government of the country, a war, the collapse of a company, technological change or a fire.

Key learning points

- An **average** is a **measure of central tendency**. The three main types of average are:
  - the arithmetic mean
  - the mode
  - the median

- The **arithmetic mean** is widely understood and well suited to further statistical analysis. The value of every item is included in the computation of the mean.

- The **mode** is a more appropriate average to use than the mean where it is useful to know the most common value.

- The **median** is of interest only where there is a range of values and the middle item is of some significance.

- **Weighted averages** take account of the relative importance of the items being averaged.

- A **time series** is a series of figures or values recorded over time.

- A **graph** of a time series is called a **historigram**.

- The **trend** in a time series is the underlying long term movement over time in the values of the data recorded. Trends must always be interpreted with care.

- **Seasonal variations** are short-term fluctuations in recorded values, resulting from different circumstances which affect results in different periods.

- **Cyclical variations** are medium-term changes resulting from circumstances which repeat in cycles.

- The trend, seasonal variations and cyclical variations need to be distinguished from **random** or **one-off variations** in a set of results over a period of time.

Quick quiz

1. What is the median of the following numbers?

   23 21 20 32 71 50 23 19 19

2. What are the main advantages of the arithmetic mean?

3. What are the main disadvantages of the mode?

4. What is the weighted average of the following books?

   > 12 × Great Britain Road Atlas (£10 each)
   > 3 × Price and Prejudice (£7 each)
   > 9 × The Little Book of Calm (£2 each)

5. What is the name of the graph of a time series?

6. What are the main identifiable features of a time series?

7. What is a moving average?

8. What are seasonal variations?

9. What are cyclical variations?

Answers to quick quiz

1. 23

2. - It is widely understood
   - The value of every item is included in the computation of the mean
   - It is well suited to further statistical analysis

3. - It ignores dispersion around the modal value
   - It does not take every value into account
   - It is unsuitable for further statistical analysis

4    $\dfrac{[(12 \times £10) + (3 \times £7) + (9 \times £2)]}{12 + 3 + 9}$ = $\dfrac{120 + 21 + 18}{24}$

= $\dfrac{£159}{24}$ = £6.625

5   Historigram

6   • A trend
     • Seasonal variations or fluctuations
     • Cycles or cyclical variations
     • Non-recurring, random variations

7   An average of the results of a fixed number of periods.

8   Short-term fluctuations in recorded values, due to different circumstances which affect results at different times of the year, on different days of week and so on.

9   Changes in results caused by circumstances which repeat in cycles.

Answers to activities

Answer 6.1

The mid point of the range 'under £60' is assumed to be £55, since all other class intervals are £10. This is obviously an approximation which might result in a loss of accuracy; nevertheless, there is no better alternative assumption to use. Note that the mid points of the classes are half way between their end points, because wages can vary in steps of only 1p and so are virtually a continuous variable.

Mid point of class	Frequency	
x	*f*	*fx*
£		
55	3	165
65	11	715
75	16	1,200
85	15	1,275
95	10	950
105	8	840
115	6	690
	69	5,835

Arithmetic mean = $\dfrac{£5,835}{69}$ = £84.57

Answer 6.2

(a)   *The mean*

Mid point	Frequency		fx	Cumulative frequency
x	*f*			
£				
5,250	4		21,000	4
5,750	26		149,500	30
6,250	133		831,250	163
6,750	35		236,250	198
7,250	2		14,500	200
	Σf 200		Σfx 1,252,500	

Mean = $\dfrac{\Sigma fx}{\Sigma f}$

= $\dfrac{1,252,500}{200}$ = £6,262.50

(b)   The median value is the value of the 100th item.

$$\text{Median} = L + \left(\frac{R}{f} \times c\right)$$

$$= \pounds6,000 + \left(\frac{100 - 30}{133} \times \pounds500\right)$$

$$= \pounds6,000 + \pounds263.16$$

$$= \pounds6,263.16$$

(c)   The modal value is in the range £6,000 and less than £6,500. It is estimated as follows.

$$\text{Mode} = L + \frac{(F_1 - F_0) \times c}{2F_1 - F_0 - F_2}$$

$$= \pounds6,000 + \frac{(133 - 26) \times \pounds500}{(2 \times 133) - 26 - 35}$$

$$= \pounds6,000 + \frac{\pounds53,500}{205}$$

$$= \pounds6,260.98$$

Answer 6.3

In order to calculate the mean handling time, we need to work with the frequency distribution for handling time.

Handling time		Mid-point of range	Frequency	fx
At least	Less than			
			(x)	(f)
-	10	5	240	1,200
10	20	15	340	5,100
20	40	30	150	4,500
40	60	50	120	6,000
60	90	75	20	1,500
90	120	105	20	2,100
120	180	150	10	1,500
			900	21,900

So the mean handling time is given by:

$$\bar{x} = \frac{\Sigma fx}{\Sigma f} = \frac{21,900}{900} = 24.33 \text{ minutes}$$

Answer 6.4

(a)   The estimated number of minutes spent handling stock each week is $\Sigma fx = 21,900$ minutes. Therefore the estimated number of hours is given by:

$$\frac{21,900}{60} = 365 \text{ man hours per week}$$

(b)   There are 12 men each of whom work seven hours a day for five days a week. So the total number of hours available each week is given by:

$12 \times 7 \times 5 = 420$ hours per week

So the percentage utilisation each week (using the answer to part (a)) is:

$$\frac{365}{420} \times 100\% = 86.9\%$$

Answer 6.5

When a time series is given, an average may be taken of n consecutive values at a time (such as values for four quarters or for five years). The first n values are averaged, then the n values starting with the second value, and so on. Thus the average moves forward through the time series, and is called a moving average.

117

Moving averages can be used to smooth out short-term variations, and thus disclose the trend.

Answer 6.6

Year	Sales £	3-year total £	3-year moving average £
1	100		
2	110	318 (yrs 1, 2, 3)	106
3	108	330 (yrs 2, 3, 4)	110
4	112	326 (yrs 3, 4, 5)	109
5	106		

Answer 6.7

The underlying trend is the trend which is revealed by removing the effect of cyclical, seasonal and random variations in time series data.

Answer 6.8

Tutorial note. A five year moving average is found simply by adding figures five at a time and dividing the result by five. Because five is an odd number, the averages are automatically centred on actual years.

The five year moving average must first be calculated.

Year	Sales	Five year total	Five year average
1985	55		
1986	52		
1987	45	265	53
1988	48	280	56
1989	65	290	58
1990	70	300	60
1991	62	310	62
1992	55	320	64
1993	58	330	66
1994	75	345	69
1995	80	345	69
1996	77	360	72
1997	55	370	74
1998	73	380	76
1999	85		
2000	90		

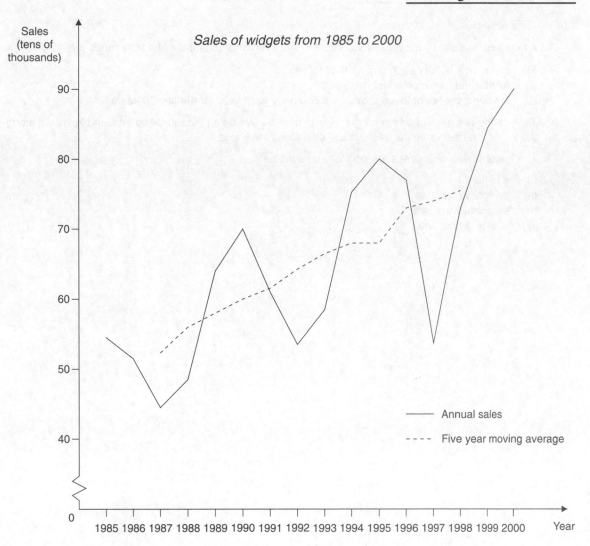

Sales of widgets from 1985 to 2000

Answer 6.9

(a)   *The mean*

The *arithmetic mean* is the best known and most widely used average. The arithmetic mean of some data is the sum of the data, divided by the number of items in the data. It is widely used because it gives a convenient and readily understood indication of the general size of the data, it takes account of all items of data and it is suitable for further mathematical analysis. On the other hand, its value can be unduly influenced by a few very large or very small items of data.

(b)   *The median*

The median is the value of the middle member of a set of data, once the data have been arranged in either ascending or descending order. It is one sort of average and it has the following properties.

(i)   It is fairly easy to obtain.
(ii)   It is not affected very much by extreme values.
(iii) It is not generally suitable for further statistical analysis.

The median may be more useful than the arithmetic mean in certain circumstances, for instance when determining the average salary of the employees in a company. Since a few employees might have very high salaries, the arithmetic mean could be drawn upwards by these, out of the range of salaries earned by most employees. The mean would then not be representative. The median, however, would be the item in the middle of the ranking, which would be within the range of salaries earned by most employees.

(c)   *Time series*

A time series is simply a series of values recorded over time. Examples of a time series are:

(i)   output at a factory each day for the last month;
(ii)   monthly sales over the last two years;
(iii)   the number of people employed by a company each year for the last 20 years.

Time series are often shown on a graph, with time always being the independent variable shown along the x axis, and the values at each time shown along the y axis.

The features of a time series are normally taken to be:

(i)   a trend;
(ii)   cyclical variations;
(iii)   seasonal variations;
(iv)   random variations.

Chapter 7   Allowing for changing price levels

Chapter topic list

1   Indexation
2   Multi-item price indices
3   Chain based index numbers
4   Limitations of index numbers
5   Using index numbers in comparing results

Learning objectives

On completion of this chapter you will be able to:

	Performance criteria	Range statement
• use an appropriate method that allows for changing price levels when comparing results over time	7.1.3	7.1.1
• *use index numbers*	n/a	n/a

Italicised objectives are areas of knowledge and understanding underlying the elements of competence for Unit 7.

1 INDEXATION

The need for index numbers

1.1 If we are making comparisons of costs and revenues over time to see how well an organisational unit is performing, we need to take account of the fact that the unit is operating within an economic environment in which general shifts in costs (ie prices) take place. If a business achieves an increase in sales of 10% in monetary (cash) terms over a year, this result becomes less impressive if we are told that there was general price inflation of 15% over the year. If the business has raised its prices in line with this inflation rate of 15%, then a 10% increase in sales in cash terms indicates a fall in the physical volume of sales. The business is now selling less at the new higher prices.

1.2 In the financial accounting field, there has been much debate over whether the financial results declared in the annual report of companies should be adjusted to reflect inflation. Understandably, the amount of debate on this subject has tended to be greater in periods of high inflation.

1.3 When results of a business are being compared over a period of time for internal management purposes, it is up to managers of the business to agree and use an appropriate method of allowing for changing price levels. The usual method is to use a series of **index numbers**.

What is an index number?

> **KEY TERM**
>
> An **index** is a measure, over a period of time, of the average changes in the values (prices or quantities) of a group of items.

1.4 An example is the **'cost of living'** index. This is made up of a large variety of items including bread, butter, meat, rent, insurance and so on. The raw data giving the prices of each commodity for successive years would be confusing and useless to most people; but a **simple index** stating that the cost of living index is 145 for 1999 compared with 100 for 1993 is easily understood.

Price indices and quantity indices

1.5 An index may be a **price index** or a **quantity index**.

> **KEY TERM**
>
> A **price index** measures the change in the money value of a group of items over a period of time.

(a) Perhaps the most well-known price index in the UK is the Retail Prices Index (RPI) which measures changes in the costs of items of expenditure of the average household, and which used to be called the 'cost of living' index. Another example which you may have heard reported in the news is the FT-SE (or 'footsie') 100 share index, which measures how the top 100 share prices in general have performed from one day to the next.

> **KEY TERM**
>
> A **quantity index** measures the change in the non-monetary values of a group of items over a period of time.

(b) A well-known example is a productivity index, which measures changes in the productivity of various departments or groups of workers.

As we shall see, a suitable price index provides a method of allowing for changing price levels when comparing costs or revenues over time.

Index points

1.6 The term '**points**' is used to measure the difference in the index value in one year with the value in another year. In the example given above the cost of living index rose 45 points between 1993 and 1999 (ie rose from an index of 100 to 145).

1.7 Points are used for measuring changes in an index because they provide an easy method of arithmetic. The alternative is to use percentages, because indices are based on percent-ages, as we shall see.

The base period, or base year

1.8 Index numbers are normally expressed as **percentages**, taking the value for a **base date** as 100. The choice of a base date or base year is not significant, except that it should normally be 'representative'. In the construction of a **price index**, the base year preferably should not be one in which there were abnormally high or low prices for any items in the 'basket of goods' making up the index.

Calculation of an index

1.9 Suppose sales for a company over the last five years were as follows.

Year	Sales (£'000)
20X5	35
20X6	42
20X7	40
20X8	45
20X9	50

The managing director decided that he wanted to set up a sales index (ie an index which measures how sales have done from year to year), using 20X5 as the base year. The £35,000 of sales in 20X5 is given the index 100%. What are the indices for the other years?

1.10 If £35,000 = 100%, then:

(a) £42,000 $= \dfrac{42,000}{35,000} \times 100\% = 120\%$

(b) £40,000 $= \dfrac{40,000}{35,000} \times 100\% = 114\%$

(c) £45,000 $= \dfrac{45,000}{35,000} \times 100\% = 129\%$

(d) £50,000 $= \dfrac{50,000}{35,000} \times 100\% = 143\%$

1.11 Now the table showing sales for the last five years can be completed, taking 20X5 as the base year.

Year	Sales (£'000)	Index
20X5	35	100
20X6	42	120
20X7	40	114
20X8	45	129
20X9	50	143

1.12 EXAMPLE: PRICE INDEX

If the price of a cup of coffee in the Café Frederick was 40p in 20X0, 50p in 20X1 and 76p in 20X2, using 20X0 as a base point the price index numbers for 20X1 and 20X2 would be:

$$\text{20X1 price index} = \frac{50}{40} \times 100 = 125$$

$$\text{20X2 price index} = \frac{76}{40} \times 100 = 190$$

1.13 EXAMPLE: QUANTITY INDEX

Similarly, if the Café Frederick sold 500,000 cups of coffee in 20X0, 700,000 cups in 20X1, and 600,000 in 20X2, then quantity index numbers for 20X1 and 20X2, using 20X0 as a base year, would be:

$$\text{20X1 quantity index} = \frac{700,000}{500,000} \times 100 = 140$$

$$\text{20X2 quantity index} = \frac{600,000}{500,000} \times 100 = 120$$

Activity 7.1

Fill in the words missing from the following.

The period for which the value of an index is taken to be 100 (or 1,000 or 1.00) is called the _____ period. Changes in the prices faced by UK manufacturers are tracked by the _____ indices published by the Office for National Statistics.

Activity 7.2

The price index of a company's major raw material is:

1995	1996	1997	1998	1999
100	110	112	106	120

Recalculate the index for the years 1998 and 1999 using 1997 as the base year. (Answers to the nearest whole number.)

Activity 7.3

A price index measuring the price of a litre of milk over the period 20X0-20X3 is as follows.

Year	Index
20X0	96
20X1	98
20X2	100
20X3	113

Tasks

(a) What year has been chosen for the base year of this index, as far as you can tell from the table above? 20X2

(b) By how many points has the index risen between 20X0 and 20X2? 4

(c) By what percentage has the index risen between 20X0 and 20X2? 4

(d) If a litre of milk cost £0.54 in 20X1, how much did it cost in 20X3? $\frac{54}{98} \times 113 = £0.62$

2 MULTI-ITEM PRICE INDICES

2.1 In the examples we have seen so far in this chapter, it is not really necessary to calculate an index, because only one product or item has been under consideration. Knowing that sales have risen by 20% from £35,000 to £42,000, for instance, is just as informative as knowing that the index has risen 20 points (from 100 to 120). There was no real need to calculate the index.

2.2 Most practical indices are made up of more than one item. For example, suppose that the cost of living index is calculated from only three commodities: potatoes, coffee and beef and that the prices for 20X1 and 20X5 were as follows.

	20X1	*20X5*
Potatoes	20p a bag	40p a bag
Coffee	25p a jar	30p a jar
Beef	450p a kilo	405p a kilo

2.3 An examination of these figures reveals three main difficulties.

(a) Two prices have gone up and one has gone down. The index number must be a compromise.

(b) The prices are given in different units.

(c) There is no indication of the relative importance of each item.

Nothing can be done about difficulty (a) - it is a feature of index numbers and must always be borne in mind - but (b) and (c) can be overcome by **weighting**, which we saw in Chapter 6 when we were looking at averages.

Weighting the index

2.4 To decide the **weighting** of different items in an index it is necessary to obtain information, perhaps by market research, about the **relative importance** of each item. In our example of a simple cost of living (or retail price) index, it would be necessary to find out how much the average person or household spends per week (or month) on each item in the 'basket' of goods.

2.5 Research may suggest that the average spending by each household in a week was as follows in 20X1 (rounding to the nearest penny).

	Quantity	Price per unit £	Total spending £	% of total spending = weighting factor
Potatoes	6 pounds	20p	1.20	60
Coffee	2 jars	25p	0.50	25
Beef	0.067 kilos	450p	0.30	15
			2.00	100 %

The weighting factor of each item in the index will depend on the proportion of total weekly spending taken up by the item. In our example, the weighting factors of potatoes, coffee and beef would be 60%, 25% and 15% respectively.

2.6 If 20X1 is a base year, the index for 20X5 is obtained as follows.

(a) Calculate the price of each item in 20X5 as a percentage of the price in 20X1. This percentage figure is called a **price relative**, because it shows the new price level of each item relative to the base year price.

(b) Multiply the price relative by the weighting factor for each item in the 'basket of goods' to give a weighted average for each item. The result for all items is added together to give a weighted average total for 20X5.

(c) Make a similar weighted average total for the base year (the price relative for each item will be 100 as it is the base year).

(d) As the base year index = 100, the 20X5 index is:

$$\frac{\text{Weighted average total in 20X5}}{\text{Weighted average total in 20X1}} \times 100$$

2.7 There are two important assumptions.

(a) That the relative quantities of potatoes, coffee and beef consumed each week by the average household did not change between 20X1 and 20X5.

(b) That the 'basket of goods' - ie potatoes, coffee and beef - is still representative of the average household's consumption pattern in 20X5 and in 20X1.

2.8 In our example:

(a) 20X5 price relatives (ie 20X5 prices as a percentage of 20X1 prices):

(i) Potatoes $\dfrac{40p}{20p} \times 100 = 200$

(ii) Coffee $\dfrac{30p}{25p} \times 100 = 120$

(iii) Beef $\dfrac{405p}{450p} \times 100 = 90$

(b) Multiply the 20X5 price relative of each item by the weighting factor of the item to give a weighted average for each item.

Item	Weighting factor	Price relative	Weighted average
Potatoes	60%	200	120
Coffee	25%	120	30
Beef	15%	90	13.5
	100%		163.5

(c) Calculate the weighted averages for the base year 20X1 (total is always 100).

Item	Weighting factor	Price relative	Product
Potatoes	60%	100	60
Coffee	25%	100	25
Beef	15%	100	15
	100%		100

(d) The 20X5 index is:

$$\frac{163.5}{100} \times 100 = 163.5$$

2.9   The formula for a weighted price index of this type may be shown as follows.

KEY TERM

Price index $= \dfrac{\Sigma p_1 w}{\Sigma p_0 w} \times 100$

where p_1 represents prices in the 'new' year

p_0 represents prices in the base year

w is the weighting factor (same for both years).

2.10 A quantity index measures the change in the **non-monetary** values of a group of items. It is calculated in much the same way as a price index, but because it deals with non-monetary values, it ignores any changes in price: there is no need to work out price relatives when calculating a quantity index. We do not look at quantity indices further here.

Activity 7.4

Sales for a company over a five year period were as follows.

Year	Sales £'000
20X5	35
20X6	42
20X7	40
20X8	45
20X9	50

Task

Work out a sales index based on the sales for 20X6 (20X6 sales = 100).

3 CHAIN BASED INDEX NUMBERS

3.1 In all the previous examples in this chapter, we have used a **fixed base** method of indexing, whereby a base year is selected (index 100) and all subsequent changes are measured against this base.

3.2 The **chain base** method of indexing is an alternative approach, whereby (in a price index), the changes in prices are taken as a percentage of the period immediately before.

3.3 This method is suitable where weightings are changing rapidly, and new items are continually being brought into the index and old items taken out.

3.4 EXAMPLE: THE CHAIN BASE METHOD

The price of a particular model of car varied as follows over the years 20X5 to 20X8.

Year	20X5	20X6	20X7	20X8
Price	£10,000	£11,120	£12,200	£13,880

Tasks

(a) Construct a fixed base index for the years 20X5 to 20X8, using 20X6 as the base year.

(b) Construct a chain base index for the years 20X5 to 20X8.

Round all answers to the nearest index point.

3.5 SOLUTION

(a) Constructing a fixed base index is exactly the same sort of problem we have already met in this chapter.

Year		Index
20X5	$\dfrac{10,000}{11,120} \times 100 =$	90
20X6		100
20X7	$\dfrac{12,200}{11,120} \times 100 =$	110
20X8	$\dfrac{13,880}{11,120} \times 100 =$	125

(b) Constructing a chain base index is almost the same, except that the index is always calculated using the percentage increase (or decrease) on the previous year, rather than on a base year.

Year		Index
20X5		100
20X6	$\dfrac{11,120}{10,000} \times 100 =$	111
20X7	$\dfrac{12,200}{11,120} \times 100 =$	110
20X8	$\dfrac{13,800}{12,200} \times 100 =$	114

3.6 The chain base index shows the rate of change in prices from year to year, whereas the fixed base index shows the change more directly against prices in the base year.

DEVOLVED ASSESSMENT ALERT

Remember that the index number of the base year is normally 100. The base year should not be a year in which prices were abnormally high or low, so if you are asked to select a base year in an assessment, make sure that your choice of year is 'representative' and that you can give reasons for your choice.

Activity 7.5

Bone is a popular brand of dog food. It is produced by mixing the four ingredients B, O, N and E, in the proportions 6, 5, 4 and 3 respectively.

Indices of the cost prices of the four ingredients for the years 20X5 to 20X8, using 20X4 as the base year are as follows.

	20X5	20X6	20X7	20X8
B	103	107	115	120
O	104	111	118	123
N	107	113	117	121
E	102	106	110	118

Tasks

(a) For each of the years 20X5 to 20X8, calculate the material cost index of Bone.
(b) For 20X8, calculate the material cost index using 20X7 as the base year.

Activity 7.6

A chart like that below was published to show sales per employee of the supermarket chain Tesco, which rose from £77,200 in 1986 to £99,400 in 1990.

Tesco: sales per employee

The average Retail Prices Index in the years 1986 to 1990 was as follows (January 1987 = 100).

	RPI
1986	97.8
1987	101.9
1988	106.9
1989	115.2
1990	126.2

Task

Comment on the significance of the data and on the way in which it has been presented.

---

4   LIMITATIONS OF INDEX NUMBERS

4.1   Index numbers are easy to understand and fairly easy to calculate, so it is not surprising that they are frequently used. However, they are not perfect and it is as well to bear in mind the following points.

(a)   **Index numbers are usually only approximations** of changes in price (or quantity) over time, and must be interpreted with care and reservation.

(b)   **Weighting factors become out of date as time passes**. Unless a chain base index is used, the weightings will gradually cease to reflect the current 'reality'.

(c)   **New products or items may appear, and old ones cease to be significant.** For example, spending has changed in recent years, to include new items such as mobile phones, PCs and video recorders, whereas the demand for large black and white televisions and spin dryers has declined. These changes would make the weightings of a retail price index for consumer goods out of date and the base of the index would need revision.

(d)   **Sometimes, the data used to calculate index numbers might be incomplete, out of date, or inaccurate.** For example, the quantity indices of imports and exports are based on records supplied by traders which may be prone to error or even falsification.

(e)   The base year of an index should be a 'normal' year, but there is probably no such thing as a perfectly normal year. **Some error in the index will be caused by untypical values in the base period.**

(f)   **The 'basket of items' in an index is often selective.** For example, the Retail Prices Index (RPI) is constructed from a sample of households and, more importantly, from a basket of only about 600 items.

(g)   **A national index cannot necessarily be applied to an individual town or region.** For example, if the national index of wages and salaries rises from 100 to 115, we cannot state that the following statements are necessarily true.

(i)   The wages and salaries of people in, say, Birmingham, have gone up from 100 to 115.

(ii)   The wages and salaries of each working individual have gone up from 100 to 115.

(h)   **An index may exclude important items,** for example, the RPI excludes payments of income tax out of gross wages.

Misinterpretation of index numbers

4.2 You must be careful not to misinterpret index numbers. Several possible mistakes will be explained using the following example of a retail price index.

20X0		*20X1*		*20X2*	
January	340.0	January	360.6	January	436.3
		February	362.5	February	437.1
		March	366.2	March	439.5
		April	370.0	April	442.1

(a) It would be wrong to say that prices rose by 2.6% between March and April 20X2. It is correct to say that prices rose 2.6 **points,** or

$$\frac{2.6}{439.5} = 0.6\%$$

(b) It would be wrong to say that because prices are continually going up, then there must be rising inflation. If prices are going up, then there must be **inflation**. But is the rate of price increases going up, or is the rate slowing down? In our example, it so happens that although the trend of prices is still upwards, the rate of price increase (inflation) is slowing down. For example:

(i) Annual rate of inflation, March 20X1 to March 20X2

$$\frac{439.5 - 366.2}{366.2} \times 100 = 20\%$$

(ii) Annual rate of inflation, April 20X1 to April 20X2

$$\frac{442.1 - 370.0}{370.0} \times 100 = 19.5\%$$

The **rate of inflation** has dropped from 20% per annum to 19.5% per annum between March and April 20X2, even though prices went up in the month between March and April 20X2 by 0.6%.

(c) It is also wrong to state that the average annual rate of inflation between January 20X0 and January 20X2 is:

$$\frac{1}{2} \text{ of } \frac{436.3 - 340.0}{340.0} = 14.2\% \text{ per annum}$$

The reason for this is that the annual increase has been compounded, ie it has been multiplied by itself. To calculate the average annual increase over the two years we must use a square root.

$$\text{Average annual increase} = (\sqrt{\frac{436.3}{340.0}} - 1) \times 100 = 13.3\% \text{ per annum}$$

5 USING INDEX NUMBERS IN COMPARING RESULTS

5.1 For the purpose of internal management reporting, results recorded over a number of periods can be adjusted using an appropriate price index to convert the figures from money terms to '**real' terms**.

5.2 As well as the Retail Prices Index (RPI) - also known as the General Index of Retail Prices - which measures the average level of prices of goods and services purchased by most households in the United Kingdom, the Office for National Statistics publishes a large number of producer price indices for different sectors of industry as well as index numbers

BPP
PUBLISHING

of agricultural prices. These indices track changes in prices facing businesses in different industries. Annual average figures for these indices covering the previous five years are published in the *Annual Abstract of Statistics*. Someone needing to track the trend in prices of raw material inputs could use the Index of Producer Prices: Materials and Fuels, which measures prices of goods as they enter the factory. The price of finished manufactured goods is tracked by the Index of Producer Prices: Manufactured Products, which is sometimes called a measure of 'factory gate prices'.

5.3　The various price indices for specific industry sectors will usually provide a more useful way of comparing results in different periods than more general indices such as the RPI. The RPI measures price changes over a varied 'basket' of retail goods and services, including housing costs. The price trends facing a wholesaler or producer in any particular industry may be very different.

5.4　Once the index to be used is agreed, the index is 'rebased' to the period required and the various data are adjusted by the rebased index.

5.5　EXAMPLE: USING INDEX NUMBERS (1)

Fuchsias Unlimited is a garden centre that specialises in all varieties of fuchsia. The following information is available for the years 20X5-20X9.

	20X5	20X6	20X7	20X8	20X9
Sales value (£)	20,000	26,000	30,780	28,710	36,000
Selling price per fuchsia (£)	1.25	1.30	1.35	1.45	1.60
UK Retail Price Index	125.1	127.4	129.6	133.0	136.9

Calculate the number of fuchsias sold in the years 20X5-20X9 and the sales values at 20X9 prices (to 2 decimal places).

5.6　SOLUTION

	20X5	20X6	20X7	20X8	20X9
Number of fuchsias sold					
(Sales value ÷ selling price)	16,000	20,000	22,800	19,800	22,500
Sales value at 20X9 prices (£)	21,886.49	27,938.78	32,513.75	29,551.87	36,000

Sales value at 20X9 prices

$$20X5 \quad = \quad £20,000 \times \frac{136.9}{125.1} \quad = \quad £21,886.49$$

$$20X6 \quad = \quad £26,000 \times \frac{136.9}{127.4} \quad = \quad £27,938.78$$

$$20X7 \quad = \quad £30,780 \times \frac{136.9}{129.6} \quad = \quad £32,513.75$$

$$20X8 \quad = \quad £28,710 \times \frac{136.9}{133.0} \quad = \quad £29,551.87$$

$$20X9 \quad = \quad £36,000 \times \frac{136.9}{136.9} \quad = \quad £36,000$$

5.7　Let us now look at an example which considers the way in which index numbers may be used to compare the results over several years of a particular model of lawnmower.

5.8 EXAMPLE: USING INDEX NUMBERS (2)

(a) Loving Lawns Ltd manufactures a range of lawnmowers. The sales for one of its most popular models, the Baritone for the periods 20X5 to 20Y0 were as follows.

	£'000
20X5	3,422
20X6	3,608
20X7	3,862
20X8	4,036
20X9	4,072
20Y0	4,114

(b) The trend in Baritone sales is to be expressed at 20Y0 prices, using the producer price index numbers for lawnmowers set out below (the base year is 20X5). The year-on-year 'real' change in sales is then to be calculated.

	Producer price index
20X5	100.0
20X6	106.3
20X7	110.4
20X8	115.4
20X9	120.1
20Y0	125.7

5.9 SOLUTION

(a)

	Rebased index (20Y0=100)	*Sales* £'000	*Sales at 20Y0 Prices* £'000	*Real year-on-year increase* %
20X5	79.6	3,422	4,299	
20X6	84.6	3,608	4,265	– 0.8
20X7	87.8	3,862	4,399	+ 3.1
20X8	91.8	4,036	4,397	0.0
20X9	95.5	4,072	4,264	– 3.0
20Y0	100.0	4,114	4,114	– 3.5

(b) Each index number is rebased to 20Y0 by dividing it by the 20Y0 index number and multiplying by 100. For example:

$$20X9: \frac{120.1}{125.7} \times 100 = 95.5$$

(c) Sales at 20Y0 prices are calculated by dividing the sales figures in cash terms by the rebased index and multiplying by 100. The real year-on-year increase is the percentage change in sales at 20Y0 prices over the previous year.

(d) Costs in a business may be adjusted in a similar way, using an appropriate index.

DEVOLVED ASSESSMENT ALERT

It is unlikely that you will be required to calculate index numbers in an assessment, but you will almost certainly be required to **use** them. It is most likely that you will be given a series of indices covering a number of periods, and that you will need to make adjustments to financial data using the given index numbers. The example in Paragraph 5.6 gives an indication of the way in which you might be required to **use** index numbers in a devolved assessment.

5.10 EXAMPLE: DEFLATION

Mick Payne works for Eastleigh Ltd. Over the last five years he has received an annual salary increase of £500. Despite his employer assuring him that £500 is a reasonable annual salary increase, Mick is unhappy because, although he agrees £500 is a lot of money, he finds it difficult to maintain the standard of living he had when he first joined the company.

Consider the figures below.

Year	(a) Wages £	(b) RPI	(c) Real wages £	(d) Real wages index
1	12,000	250	12,000	100.0
2	12,500	260	12,019	100.2
3	13,000	275	11,818	98.5
4	13,500	295	11,441	95.3
5	14,000	315	11,111	92.6

(a) This column shows Mick's wages over the five-year period.

(b) This column shows the current RPI.

(c) This column shows what Mick's wages are worth taking prices, as represented by the RPI, into account. The wages have been deflated relative to the new base period (year 1). Economists call these deflated wage figures **real wages**. The real wages for years 2 and 4, for example, are calculated as follows.

Year 2: £12,500 × 250/260 = £12,019

Year 4: £13,500 × 250/295 = £11,441

(d) This column is calculated by dividing the entries in column (c) by £12,000, his starting salary.

$$\text{Real index} = \frac{\text{current value}}{\text{base value}} \times \frac{\text{base indicator}}{\text{current indicator}}$$

So, for example, the real wage index in year 4 $= \frac{£13,500}{£12,000} \times \frac{250}{295} = 95.3$

The real wages index shows that the real value of Mick's wages has fallen by 7.4% over the five-year period. In real terms he is now earning £11,111 compared to £12,000 in year 1. He is probably justified, therefore, in being unhappy.

Activity 7.7

The MN Company's sales over the last four years, together with the Retail Prices Index for each of the years is as follows.

	Year 1	Year 2	Year 3	Year 4
Sales £'000	27,500	29,680	32,535	34,455
Retail Prices Index	217	228	246	268

Tasks

Remove the effect of increased prices from the annual sales figures (ie deflate the sales figures) and comment on the result.

Activity 7.8

Your company wishes to construct a price index for three commodities, A, B and C. The prices in 20X0 were £2, £3 and £5 respectively and quantities consumed in the same period were 5,000, 6,000 and

3,000 respectively. The prices for 20X1 and 20X2 are given as percentages of 20X0 prices.

	20X1	*20X2*
A	100	110
B	108	115
C	90	100

Task

You are required to construct a price index using 20X0 as a base point.

Activity 7.9

The following information relates to Lily Ltd's sales figures for the four quarters in 20X9.

	20X9			
	Quarter 1	*Quarter 2*	*Quarter 3*	*Quarter 4*
	£	£	£	£
Sales revenue	533,280	495,700	525,400	506,210

The sales director has requested that in addition to reporting quarterly sales figures in the sales report, he would like the accounting technician to adjust these sales figures to take account of price rises. He has identified suitable indices as follows.

First quarter 20X8 (Base period)	=	179.1
First quarter 20X9	=	184.2
Second quarter 20X9	=	189.4
Third quarter 20X9	=	185.9
Fourth quarter 20X9	=	187.6

Calculate the adjusted sales figures to be included in the sales report (to the nearest whole number).

Activity 7.10

The mean weekly take-home pay of the employees of Staples Ltd and a price index for the 11 years from 20X0 to 20Y0 are as follows.

Year	*Weekly wage*	*Price index (20X0 = 100)*
	£	
20X0	150	100
20X1	161	103
20X2	168	106
20X3	179	108
20X4	185	109
20X5	191	112
20X6	197	114
20X7	203	116
20X8	207	118
20X9	213	121
20Y0	231	123

Task

Construct a time series of real wages for 20X0 to 20Y0 using a price index with 20X6 as the base year.

'Cash' and 'real' terms in the public sector: GDP deflator

5.11   It is recognised in public sector organisations as well as in the private sector that in order to form a judgement about what has happened to unit costs in real terms over a period of years, it may be necessary to show the past figures **on a consistent price basis by applying a price index**.

5.12   The Treasury recommends that public sector agencies use for this purpose an index called the **GDP deflator**, which measures **the extent of price change year by year** in the economy as a whole. Other indices may be used to measure **productivity**, but in accordance with long-standing mandatory government decisions, in the public sector 'real terms' applies only to figures which are 'deflated' by the GDP deflator.

5.13   A target for the unit cost of output of a public sector agency might be expressed in **cash** or in **'real' terms**. Cash figures will need to be adjusted to real terms in order to assess whether such a target has been reached.

5.14   EXAMPLE: UNIT COST TARGETS IN REAL TERMS

The Certification Agency (a fictitious government agency) has been set a target for 20X1-X2 of reducing the unit cost of issuing a certificate by 2.5% in real terms. The unit cost in cash terms was £8.62 in 20X1-X2, compared with £8.42 in 20X0-X1. The GDP deflator had an average value of 104.6 for 20X1-X2 (20X0-X1 = 100). Did the agency meet its target?

5.15   SOLUTION

	Unit cost £	GDP deflator	Real unit cost £	Real unit cost decrease
20X0-X1	8.42	100.0	8.42	
20X1-X2	8.62	104.6	8.24	2.1%

The real unit cost is shown at 20X0-X1 prices by dividing the 20X1-X2 unit cost by the GDP deflator and multiplying by 100. The real unit cost has decreased by 2.1%, but the agency has failed to meet its target of a 2.5% decrease.

Recent price index values

5.16   Examples of some of the main annual average price indices in recent years are set out in the table below.

Year	General Index of Retail Prices	Producer prices Materials and fuels by manufacturing industry
1987	100.0	
1988	106.9	95.4
1989	115.2	100.7
1990	126.1	100.0
1991	133.5	97.9
1992	138.5	97.4
1993	140.7	101.8
1994	144.1	100.4
1995	149.1	114.4
1996	152.7	113.1

Source: *Annual Abstract of Statistics*, 1998 edition

Key learning points

- **Index numbers** are used to make comparisons of costs and revenues over time, in order to see how well an organisational unit is performing.

- An index may be a **price index** or a **quantity index.**

- The index number for a **base year** is normally 100. The base year is chosen as a representative year.

- Index numbers are easy to calculate and understand. They do however have a number of limitations.

- **Weighting** is used to reflect the importance of each item in the index.

- Index numbers are used to compare the results of a business recorded over a number of periods.

Quick quiz

1   What is an index?

2   Which value is the base year normally assigned when calculating index numbers?

3   What does a quantity index measure?

4   List four limitations of index numbers.

5   What is the name of the index used by public sector agencies in order to show past figures on a consistent price basis?

Answers to quick quiz

1   A measure over a period of time of the average changes of a group of items.

2   100.

3   The change in the non-monetary values of a group of items.

4   (a)   Usually only approximations of changes in price or quantity.

   (b)   Weighting factors often become out of date with time.

   (c)   Spending on products may change. This would result in weightings of a retail price index for consumer goods to become out of date.

   (d)   Data used to calculate index numbers may be incomplete, out-of-date or inaccurate.

   (e)   See paragraph 4.1 for complete list.

5   The GDP deflator.

Answers to activities

Answer 7.1

Base period; producer price indices.

Answer 7.2

1998 $\dfrac{106}{112} \times 100 = 94.6$, rounded to 95

1999 $\dfrac{120}{112} \times 100 = 107.1$, rounded to 107

Answer 7.3

(a) The base year appears to be 20X2, because the index is 100. We cannot be absolutely sure about this, because the base year *could* be before 20X0 or after 20X3, and the price of a litre of milk in 20X2 just happened to be the same as in the base year.

(b) The index has moved from 96 points to 100 points, a rise of 4 points.

(c) $\dfrac{4}{96} \times 100\% = 4.17\%$

(d) $0.54 \times \dfrac{113}{98} = £0.62$

Answer 7.4

Year	Sales (£'000)		Index
20X5	35	$\dfrac{35}{42} \times 100$	= 83
20X6	42		100
20X7	40	$\dfrac{40}{42} \times 100$	= 95
20X8	45	$\dfrac{45}{42} \times 100$	= 107
20X9	50	$\dfrac{50}{42} \times 100$	= 119

Answer 7.5

Tutorial note. An index covering the prices of several items is an indication of the average of changes in the prices, with weights being used to allow for the relative importance of the different items.

Ingredient	Weight	20X5 Index	W'ted	20X6 Index	W'ted	20X7 Index	W'ted	20X8 Index	W'ted
B	6	103	618	107	642	115	690	120	720
O	5	104	520	111	555	118	590	123	615
N	4	107	428	113	452	117	468	121	484
E	3	102	306	106	318	110	330	118	354
	18		1,872		1,967		2,078		2,173

(a) Material cost index

(20X4 = 100) 104   109   115   121

Each total is divided by 18 (the sum of the weights) to derive the index number.

(b) Using 20X7 as the base year, the index for 20X8 is

$$\dfrac{2,173 \times 100}{2,078} = 105.$$

Answer 7.6

Figures for sales per employee provide one indication of how efficient a supermarket chain is. This does not necessarily translate into profitability terms, since if margins (or price mark-ups) are reducing then the business may be becoming less profitable.

Over the period 1986 to 1990, sales per employee rose by 29% from £77,200 to £99,400. However, this is a rise in money terms. There was also a general rise in prices over this period of approximately 29%, using average RPI figures for the calendar years 1986 and 1990. Thus, in real terms, sales per employee have not changed much between 1986 and 1990. This means that the 'physical volume' of sales per employee has not changed much over the period.

The chart shows sales per employee in money terms. A chart such as this is intended as a visual aid to the reader: alternatively, just the figures could be included in a report. The chart gives the visual impression that there has been a significant rise in sales per employee.

Two features of the chart help to give this visual impression.

(a)   The y-axis starts at 75 and not at zero.
(b)   The chart is based on sales figures in money terms rather than real terms.

As commented above, the rise does not appear to have been significant in real terms and it is the figures for sales per employee in real terms which matter.

Answer 7.7

Sales expressed in terms of Year 1 prices

		£'000
Year 1		27,500
Year 2	29,680 × 217/228	28,248
Year 3	32,535 × 217/246	28,700
Year 4	34,455 × 217/268	27,898

Although sales have increased each year in absolute terms, when the effect of inflation is removed it can be seen that, in real terms, sales rose in year 2 and year 3 but fell in year 4.

Answer 7.8

The values of items consumed in the base period are:

A   £10,000
B   £18,000
C   £15,000

These can be cancelled down to give weights of 10, 18 and 15.

	Price relative × weight			
Period	*A*	*B*	*C*	*Total*
20X0	1,000	1,800	1,500	4,300
20X1	1,000	1,944	1,350	4,294
20X2	1,100	2,070	1,500	4,670

$$\text{Price index for 20X1} = \frac{4,294}{4,300} \times 100 = 99.9$$

$$\text{Price index for 20X2} = \frac{4,670}{4,300} \times 100 = 108.6$$

Answer 7.9

	Quarter 1 £	*Quarter 2* £	*Quarter 3* £	*Quarter 4* £
Adjusted sales revenue	518,515 [1]	468,743 [2]	506,181 [3]	483,274 [4]

(1) $£533,280 \times \dfrac{179.1}{184.2} =$ £518,515

(2) $£495,700 \times \dfrac{179.1}{189.4} =$ £468,743

(3) $£525,400 \times \dfrac{179.1}{185.9} =$ £506,181

(4) $£506,210 \times \dfrac{179.1}{187.6} =$ £483,274

Answer 7.10

The index number for each year with 20X6 as the base year will be the original index number divided by 1.14, and the real wages for each year will be (money wages × 100)/index number for the year.

Year	Index	Real wages £
20X0	88	170
20X1	90	179
20X2	93	181
20X3	95	188
20X4	96	193
20X5	98	195
20X6	100	197
20X7	102	199
20X8	104	199
20X9	106	201
20X0	108	214

Chapter 8   Writing reports and completing forms

Chapter topic list

1   Written reports

2   Planning a report

3   General points on style

4   The format of formal and informal reports

5   Information for your reports

6   Standard forms

Learning objectives

On completion of this chapter you will be able to:

	Performance criteria	Range statement
• prepare reports in the appropriate form and present them to management within required timescales	7.1.6	
• identify, collate and present relevant information in accordance with the conventions and definitions used by outside agencies	7.2.1	7.2.1
• present reports and returns in accordance with outside agencies' requirements and deadlines	7.2.4	7.2.1

BPP PUBLISHING

1   WRITTEN REPORTS

Introduction

1.1   The standards of competence for Unit 7: *Preparing reports and returns* require you to be able to prepare **written reports** in a clear and intelligible form. The term 'reports' here embraces the **periodic performance reports** of an enterprise which you may be required to prepare in your workplace. **External agencies** of various kinds, such as grant-awarding agencies, may also require written reports, as well as forms and other returns, to be submitted to them. The standards of competence expect you to be able to deal with written reports on specific issues as well as reports of a more routine nature.

1.2   Sections 1 to 5 of this chapter are designed to guide you in the effective marshalling and presentation of information in a **written report format**. We go on to look at the completion of forms in Section 6.

What is a report?

> **KEY TERM**
>
> **Report** is a general term and one that may suggest a wide range of formats. If you give someone a verbal account, or write him a message in a letter or memorandum informing him of facts, events, actions you have taken, suggestions you wish to make as a result of an investigation and so on, you are 'reporting'. In this sense the word means simply 'telling' or 'relating'.

1.3   There will be variety in the format and style of a report.

(a)   **Formal or informal.** You may think of reports as huge documents with sections, subsections, paragraphs, subparagraphs, indexes, appendices and so on. There *are* extensive, complex reports like this, but a single sheet ordinary memorandum may be sufficient in many contexts.

(b)   **Routine** reports are produced at regular intervals. Examples of routine reports are as follows.

•   Budgetary control reports
•   Sales reports
•   Progress reports.

Occasional reports include an **accident report** or a **disciplinary report**. **Special** reports may be commissioned for 'one-off' planning and decision-making such as a **market research report**, or a report on a **proposed project** or particular issue.

(c)   Reports may be **professional,** or for a **wider audience** of laymen or people from other backgrounds, who will not necessarily understand or require the same information or language.

1.4   Reports are meant to be **useful**. There should be no such thing as 'information for information's sake' in an efficient organisation: information is stored in files and retrieved for a purpose. The information contained in a business report might be used in several ways.

(a)   **To assist management.** Higher levels of management rarely have time to carry out their own detailed investigations into the matters on which they make decisions; their time, moreover, is extremely expensive. If all (and only) the information relevant to their needs can be gathered and 'packaged' by report writers, managerial time and money will be saved.

A report may consist of the following.

(i) **Information**, retrieved from files or other sources as a basis for management activity

(ii) **Narrative** or **description**, for example of one-off events or procedures, such as an accident, or the installation of new equipment

(iii) **Analysis**, which means making a further processing of information to render it more useful

(iv) **Evaluation** and **recommendation**, directly assisting in the decision-making process

(b) **As a permanent record and source of reference**, should details need to be confirmed or recalled in the future.

(c) **To convey information** or suggestions/ideas to other interested parties (eg in a report on a presentation, for a staff journal, for a committee or for a grant awarding agency).

1.5 As a report writer you should be aware that there are **different types of information** that might be given in a report.

(a) **Descriptive or factual information**

This consists of a **description of facts** and is objective: inferences can be drawn from the facts, but they must be logical and unbiased.

(b) **Instructive information**

This is information that tells the report user **how** to do something, or **what** to do. A recommendation in a report is a form of advice, and is therefore instructive information.

(c) **Evaluative information**

This consists of **opinions** and **ideas**, based on an objective assessment of the facts and with reasons explaining why these opinions and ideas have been reached.

Reports and their purpose

1.6 Reports will usually be **communications** that are intended to initiate a decision or action by the person or group receiving the report. The decisions or actions might be the following types.

(a) **Control action**. If the report describes **what has happened in the past**, it might indicate a need for control action, or alternatively it might indicate that there is no need for control action. The purpose of the report would in either case be to provide control information.

Budgetary control reports are examples of these reports. Reports that are intended to review events that have happened in the past (eg reports arising out of investigations into high labour turnover, a substantial loss on a major contract or the loss of a major customer to a competitor) are also examples of control reports.

(b) **Planning decisions**. Reports that are commissioned to **advise** on a certain course of action will include a **recommendation** about what decision should be taken.

The report and the report users

1.7 A report is usually made by someone who is instructed to do so by a superior.

   (a) A special **'one-off' report** will be commissioned by a manager, who will then expect to make a decision on the basis of what the report tells him. For example, the board of directors of a company might call for a report on the financial viability of a new product or investment, and they will expect to decide whether or not to undertake the product development or the investment on the basis of the report's findings.

   (b) **Routine reports**, such as performance reports, might be required because they are a part of established procedures. The managers receiving the reports will not have commissioned them specifically, but they will be expected to act on anything out-of-the-ordinary that the report tells them.

   (c) Some reports arise out of a particular event, on which **regulations** prescribe the writing of a report. For example, a leaving report must be written following an employee's resignation; any accident in the workplace must be reported.

   (d) **Individual responsibilities** often include the requirement to write reports - a representative on a committee, or the secretary at a meeting, will have to report to members, or other committees, the procedures and decisions taken.

1.8 Whether the report is 'one-off' or routine, there is an **obligation on the part of the person requesting the report to state the use to which it will be put**. In other words, the purpose of the report must be clear to both its writers and its users.

1.9 In the case of routine reports, the purpose of each and how it should be used ought to be specified in a **procedures manual**. 'One-offs' will require **terms of reference**, explaining the **purpose** of the report and any **restrictions** on its scope. For example, the terms of reference of a management report might be to investigate the short-term profit prospects for a particular service, with a view to recommending either the withdrawal of the service or its continuation. These terms of reference would exclude considerations of long-term prospects for the service, and so place a limitation on the scope and purpose of the report.

   Be aware of this in any assessment tasks. You do not have time to write about irrelevancies.

1.10 There is also **an obligation on the part of the report writer to communicate information in an unbiased way**. The report writer knows more about the subject matter of the report than the report user (otherwise there would be no need for the report in the first place). It is important that this information should be **communicated impartially**, so that the report user can make his own judgements. The following must therefore apply.

   (a) Any assumptions, evaluations and recommendations by the report writer should be clearly 'signalled' as such.

   (b) Points should not be over-weighted (or omitted as irrelevant) without honestly evaluating how objective the selection is.

   (c) Facts and findings should be balanced against each other.

   (d) A firm conclusion should, if possible, be reached. It should be clear how and why it was reached.

1.11 Finally, **there is an obligation on the part of the report writer to recognise the needs and abilities of the report user**.

    (a) Beware of **jargon, overly technical terms** and **specialist knowledge** the user may not share.

    (b) Keep your vocabulary, sentence and paragraph structures as **simple as possible**, for clarity (without patronising an intelligent user).

    (c) Bear in mind the type and **level of detail** that will interest the user and be relevant to his/her purpose.

    (d) In a business context, **the user may range** from senior manager to junior supervisor, to non-managerial employee (such as in the case of minutes of a meeting, or general bulletin) to complete layman (customer, press and so on). Your vocabulary, syntax and presentation, the amount of detail you can go into, the technical matter you can include and the formality of your report structure should all be influenced by such concerns.

Timeliness

1.12 As with all information, we stress again that a report may be of no use at all if it is not produced **on time**, however well researched and well presented it is. There is no point in presenting a report to influence a decision if the decision has already been made by the time the report is issued. The **timescales** within which the report user is working must be known, and the **time available** to produce the report planned accordingly.

2 PLANNING A REPORT

2.1 Whether you are completing an assignment for your course of studies, compiling a report at work or researching a hobby of your own, you will need to know how to put information together **effectively**. Unless you have an extremely orderly mind, this will take **planning**. Before you can even begin to think about what information you will need and where you will find it (that is, to formulate your information search strategy), you need to consider the following.

- Who is the user?
- What type of report will be most useful to him/her?
- What exactly does he/she need to know, and for what purpose?
- How much information is required, how quickly and at what cost?
- Do you need to give judgements, recommendations and so on (or just information)?

2.2 If you know who the user is, what he or she wants and why, and if you are aware of particular constraints imposed on you in terms of report size, time and money, you will have a good framework for going on to plan the **structure** and **content** of your report.

2.3 When you then come to plan a report in detail, you can ask yourself questions such as the following.

    (a) What information do I need to **provide**? What is **relevant** to the user's requirements?

    (b) Do I need to follow a **line of reasoning**? If so, what is the most logical way in which data can be grouped, and sequenced, to make my reasoning clear?

    (c) Do I need to include my own **personal views**? If so, at what point: final recommendation, throughout?

(d) What can I do to make the report **easier to read**?

    (i) Are there suitable **section** or **sub-headings** I can use to indicate effectively each stage of the information/argument?

    (ii) Is the subject of the report **too technical** for the users? What vocabulary should I use to help them understand?

    (iii) Do I have a **clear introduction** to 'ease' the readers in to the subject, and a **clear conclusion** that will draw everything together for them?

2.4 You could use the above questions as a **checklist** for planning your report. If you can then jot down a 'skeleton' of the headings and sub-headings you have decided to use (with notes of any particular points that occur to you as you go along) you will be ready to write. The **formal headings** of standard business reports may be useful to help you to organise your thoughts - but may not be necessary, or even advisable, if they simply act as a constraint on what you actually want to say, and how you want to 'shape' it. You should not worry at this stage about having 'Terms of Reference', 'Procedures', 'Findings' (discussed below), unless they provide a **relevant framework** for your report.

2.5 EXAMPLE: REPORT PLAN

A manager would like your views on the use of flexible working hours in your organisation. In due course, you are to write him a report considering the advantages and disadvantages to all concerned, and give your conclusions. Your task now is to prepare a plan for the report.

2.6 SOLUTION

Note: again, a hint is given as to what is required. A **brief** introduction to flexible working hours may not be amiss (as if the manager has not considered how flexi-time might work). The central section of the report might be structured: **Advantages** - Party 1, party 2, party 3. **Disadvantages** - Party 1, party 2, party 3. We have chosen to take the 'concerned' parties in turn, and consider the advantages and disadvantages for each. Don't just consider yourself and the staff, but '*all* concerned.'

The plan below is only a suggestion: the ideas for content should be your own.

REPORT PLAN

I INTRODUCTION

How flexible working hours operate (briefly), core period and flexible hours. Debit/credit of hours per week or month.

II EFFECTS

1 *Staff*

(a) *Advantages*

   (i) reduced stress: vagaries of traffic etc. no longer a major worry
   (ii) flexibility: fitting in with family patterns, shop hours etc
   (iii) morale enhanced by discretion in own work patterns
   (iv) favourable results for morale, attendance etc. in trial schemes

(b) *Disadvantages*

   (i) reduced discipline: some staff may take advantage
   (ii) fluctuating work patterns may be psychologically disruptive
   (iii) friction may result from scheduling to cover non-core periods

2 *Management*

(a) *Advantages*

   (i) morale and attendance advantages (for staff) May help management as well
   (ii) fewer idle staff (wastage) during quieter periods

(b) *Disadvantages*

   (i) planning, administering, controlling scheme
   (ii) cost of mechanical logging in/out devices

3 *Customers*

(a) *Advantages*

   (i) high morale of staff hopefully leads to better service

(b) *Disadvantages*

   (i) possible bottlenecks of work during flexi-periods: delays
   (ii) possible discontinuity of service: personnel changing through day etc.

III CONCLUSIONS

1 Disadvantages: few and can be overcome with good management.

2 Advantages: fundamental, shown to be effective elsewhere.

3 Recommend trial scheme of flexi-time with a view to introducing it later in full.

---

3 GENERAL POINTS ON STYLE

3.1 There are certain stylistic requirements in the writing of reports, formal or informal.

(a) **Objectivity and balance.** Even in a report designed to persuade as well as inform, subjective value judgements and emotions should be kept out of the content and style as far as possible: the bias, if recognised, can **undermine the credibility** of the report and its recommendations.

(i)   Emotional or otherwise loaded words should be avoided.

(ii)   In more formal reports, **impersonal constructions** should be used rather than 'I', 'we' etc., which carry personal and possibly subjective associations. In other words, first person subjects should be replaced with third person.

	It became clear that...
I/we found that...	(Your name) found that...
	Investigation revealed that...

(iii)   **Colloquialisms** and **abbreviated forms** should be avoided in formal written English: colloquial (informal) 'I've', 'don't' and so on should be replaced by 'I have' and 'do not'. You should not use expressions like 'blew his top': formal phrases should be used, such as 'showed considerable irritation'.

(b) **Ease of understanding**

(i)   This will involve **avoiding technical language** and complex sentence structures for non-technical users.

(ii)   The material will have to be **logically organised**, especially if it is leading up to a conclusion or recommendation.

(iii)   **Relevant themes** should be signalled by appropriate headings or highlighted for easy scanning.

(iv)   The layout of the report should **display data clearly** and **attractively**. Figures and diagrams should be used with discretion, and it might be helpful to highlight key figures which appear within large tables of numbers.

3.2   Various **display techniques** may be used to make the content of a report easy to identify and digest. For example, the relative importance of points should be signalled, each point may be referenced, and the body of text should be broken up to be easy on the eye. These aims may be achieved as follows.

(a) **Headings**

Spaced out or enlarged CAPITALS may be used for the main title.

Important headings, eg of sections of the report, may be in CAPITALS.

Underlining or *Italics* may be used for subheadings.

(b) **References**

Each section or point in a formal report should have a code for easy identification and reference.

Use different labelling for each type of heading	*Alternatively a 'decimal' system may be used:*	
Main section headings		
I,II,III,IV,V etc.	1	Heading 1
A,B,C,D,E etc.	1.1	Subheading 1
Subsections	1.1.1	Subheading 1, Point 1
1,2,3,4,5 etc.	1.1.2	Subheading 1, Point 2
	1.2	Subheading 2
Points and subpoints	1.2.1	(a) Subheading 2, Point 1, Subpoint (a),
(a), (b), (c) etc.	2	Heading 2
(i), (ii), (iii) etc.		

(c) **Spacing**

Intelligent use of spacing separates headings from the body of the text for easy scanning, and also makes a large block more attractive and 'digestible'.

4 THE FORMAT OF FORMAL AND INFORMAL REPORTS

General principles

4.1 When a formal request is made by a superior for a report to be prepared, such as in a formally worded memorandum or letter, the **format** and **style** of the report will obviously have to be formal as well: it will be strictly **schematic**, using impersonal constructions and **avoiding emotive or colloquial expressions**.

4.2 An informal request for a report - 'Can you jot down a few ideas for me about...' or 'Let me know what happens, will you?' - will result in an **informal report**, in which the structure will be less rigid, and the style slightly more personal (depending on the relationship perceived to exist between the writer and user).

If in doubt, it is better (more courteous and effective) to be too formal than overfamiliar.

4.3 The purpose of reports and their subject matter vary widely, but there are certain **generally accepted principles** of report writing that can be applied to most types of report.

(a) **Title**. The report should have a title, and the title should be:

(i) **explicit**. In other words, the title should indicate clearly what the report is about;

(ii) **brief**. The title should be as short as possible whilst being explicit at the same time.

(b) **Identification of report writer, report user and date**. Reports should indicate in a clear place, possibly before the title itself, whom they are directed at, who has written them and the date of their preparation.

(c) **Confidentiality**. If the report is confidential or 'secret' this fact must be printed at the top of the report and possibly on every page.

(d) **Contents page**. If the report is extensive, it should open with a list of contents.

(e) **Terms of reference**. The introductory section of the report should explain why the report has been written and the terms of reference. The terms of reference will explain not only the **purpose** of the report but also any **restrictions on its scope**. For example, an internal auditing report might state that its terms of reference have been to investigate procedures in the credit control section of the accounts department, with a view to establishing whether the existing internal checks are adequate.

Similarly, the terms of reference of a management accounting report might be to investigate the short-term profit prospects for a particular product, with a view to recommending either the closure of the product line or its continued production. These terms of reference would exclude considerations of long-term prospects for the product, and so place a limitation on the scope of the report.

When timescale is important, this should be specified in the terms of reference. For example, the board of directors might call for a report so that they can take a decision by a certain cut-off date, eg whether to put in a tender for a major contract and if so at what price, in a situation where a customer has invited tenders which must be submitted by a certain date.

(f) **Sources of information.** If the report draws on other sources for its information, these sources should be acknowledged in the report. Alternatively, if the report is based on primary research, the nature of the fact-finding should be explained, perhaps in an appendix to the report.

If there is an extensive series of documents referring to one matter, a summary of the history may be provided in the **appendix**. If the literature includes a lot of correspondence, a uniform code should be used to refer to letters in the summary: for example letters between the Company Secretary and the Companies Registry might be referenced as CS/Reg [date].

(g) **Sections.** The main body of the report should be divided into sections. The sections should have a **logical sequence**, and each section should ideally have a **clear heading**. These headings (or sub-headings) should if possible be **standardised** when reports are produced regularly (eg audit reports). Paragraphs should be **numbered**, for ease of reference. Each paragraph should be concerned with just one basic idea.

(h) **Appendices.** To keep the main body of the report short enough to hold the reader's interest, detailed explanations, charts and tables of figures should be put into appendices. The main body of the report should make **cross-references** to the appendices in appropriate places.

(i) **Summary of recommendations.** A report will usually contain conclusions or recommendations about the course of action to be taken by the report user. These conclusions or recommendations should perhaps be stated at the **beginning** of the report (after the introduction and statement of terms of reference). The main body of the report can then follow, in its logically-progressive sections, and should lead the report user through the considerations that led the report writer to these conclusions.

The conclusions or recommendations should then be **re-stated at the end** of the main body of the report. For example, a management accounting report into the performance of an operating division might summarise its findings at the beginning, as follows.

	Plan	*Actual*
Sales turnover	X	X
Profit	X	X
Cash movement	X	X
Capital employed	X	X
Return on capital employed	X	X

The following sections of the report would then go on to look at each of these items **in more detail**, concluding with an assessment of the division's performance and perhaps recommendations as to how it needs to be improved.

Any assumptions, forecasts or conjectures should be signalled as such, and not passed off as fact.

(j) **Prominence of important items.** The most significant items in a report should be given prominence.

(k) **Report summaries.** Long reports should be summarised **in brief**. However, as suggested already it is often better to keep the main report itself brief, with the detail in appendices; a report summary would probably not then be necessary.

(l) **Implications for management.** Reference should be made where appropriate to costs, savings and other benefits that might accrue, and to any other implications for management in the report's recommendations (eg implications for staff recruitment, training or redundancies and so on).

(m) **Completeness**. The qualities of information - reliability, objectivity, timeliness, clarity, completeness, and relevance - have been discussed earlier in this Interactive Text. However, it is worth stressing that a report should be **logically complete** and should not overlook any item or consideration so that its recommendations are called into question.

4.4 The main types of report you might have to deal with are summarised as follows.

- The short formal report
- The short informal report
- The memorandum report

You should not feel bound to use the following headings in a report for an assessment task, but the guidelines on report sections may be helpful, should you wish to follow them.

The short formal report

4.5 The **short formal report** is used in formal contexts such as where middle management is reporting to senior management. It should be laid out according to certain basic guidelines. It will be split into logical sections, each **referenced** and **headed** appropriately.

TITLE

I	TERMS OF REFERENCE (or INTRODUCTION)		
II	PROCEDURE (or METHOD)		
III	FINDINGS		
	1	Section heading	
	2	Section heading	if required
		(a) sub heading	
		(i) sub point	
IV	CONCLUSIONS		
V	RECOMMENDATIONS	if asked for	

SHORT FORMAL REPORT

TITLE   At the top of every report (or on a title page, for lengthy ones) appears the title of the report (its subject) and, as appropriate, *who* has prepared it, *for whom* it is intended, the *date* of completion, and the *status* of the report ('Confidential' or 'Urgent').

I   TERMS OF REFERENCE or INTRODUCTION

Here is laid out the scope and purpose of the report: what is to be investigated, what kind of information is required, whether recommendations are to be made etc. This section may more simply be called 'Introduction', and may include the details set above under 'Title'. The title itself would then give only the subject of the report.

II   PROCEDURE or METHOD

This outlines the steps taken to make an investigation, collect data, put events in motion etc. Telephone calls or visits made, documents or computer files consulted, computations or analyses made etc. should be briefly described, with the names of other people involved.

III   FINDINGS

In this section the information itself is set out, with appropriate headings and sub-headings, if the report covers more than one topic. The content should be complete, but concise, and clearly structured in chronological order, order of importance, or any other *logical* relationship.

IV   CONCLUSIONS

This section allows for a summary of main findings (if the report is complex and lengthy). For a simpler report it may include action taken or decisions reached (if any) as a result of the investigation, or an expression of the overall 'message' of the report.

V   RECOMMENDATIONS

Here, if asked to do so in the terms of reference, the writer of the report may suggest the solution to the problem investigated so that the recipient will be able to make a decision if necessary.

EXAMPLE: SHORT FORMAL REPORT

REPORT ON DISK STORAGE, SAFETY AND SECURITY

To: M Ployer, Accounts Department Manager
From: M Ployee, Senior Accounts Clerk
Status: Confidential
Date: 3 October 20X0

I   INTRODUCTION

This report details the findings of an investigation into methods of computer disk storage currently employed at the Head Office of the firm. The report, to include recommendations for the improvement of current procedure, was requested by Mr M Ployer, Accounts Department Manager, on 3rd September 19--. It was prepared by M Ployee, Senior Accounts Clerk, and submitted to Mr Ployer on 3rd October 19--.

II   METHOD

In order to evaluate the present procedures and to identify specific shortcomings, the following investigatory procedures were adopted:

1   interview of all data processing staff
2   storage and indexing system inspected
3   computer accessory firm consulted by telephone and catalogues obtained (Appendix I refers)

III   FINDINGS

1   <u>Current system</u>

    (a) Floppy disks are 'backed up' or duplicated irregularly and infrequently.

    (b) Back-up disks where they exist are stored in plastic containers in the accounts office, ie in the same room as the disks currently in use.

    (c) Disks are frequently left on desk tops during the day and even over night.

2   <u>Safety and security risks</u>

    (a) There is no systematic provision for making copies, in the event of loss or damage of disks in use.

    (b) There is no provision for separate storage of copies in the event of fire in the accounts office, and no adequate security against fire or damage in the containers used.

    (c) There appears to be no awareness of the confidential nature of information on disk, nor of the ease with which disks may be damaged by handling, the spilling of beverages, dust etc.

IV   CONCLUSIONS

The principal conclusions drawn from the investigation were that there was insufficient awareness of safety and security among the DP staff, that there was insufficient formal provision for safety and security procedure, and that there was serious cause for concern.

V   RECOMMENDATIONS

In order to rectify the unsatisfactory situation summarised above, the author of the report recommends that consideration be given as a matter of urgency to the following measures:

1   immediate backing-up of all existing disks
2   drafting of procedures for backing up disks at the end of each day's work
3   acquisition of a fire-proof safe to be kept in separate office accommodation
4   communication to all DP staff of the serious risk of loss, theft and damage arising from careless handling of computer disks

The short informal report

4.6 The **short informal report** is used for less complex and lower level information. You, as Senior Accounts Clerk (or similar) could be asked to prepare such a report for the Accounts Manager.

4.7 The structure of the informal report is **less developed**: it will be **shorter** and **less complex** in any case, so will not require elaborate referencing and layout. There will be three main sections, each of which may be headed in any way appropriate to the context in which the report is written.

TITLE

1   BACKGROUND/INTRODUCTION/SITUATION

2   FINDINGS/ANALYSIS OF SITUATION

3   ACTION/SOLUTION/CONCLUSION

SHORT INFORMAL REPORT

Title   Again, the subject title, 'to', 'from', 'date' and 'reference' (if necessary) should be provided, perhaps in the same style as memorandum headings.

1   **Background** or **Situation** or **Introduction**

This sets the context of the report. Include anything that will help the reader to understand the rest of the report: the reason why it was requested, the current situation, and any other background information on people and things that will be mentioned in the following detailed section. This section may also contain the equivalent of 'terms of reference' and 'procedure' ('method').

2   **Findings** or **Analysis of the situation**

Here is set out the detailed information gathered, narrative of events or other substance of the report as required by the user. This section may or may not require subheadings: concise prose paragraphs may be sufficient.

3   **Action** or **Solution** or **Conclusion**

The main thrust of the findings may be summarised in this section and conclusions drawn, together with a note of the outcome of events, or action required, or recommendations as to how a problem might be solved.

EXAMPLE: SHORT INFORMAL REPORT

REPORT

<u>Confidential</u>

To: M Ployer, Accounts Manager
From: M Ployee, Senior Accounts Clerk
Date: 13 June 20X0
Subject: Customer complaint by F R Vessent

1 Background

I have thoroughly investigated the situation with regard to Mr Vessent, and the correspondence provided. Mr Vessent is Accounts Clerk for Dibbin & Dobbs Ltd. who have had an account with us since June 19--: account number 39867. Credit terms were agreed with the firm whereby 10% discount is credited to their account for payment within two weeks of the statement date, payment in any case to be made within 30 days.

I have questioned the Accounts Clerk concerning the Dibbin & Dobbs account for April, and we have together consulted the records. In addition I telephoned the third party, Doobey & Sons to make enquiries about payments received from them.

2 Findings

The substance of Mr Vessent's complaint was that he had received from us a reminder that an amount of £1,306.70 was outstanding on the Dibbin & Dobbs account for April: according to Mr Vessent, a cheque payment for that amount had been sent on the 12th April, ie within 10 days of receiving the statement on 3rd April.

Records show no payment credited to the Dibbin & Dobbs account. However, an amount of £1,306.70 was credited to the account of Doobey & Sons on the same day, and payment duly acknowledged. Doobey & Sons when consulted admitted to having been puzzled by the acknowledgement of a payment they had never made.

The Accounts Clerk was absent through illness that week, and a temporary Clerk employed.

3 Conclusion

It would appear that the temporary Clerk credited the payment to the wrong account.

The entries have been duly corrected, and 10% prompt payment discount credited to Dibbin & Dobbs as usual.

I am writing an appropriate letter of apology and explanation to Mr Vessent.

Obviously this is a matter of some concern in terms of customer relations. I suggest that all clerks be reminded of the need for due care and attention, and that temporary staff in particular be briefed on this matter in the future.

Activity 8.1

(a) Where in a report might its conclusions be set out?
(b) What is meant by 'the terms of reference' of a written report?
(c) For what reasons might parts of a report be contained in appendices?

Activity 8.2

(a) List the headings you might use as a framework for a:

    (i)   short formal report;

    (ii)   short informal report.

(b) List ten words you might use instead of 'said' to report someone's speech ('He said that...')

(c) How would you rephrase the following so that they were suitable for a formal report, and why?

    (i)   I investigated the matter.

    (ii)   'I will investigate further', Mr Harris told me.

    (iii) 'There must be a problem in Accounts,' he said, 'since it obviously isn't our fault'.

    (iv) Accounts pretended not to have received the complaint.

    (v)   'It is outrageous, what those layabouts in Accounts are getting away with!' fumed Mr Harris.

    (vi) I said I'd give it a go myself, if they weren't sufficiently on the ball.

The memorandum report

4.8   In informal reporting situations within an organisation, the 'short informal report' may well be presented in **A4 memorandum format**, which incorporates **title headings** and can thereafter be laid out at the writer's discretion. An ordinary memorandum may be used for flexible, informal reports: aside from the convenient title headings, there are no particular requirements for structure, headings or layout. The writer may consider whatever is **logical, convenient** and **attractive** for the reader.

Form reports

4.9   Some commonly prepared reports have certain standard content requirements, and can therefore be **preprinted** with appropriate format and headings and filled in when the need arises: an **accident report form**, for example, or a **damaged goods report** (for incoming orders found to be faulty). Another example is the **personnel profile** (like a curriculum vitae). Pre-printed forms allow the details of the report to be presented under the relevant headings, and in the space available. (This is largely a matter of common sense, plus the **ability to summarise information** within formal constraints.) Even if an organisation does not have formatted reports pre-printed, and each report has to be drafted for the occasion, the common elements will still be required.

Producing a report for assessment

4.10 When you need to produce a report for assessment, remember the following key points.

    (a) **Format and layout.** *All* reports should include the following.

- A title
- Names of recipients
- Author (you)
- A date
- A clear structure with headings

    An informal report should have at least three headings or sections: introduction/purpose/situation, findings and conclusions/recommendations. A formal report will have more sections, but these three are the meat of the matter.

    (b) **Style.** The tone should be **clear** and **objective**. Even an informal report should avoid colloquialism. By definition you are reporting information which will be 'on the record'

and which will be read and used by people who do not have as much detailed knowledge as yourself. You do not want to go 'on record' as a muddled thinker or as someone who does not understand the importance of clear communication.

(c) **Relevance**. Particularly where you are preparing a report on a workplace situation for devolved assessment, you need to keep information in the report ruthlessly relevant. It is easy to get bogged down in detail and find your terms of reference section taking three sides as you explain the background of a situation! The trick is to sort your information and **summarise** it in the report, referring to appendices where you think the users really need to see the information unsummarised.

(d) **Completeness**. The important thing when producing any report is to ensure that the purpose of the report is fulfilled. In a central assessment, if you are asked to 'prepare a report for the Chief Accountant with your recommendations on this matter', you will lose out on marks if you do not include recommendations or a conclusion of some sort, even if this is simply 'more information-gathering should be performed'.

DEVOLVED ASSESSMENT ALERT

You are very likely to be asked to produce a report as part of the devolved assessment procedures in your AAT studies, for example, you may be asked to produce a report on a situation which exists in your workplace or which has developed in a simulation. You must therefore pay good attention to the principles and procedures of report writing.

4.11 In the next section we shall look at how information for a report should be **gathered** and **put across**.

5 INFORMATION FOR YOUR REPORTS

5.1 Because your report is a vehicle for conveying information, it should pay attention to the qualities of good information which we saw in Chapter 2.

- Relevance
- Accuracy
- Reliability
- Timeliness
- Appropriateness of communication
- Cost effectiveness

5.2 The information contained in your report can come from one of the two sources which we saw in Chapter 3.

(a) **External sources**. There is a wealth of places outside your organisation from which information can be gained.

  (i) **Primary data** are gathered as **raw data** from, for example, customers. A company may employ researchers to compile a survey of customers in order to find out *exactly* what the company wants to know - for example, exactly what qualities customers are looking for in, say, a new women's magazine.

  (ii) **Secondary data** come from **published sources** which convey information gathered for general use. To continue the example, the magazine company may look at the ONS's *Economic Trends* publication to see how much more disposable income young women have now compared to three years ago. This will help it to decide whether the world is ready for yet another new women's magazine - but since the data were not gathered specifically for the purpose of helping to make this decision, they must be handled with care.

(b) **Internal sources.** For example, management accounts, reports from management meetings, sales data and so on. The amount of information **already existing but not used properly** in most organisations is huge. It is often the best source but again the data must be handled and interpreted carefully, and you may find your access to it is restricted at times.

Activity 8.3

Your company is considering the possibility of exporting its products to Russia, and a report is to be prepared for management.

Task

Write out the information given in the table below in narrative form, using approximately 100 words, for inclusion in the report as a subsection entitled 'Russia: country data'. (The information given is considered to be sufficiently recent for this purpose.)

Russia	
Area (1,000 sq km)	17,075
% of former Soviet Union (FSU) territory	76
Population 1990 mid-yr (millions)	148.3
% of total population of FSU	51
Growth rate 1980-90 (percent)	0.4
Density 1990 (per sq km)	8.7
GDP, at current market prices, 1989 (bn roubles)	573.1
Industry as % of total GDP	46.6
Services as % of total GDP	37.8
Agriculture as % of total GDP	15.6
Exports in 1989 (bn roubles)	140.9
Oil and gas exports as % of total	31.2

Source: World Bank

(GDP = Gross Domestic Product)

Activity 8.4

You have been asked to contribute to a section of a report on the effects of regulations on the activities of public enterprises in the period before privatisation. (You do not need to have worked in the public sector to complete this Exercise.)

The table below identifies the main changes to the competitive environment faced by the largest enterprises in the nationalised industry sector from the late 1970s to 1990.

Enterprise	*Main changes to competitive environment*
British Airways	Routes liberalised: North Atlantic (1977); UK (1982); Europe (1984 onwards).
British Coal	Better defined contracts for supply to electricity generators (1989); reduced protection from imports of coal and from gas.
British Gas	Gas Act (1985); partial competition in supply to industrial customers.
British Rail	Increased competition from deregulated buses (1986), coaches (1980) and domestic aviation (1982).
British Steel	Unwinding of EC steel quotas (1980 onwards).
British Telecom	Liberalisation of apparatus (1981); value added services (1981) and second terrestrial carrier (1982).
Electricity supply	Energy Act (1983): partial competition in supply. Electricity Act (1986); competition in supply (1990).
Post Office	Courier services deregulated (1981). Restructured into separate businesses.

Source: Treasury Bulletin

Task

Present the information given in the table in narrative (non-tabular) form.

6 STANDARD FORMS

6.1 In **recording data** and in **presenting routine reports** to management, accountants and others in organisations make frequent use of **standard forms**.

> ### KEY TERM
>
> A **form** can be defined as a schedule which is to be filled in with details and has a prescribed layout, arrangement and wording. Forms are standard documents which are used regularly to 'capture' data and communicate information.

6.2 Using forms, rather than collecting data or providing information on on-standard documents, has several important advantages.

(a) Forms ensure that all the information required is actually obtained, or at least that any gaps in the information can be easily recognised. In other words, they help to ensure **completeness** of the data or information when the form is initially filled in.

(b) Because they are in a standard format, they are more easily **understandable**. Users of forms know where to look on the form for items of information, and if there is anything they do not understand, they can check the meaning in an office procedures manual, which should describe the functions of forms used by the organisation.

(c) Using forms helps management to **regulate the flow of information** within the organisation, by planning what forms there should be, who should fill them in, how frequently they should be filled in and who should receive and use them.

General principles of good form design

6.3 For Unit 7 *Preparing reports and returns* you are expected to be able to **complete standard forms**. Competent handling of standard forms will be easier if you are aware of some of the basic principles of **form design**.

6.4 Form design, like form filling, is largely a matter of **common sense** and **experience**, but there are certain principles that should be applied to ensure that there are suitable well-designed forms in use within the organisation. The purpose served by a form is to ensure the **effective transmission of necessary information**.

6.5 A good form is one which is designed as follows.

(a) The layout of the form and instructions on how to fill it in should be **clear** to the user. As much information as possible should be pre-printed to avoid error and reduce the work-load and sentence completion, tick boxes and deletion used where possible to cut down on the amount of writing required. Forms should request and contain all the data required, but no more. In other words the form must be easy to use so that **information can be easily obtained**.

(b) The form must be capable where necessary of easy handling so that information can be **easily transmitted**.

(c) The layout of information on the form must be in a **clear, logical sequence** so that it can be readily understood by the reader. Related items should be grouped together and separated from other areas. A good title will help, and colour coding and typeface may also clarify the purpose of the form and each of its sections so that the information may be **easily interpreted**.

159

(d) The size of filing cabinets or trays should be considered for forms stored for a long period as hard copy. Each document should have a clear title, and usually a code or identifying colour or number so that information can be **easily filed.**

(e) The problems of retrieving a form from file should also be considered. The position of the serial number or identification of the record may be important. Information must therefore be able to be **retrieved easily.**

Form filling

6.6 A well designed form should be **easy to fill in.** It may not *look* very easy, if it requires a large amount of complex information, but you should find the required items indicated for you, and sufficient instruction to enable you to insert the desired data in the right place and manner. Many forms do the work for you, leaving you only with small insertions, crosses or ticks in 'choice' boxes, either/or deletions and so on.

As noted above under 'form reports', however, some forms do simply leave space and ask you to 'give details of....': summarising will be necessary here, since you will probably not have as much space as you initially think you need.

6.7 Some hints for form-filling include the following.

(a) **Scan the form first,** for main headings and topic areas. That way, you will not put into Section A information that more properly fits into Section D later on.

(b) **Obey any instructions about what to include.** For example, the rubric on an accident report might be: 'Give a full account of the accident explaining as far as possible how it happened and how those killed or hurt received their injuries. Give name and type of any plant, equipment, machinery or vehicle involved and note whether it was in motion.'

(c) **Obey instructions about how to provide data**

  (i) **The level or type of detail required:** 'Precise place eg South Warehouse, No 2 Machine Shop, canteen kitchen'

  (ii) **The method of entry:** 'Please complete in block capitals', 'tick the appropriate box' etc

(d) **Plan any prose descriptions or narratives requested.** Forms will usually offer you the chance to use 'continuation sheets' if required, but you should practise providing necessary information within the constraints of formality and limited space. Draft an account with all the details you want to include, then delete any items that seem irrelevant to the purpose of the form. Finally, **do not use more words or expressions** than are necessary. Then you will be able to write the information 'clean' into the form.

(e) **Remember who is going to use the information and why.** This will help you to keep to a relevant content and clear written style.

Forms in computer systems

6.8 In computer systems source documents may have to be transcribed into a **machine readable medium** (eg magnetic disk or tape) but they may have other functions than merely data capture for computer processing. For example, a sales invoice has to function as a sales invoice and so its contents may contain data which is not required for computer processing. The layout of the invoice must do the following.

(a) Give a **clear indication** of which data is to be transcribed for computer input.

(b) Make sure that the data required is **entered on the invoice in keying-in sequence** (eg from left to right, top to bottom of the sheet). The keying-in sequence should preferably be the sequence in which the data will be used by the computer program.

6.9 **Computer-produced forms** or even other printed forms might be turn-round documents - which start by providing output to a user, are then used (filled in) and re-input to a computer, and so re-processed. Examples of turn-round documents are **bank giro payment slips** (as at the bottom of telephone bills and electricity bills).

Timeliness

6.10 Like reports, returns made on standard forms must be **presented on time**. In the case of a form for an external agency, there will usually be a **deadline** by which the form must be submitted. As with reports, lateness may make a standard return worthless or may lead to **sanctions** for late submission being exercised. For example, a late VAT return may attract **penalties,** and a late grant application might **not be accepted** at all.

Activity 8.5

(a) How many forms do you handle or have to fill in at work, at school or college, or in connection with other matters? List as many sorts of forms as you can think of.

(b) Get hold of any copies of forms that you might have filled and kept: you might also be able to get samples of forms you use regularly at work, or bank or Post Office forms (eg opening an account, insurance, redirection of mail, application for driving test). If you really cannot find any, there may be subscription or order forms in a newspaper or magazine that you could cut out.

Study them.

Are they easy to fill in? Are all the items to be input clearly identified and explained?

What features do they have in common? Are they good forms, do you think?

Try drafting your own version, if you think you could 'iron out the bugs'. Improvement?

BPP PUBLISHING

Key learning points

- **Report** means 'telling' or 'relating'. Reports may be **formal, informal, routine, occasional** or **special.**

- Information contained within a business report might be used as follows.
    - To assist management
    - As a permanent record and source of reference
    - To convey information

- Different types of information contained within a report are as follows.
    - Descriptive or factual
    - Instructive
    - Evaluative

- Whether a report is '**one-off**' or **routine**, the following apply.
    - There is an obligation on the part of the person requesting the report to state the use to which it will be put
    - There is an obligation on the part of the report writer to communicate information in an unbiased way
    - There is an obligation on the part of the report writer to recognise the needs and abilities of the report user

- The main types of report are: the **short formal** report; the **short informal** report; and the **memorandum** report.

- The key points to note when producing a report are the following.
    - Format and layout
    - Style
    - Relevance
    - Completeness

- A **form** is a schedule which is filled in with details and has a prescribed layout, arrangement and wording. Forms are standard documents which are used regularly to 'capture' data and communicate information.

Quick quiz

1   What is the nature of a report which is produced at regular intervals and give three examples?

2   What does evalutive information consist of?

3   What is the purpose of 'terms of reference' as found in some reports?

4   What is the first thing you should do when writing a report?

5   How can you make your report easy to understand?

6   What sort of report is likely to be used where middle management is reporting to senior management?

7   List the five hints which should be noted when filling in forms.

Answers to quick quiz

1   Routine report. Budgetary control report, sales report, progress report.

2   Opinions and ideas based on an objective assessment of facts (with reasoning).

3   In order to explain the purpose of the report and any restrictions on its scope.

4   Produce a plan.

5   • Avoid technical language
    • Organise the report material in a logical fashion
    • Relevant themes should be highlighted
    • Data should be displayed clearly and attractively

6   The short formal report.

7   •   Scan the form first
        •   Obey any instructions about **what** to include
        •   Obey any instructions about **how** to provide data
        •   Plan any prose descriptions or narratives requested
        •   Remember who is going to use the information and why

Answers to activities

Answer 8.1

(a)   The conclusions of a report might be positioned either at the end (perhaps before a 'recommendations' section and any lists of sources) or alternatively after the introduction.

(b)   The terms of reference of a report are an explanation of the purpose of the report and of any limitations on its scope.

(c)   To keep the main body of the report short enough to hold the reader's interest, detailed explanations and tables of figures may be put into appendices to which the main body of the report cross refers.

Answer 8.2

(a)   *Tutorial note.* In essence, the informal report is more flexible about the kind of headings you can use. It is also less scrupulous about setting out the formal purposes and methodology of the investigation and report.

        Short formal report

        I   Terms of reference/Introduction
        II   Procedure/Method
        III   Findings/Information
        IV   Conclusions/Summary
        V   Recommendations (if required)

        Short informal report

        I   Background/Introduction/Situation
        II   Findings/Analysis/Information
        III   Action/Solution/Conclusion/Summary
        IV   Recommendations (if required)

(b)   *Tutorial note.* Even the formal requirements of a report need not make it stiff and uninteresting to read.

        Any ten of:

Stated	Affirmed
Asserted	Proposed
Commented	Argued
Suggested	Replied
Claimed	Insinuated
Remarked	Repeated
Emphasised	Stressed
Agreed	Promised
Indicated	Alleged
Told (x) that	Informed (x) that

(c)   (i)   Your Name investigated the matter.   *or*

                The matter was investigated.

                (In a formal report, the first person should be avoided, and third person or impersonal constructions used.)

        (ii)   Mr Harris indicated [to Your Name] that he would investigate further.

                (Direct speech should not be used, and should be changed to indirect or reported speech. It is optional whether you include the fact that Mr Harris told *you* specifically: this can be assumed, since you are the author of the report.)

(iii)   He surmised [suggested/assumed] that there was a problem in the Accounts Department, since it seemed [he considered/felt/believed] that the fault did not lie with his own department.

(Direct speech becomes indirect, with the clarifying details that that requires - eg 'our' becomes 'his own department'. Just as importantly, the speaker is using words like 'must be' and 'obviously', indicating that he is making certain assumptions and is stating an *opinion* or viewpoint of his own. In a formal report, any assumptions or potential bias must be made clear so that the account is objective: verbs like 'surmised', 'assumed' and 'believed' show clearly that what follows is a *subjective* statement, not objective fact.)

(iv)   Accounts appeared not to have received the complaint.

(Viewed objectively, the facts are that Accounts say they have not received the complaint: that they might be lying about this is an assumption - and accusation - on the part of the writer and should be kept out of the formal report, especially since 'pretended' is a rather loaded word.)

(v)   Mr Harris considered the latitude given to the Accounts Department to be deplorable.

(Emotionally loaded words like 'outrageous', 'layabouts', 'getting away with' and 'fumed' should be avoided in favour of a more impersonal, 'calmer' style.)

(vi)   Your Name indicated that he would himself undertake the task, if they lacked the initiative to do so.

(Avoid colloquial abbreviations – I'd, weren't etc - and expressions in formal written English.)

Answer 8.3

Russia: country data

Russia covers an area of 17.1 million square kilometres. The country comprises 76% of the territory of the former Soviet Union (FSU) but, with 148.3 million inhabitants in mid-1990, only 51% of the total population of the FSU. Average annual population growth was 0.4% during the 1980s and population density was 8.7 per square kilometre in 1990.

Russia's Gross Domestic Product at current market prices was 573.1 billion roubles in 1989. Industry accounted for 46.6% of this total, services accounted for 37.8% and agriculture accounted for 15.6%.

The value of Russia's exports was 140.9 billion roubles in 1989, of which oil and gas represented 31.2%.

Answer 8.4

Tutorial note. Additional knowledge of the subject matter is not required in order to summarise the information for a written report, as below. The table listed the enterprises in alphabetical order: note that a different order of presentation has been used below.

Important changes occurred in the competitive environment facing the largest public enterprises from the late 1970s up to 1990.

Changes for the Post Office were the deregulation of courier services in 1981 and the restructuring of the enterprise into separate businesses. British Telecom (BT) was affected by the liberalisation of apparatus (1981), value added services (1981) and a second terrestrial carrier in 1982.

British Coal had better defined contracts for supply to electricity generators from 1989 and reduced protection from imports of coal and from gas. British Steel was affected by the unwinding of European Community steel quotas from 1980 onwards.

Important legislation in the energy supply industries were the Energy Act (1983), the Gas Act (1985) and the Electricity Act (1986). British Gas faced partial competition in the supply of gas to industrial consumers; partial competition was also introduced in the electricity supply industry, with fuller competition in electricity supply being introduced in 1990.

The main competitive change for British Airways was route liberalisation which was introduced on North Atlantic routes in 1977, UK routes in 1982 and European routes from 1984 onwards. Domestic aviation presented increased competition for British Rail from 1982, as did the deregulation of bus services in 1986 and coach services from 1980.

Answer 8.5

(a)   Your answer might have included the following.

Enrolment and application forms of many different sorts
Order forms for goods
Payment or paying-in forms at the bank
Complaint forms
Parking tickets

(b)   The answer will depend upon the forms you have obtained. Look back at the interactive text if you need guidance on the general features of 'good' forms.

BPP
PUBLISHING

Chapter 9   Costs, standard costs and performance

Chapter topic list

1   Cost accounting
2   Direct costs and overheads (indirect costs)
3   Functional costs
4   Cost centres and cost units
5   Cost codes
6   Standard costs
7   Standard costing as a cost accounting system
8   Productivity ratios

Learning objectives

On completion of this chapter you will be able to:

	Performance criteria	Range statement
• consolidate information derived from different units of the organisation into the appropriate form	7.1.1	7.1.1
• correctly reconcile information derived from different systems within the organisation	7.1.2	7.1.1
• calculate ratios and performance indicators accurately and in accordance with the organisation's procedures	7.1.5	7.1.1
• calculate ratios and performance indicators accurately	7.2.2	
• *be aware of relevant performance and quality measures*	N/a	n/a
• *use standard units of inputs and outputs*	N/a	n/a
• *understand performance indicators of productivity, cost per unit, resource utilisation and profitability*	N/a	n/a

Italicised objectives are areas of knowledge and understanding underlying the elements of competence for Unit 7.

1   COST ACCOUNTING

1.1   To measure performance effectively the managers of a business must be provided with sufficiently accurate and detailed information - ie periodic performance reports - and the cost accounting system should provide this.

> ## KEY TERM
>
> **Cost accounting** is a management information system which analyses past, present and future data to provide the basis for managerial action.

In this chapter we introduce some of the basic concepts of cost accounting. Various aspects of this subject are dealt with in Unit 6: *Recording Cost Information*.

1.2   The cost accountant is interested in providing the answers to the following types of question.

   (a)   **What has been the cost of goods produced or services provided?**

   What has been the cost of a department or work section?

   What have revenues been?

   Knowing about costs and revenues that are being/have been incurred and earned enables management to do the following.

   (i)   **Assess the profitability** of a product, a service, a department, or the organisation in total.

   (ii)   Perhaps, **set selling prices** with some regard for the costs of sale.

   (iii)   **Put a value to stocks** of goods (raw materials, work in progress, finished goods) that are still held in store at the end of a period, for preparing a balance sheet of the company's assets and liabilities.

   (b)   **What are the future costs of goods and services likely to be?** Costing is an integral part of budgeting (planning) for the future.

   (c)   **How do actual costs compare with budgeted costs?** If an organisation plans for its revenues and costs to be a certain amount, but they actually turn out differently, the differences can be measured and reported. Management can use these reports as a guide to whether corrective action (or 'control' action) is needed to sort out a problem revealed by these differences between budgeted and actual results. This system of control is often referred to as budgetary control.

   (d)   **What information does management need in order to make sensible decisions about profits and costs?**

1.3   It would be wrong to suppose that cost accounting systems are restricted to manufacturing operations, although they are probably more fully developed in this area of work. Service industries, government departments and welfare activities can all make use of cost accounting information. Within a manufacturing organisation, the cost accounting system should be applied not only to manufacturing but also to administration, selling and distribution, research and development and so on.

The work of the cost department

1.4   The cost department is responsible for keeping the cost accounting records.

(a) These records should analyse production, administration, marketing costs and so on in such a way as to fulfil all of the requirements set out in paragraph 1.2 above.

(b) The systems should cater for the production of regular performance statements which are necessary to management for control purposes.

(c) The system should also be capable of analysing the following.

- Past costs (for profit measurement, stock valuation)
- Present costs (for control, comparing current results against the budget)
- Future costs (for budgeting and decision making)

1.5 If a company did not have a costing system, management would not have adequate information on the following.

- The profitability of individual products, services or jobs.
- The profitability of different departments or operations.
- The cost behaviour of the various items of expenditure in the organisation.
- The differences between actual results and expected results.
- How to set prices so as to cover costs and generate an acceptable level of profit.
- The effect on profits of increases or decreases in output.

The relationship with financial accounting

1.6 The **financial accounting** and **cost accounting** systems in a business both record the same basic data for income and expenditure, but each set of records may analyse the data in a different way. This is because each system has a different purpose.

(a) Financial accounting is primarily **a method of reporting the results and financial position of a business**. Although the financial accounts may be of interest to management, their principal function is to satisfy the information needs of persons not involved in the day-to-day running of the business.

(i) Shareholders, for instance, may use them to assess how well the directors have carried out their stewardship function.

(ii) Other outsiders whose information needs are satisfied wholly or in part by the financial accounts are suppliers, customers, employees and the Inland Revenue.

In addition, the financial accounts must be prepared in accordance with **strict guidelines** which are laid down in **company law** and in **accounting standards**.

(b) Cost accounting is an **internal reporting system for the organisation's own management**. It provides them with the information which they need to manage the business. Outsiders will not see this information, and there are no strict rules which govern the way in which cost accounting information should be prepared and presented. Each organisation can develop the system which is best suited to its needs.

1.7 Since the cost accounting system and the financial accounting system have different purposes and analyse the data in different ways, they are often kept separately in two sets of accounts. However, it is possible to maintain a **single integrated set of accounts** containing both cost and financial accounting information.

1.8 Finally, there is a **legal requirement** for a financial accounting system. Companies are obliged to prepare annual accounts for **external reporting purposes**. There is no legal requirement for a costing system, which is only necessary if management believes that cost information will help them to **plan** and **control** the resources of the organisation more efficiently than if no formal costing system existed. There is no point in having a costing system if its costs outweigh the benefits it provides.

2 DIRECT COSTS AND OVERHEADS (INDIRECT COSTS)

2.1 Total costs of a product or service consist of the following costs.

(a) The **cost of materials consumed** in making the product or providing the service.

(b) The **cost of the wages and salaries** of employees of the organisation, who are directly or indirectly involved in producing the product or providing the service.

(c) The **cost of other expenses**, apart from materials and labour costs. These include items such as the following.

- Rent and rates
- Electricity bills
- Gas bills
- Depreciation
- Interest charges
- The cost of contractors' services (for example sub-contractors and office cleaners)
- Telephone bills

2.2 Materials, labour costs and other expenses can be classified as **direct costs** or as **indirect costs**.

KEY TERM

A **direct cost** is a cost that can be traced in full to the product or service (or department) that is being costed.

(a) **Direct materials** costs are the costs of materials that are known to have been used in making and selling a product (or providing a service), ie 'the cost of materials entering into and becoming constituent elements of a product or saleable service, and which can be identified separately in product cost'.

(b) **Direct labour** costs are the specific costs of the workforce used to make a product or provide a service, for the 'remuneration for employees' effort and skills applied directly to a product or saleable service and which can be identified separately in product cost'. Direct labour costs are established by measuring the time taken for a job, or the time taken in 'direct production work'. Traditionally, direct labour costs have been restricted to wage-earning factory workers, but in recent years, with the development of systems for costing services ('service costing') the costs of some salaried staff might also be treated as a direct labour cost.

(c) Other **direct expenses** are those expenses that have been incurred in full as a direct consequence of making a product, or providing a service, or running a department (depending on whether a product, a service or a department is being costed).

KEY TERM

An **indirect cost** is a cost that is incurred in the course of making a product, providing a service or running a department, but which cannot be traced directly and in full to the product, service or department.

2.3 Total expenditure may be analysed as follows.

Material cost	=	Direct material cost	+	Indirect material cost
+		+		+
Wages	=	Direct wages	+	Indirect wages
+		+		+
Expenses	=	Direct expenses	+	Indirect expenses
Total cost	=	Prime cost	+	Overhead

Activity 9.1

A direct labour employee's wage in week 5 consists of:

		£
(a)	basic pay for normal hours worked, 36 hours at £4 per hour =	144
(b)	pay at the basic rate for overtime, 6 hours at £4 per hour =	24
(c)	overtime shift premium, with overtime paid at time-and-a-quarter ¼ × 6 hours × £4 per hour =	6
(d)	a bonus payment under a group bonus (or 'incentive') scheme: bonus for the month =	30
	Total gross wages in week 5 for 42 hours of work	204

Which costs are direct? Are any indirect?

3 FUNCTIONAL COSTS

3.1 In a 'traditional' costing system for a manufacturing organisation, costs are classified as follows.

- Production or manufacturing costs
- Administration costs
- Marketing, or selling and distribution costs

3.2 Many expenses fall comfortably into one or other of these three broad classifications. Manufacturing costs are associated with the **factory, selling** and **distribution** costs with the **sales, marketing, warehousing** and **transport** departments and administration costs with general office departments (such as accounting and personnel).

3.3 Other expenses that do not fall fully into one of these classifications might be categorised as **general overheads** or even listed as a classification on their own (for example research and development costs).

3.4 In costing a small product made by a manufacturing organisation, **direct costs are usually restricted to some of the production costs** (although it is not uncommon to find a salesman's commission for selling the product as a direct selling cost). A common analysis of costs might look like this.

	£
Production costs	
Direct materials	A
Direct wages	B
Direct expenses (if any)	C
Prime cost	A+B+C
Production overheads	D
Full factory cost	A+B+C+D
Administration overheads	E
Selling and distribution overheads	F
Full cost of sales	A+B+C+D+E+F

Functional costs, in more detail

3.5 **Functional costs** include the following.

> **KEY TERMS**
>
> - **Production costs**: the costs which are incurred by the sequence of operations beginning with the supply of raw materials, and ending with the completion of the product ready for warehousing as a finished goods item; packaging costs are production costs where they relate to 'primary' packing (for example, boxes and wrappers).
>
> - **Administration costs**: the costs of managing an organisation, ie planning and controlling its operations, but only insofar as such administration costs are not related to the production, sales, distribution or research and development functions.
>
> - **Selling costs**, sometimes known as **marketing costs**, are the costs of creating demand for products and securing firm orders from customers.
>
> - **Distribution costs**: the costs of the sequence of operations beginning with the receipt of finished goods from the production department and making them ready for dispatch and ending with the reconditioning for re-use of returned empty containers.
>
> - **Research and development costs**
>
>   o   Research costs are the costs of searching for new or improved products.
>
>   o   Development costs are the costs incurred between the decision to produce a new or improved product and the commencement of full, formal manufacture of the product.

Activity 9.2

Within the costing system of a manufacturing company the following types of expense are incurred.

Reference
number

1	Cost of oils used to lubricate production machinery
2	Motor vehicle licences for lorries
3	Depreciation of factory plant and equipment
4	Cost of chemicals used in the laboratory
5	Commission paid to sales representatives
6	Salary of the secretary to the finance director
7	Trade discount given to customers
8	Holiday pay of machine operatives
9	Salary of security guard in raw material warehouse
10	Fees to advertising agency
11	Rent of finished goods warehouse
12	Salary of scientist in the laboratory
13	Insurance of the company's premises
14	Salary of supervisor working in the factory
15	Cost of typewriter ribbons in the general office
16	Protective clothing for machine operatives

Tasks

(a) Place each expense within the following classifications.

  Production overhead
  Selling and distribution overhead
  Administration overhead
  Research and development overhead

  Each type of expense should appear only once in your answer. You may use the reference numbers in your answer.

(b) Give three reasons why direct production labour cost might be regarded as a fixed cost rather than as a variable cost.

4   COST CENTRES AND COST UNITS

Allocation of costs to cost centres

4.1   Costs consist of the following.

  • Direct materials
  • Direct labour
  • Direct expenses
  • Production overheads
  • Administration overheads
  • General overheads

  But how does a cost accountant set about **recording** in practice the actual expenses incurred as any one of these classifications?

4.2   To begin with, all costs should be recorded as a direct cost of a **cost centre**. Even 'overhead costs' are directly traceable to an office or an item of expense and there should be an **overhead cost centre** to cater for these costs.

> **KEY TERM**
>
> A **cost centre** is a location, person or item of equipment for which costs may be
> ascertained and related to cost units for control purposes.

4.3   Suitable cost centres might be as follows.

(a)   In a **production department**: the department itself, a machine within the department
       or group of machines, a foreman's work group, a work bench and so on.

(b)   **Production 'service'** or **'back-up' departments**, such as the stores, maintenance,
       production planning and control departments.

(c)   **Administration**, **sales** or **distribution departments**, such as the personnel, accounting
       or purchasing departments; a sales region or salesman; or a warehouse or distribution
       unit.

(d)   **Shared costs** (for example rent, rates, electricity or gas bills) may require cost centres
       of their own, in order to be directly allocated. Shared cost items may be charged to
       separate, individual cost centres, or they may be grouped into a larger cost centre (for
       example factory occupancy costs, for rents, rates, heating, lighting, building repairs,
       cleaning and maintenance of a particular factory).

4.4   Charging costs to a cost centre simply involves two steps.

Step 1.   Identifying the cost centre for which an item of expenditure is a direct cost.

Step 2.   Allocating the cost to the cost centre (usually by means of a **cost code** - discussed
             below).

Cost centres, therefore, provide a **basis for collection** and then further analysis of actual
costs, and are a means of **building up estimated costs** in budgeting.

4.5   Cost centres are an essential 'building block' of a costing system. They are the starting point
       for the following.

•   Classifying actual costs incurred
•   Preparing budgets of planned costs
•   Comparing actual costs and budgeted costs, for management control information

Cost per unit

4.6   Once costs have been traced to cost centres, they can be further analysed in order to
       establish a **cost per cost unit**. Alternatively, some items of cost may be charged directly to a
       cost unit, for example direct materials and direct labour costs.

> **KEY TERM**
>
> A **cost unit** is 'a unit of product or service in relation to which costs are ascertained'.
>
>   CIMA *Official Terminology*

4.7   The unit selected must be appropriate to the business and one with which expenditure can
       be readily associated. Care must be taken in non-manufacturing operations to ensure that
       the unit is a **meaningful measure**. For instance in transport undertakings the cost per
       tonne transported may not be particularly useful. The cost per tonne carried from London

to Glasgow would probably be greater than the cost per tonne from London to Dover, and it would not be easy to make comparisons for control purposes. If the cost unit was changed to a tonne-mile (the cost of transporting one tonne for one mile) then a comparison between the two journeys would be valid.

4.8 Some examples of cost units are shown in the table below. (Source: CIMA *Official Terminology*).

Examples of cost units

Business	Cost unit
Brewing	Barrel
Brick-making	1,000 bricks
Coal mining	Tonne/ton
Electricity	Kilowatt hour (kWh)
Engineering	Contract, job
Oil	Barrel, tonne, litre
Hotel/catering	Room/cover
Professional services (accountants, architects, lawyers, surveyors)	Chargeable hour, job, contract
Education	(a) Course
	(b) Enrolled student
	(c) Successful student
Hospitals	Patient episode
Activity	
Credit control	Account maintained
Materials storage/handling	(a) Requisition unit issued/received
	(b) Material movement value issued/received
Personnel administration	Personnel record
Selling	(a) Customer call
	(b) Value of sales
	(c) Orders taken

Activity 9.3

(a) Suggest a cost unit appropriate to a hospital.
(b) Suggest *one* suitable cost unit and *two* cost centres for a college of further education.

5 COST CODES

5.1 We have seen that charging costs to a cost centre involves two steps.

- **Identifying** the cost centre for which an item of expenditure is a direct cost.
- **Allocating** the cost to the cost centre.

5.2 The allocation of the cost to the cost centre is usually by means of a **cost code.**

KEY TERM

A **code** is 'A system of symbols designed to be applied to a classified set of items to give a brief accurate reference, facilitating entry, collation and analysis'.

CIMA *Official Terminology*

5.3 In order to provide accurate management information, it is vital that costs are **allocated correctly**. Each individual cost should therefore be identifiable by its code. This is possible by building up the individual characteristics of the cost into the code.

5.4 The characteristics which are normally identified are as follows.

- The nature of the cost (materials, wages, hire charges and so on)
- The type of cost (direct or indirect and so on)
- The cost centre to which the cost should be allocated
- The department which the particular cost centre is in

Types of code

5.5 The main coding methods are listed below.

(a) **Sequence (or progressive) codes**

Numbers are given to items in ordinary numerical sequence, so that there is no obvious connection between an item and its code. For example:

000042   2" nails
000043   office stapler
000044   hand wrench

(b) **Group classification codes**

These are an improvement on simple sequence codes, in that a digit (often the first one) indicates the classification of an item. For example:

4NNNNN   nails
5NNNNN   screws
6NNNNN   bolts

(*Note.* 'N' stands for another digit; 'NNNNN' indicates there are five further digits in the code.)

(c) **Faceted codes**

These are a refinement of group classification codes, in that each digit of the code gives information about an item. For example:

(i)   The first digit: 1   Nails
    2   Screws
    3   Bolts
    etc...

(ii)   The second digit: 1   Steel
    2   Brass
    3   Copper
    etc...

(iii) The third digit: 1   50 mm
                         2   60 mm
                         3   75 mm
                         etc...

A 60mm steel screw would have a code of 212.

(d) **Significant digit codes**

These incorporate some digit(s) which is (are) part of the description of the item being coded. For example:

5000   screws
5050   50 mm screws
5060   60 mm screws
5075   75 mm screws

(e) **Hierarchical codes**

This is a type of faceted code where each digit represents a classification, and each digit further to the right represents a smaller subset than those to the left. For example:

3   =   Screws
31   =   Flat headed screws
32   =   Round headed screws
322 =   Steel (round headed) screws
and so on.

5.6 A coding system does not have to be structured entirely on any one of the above systems - **it can mix the various features according to the items which need to be coded**. But the system eventually chosen should always be simple to use and understand and it should be flexible (so that it can readily accommodate changes within an organisation, especially expansion).

5.7 For accounting purposes, the coding system most commonly used is a form of **hierarchical code**. The code will need to show whether an item is an **asset** (and what sort of an asset) or a **liability** (and what sort of a liability) and the **cost centre** to which it is attributable (if the code is to be used for cost accounting).

6   STANDARD COSTS

Definitions

> **KEY TERM**
>
> A **standard cost** is an estimated unit cost, prepared in advance and calculated from management's expectations of:
>
> - efficiency levels in the use of materials and labour;
> - the expected price of materials, labour and expenses;
> - budgeted overhead costs and budgeted volumes of activity.
>
> It is a planned cost, and so is the cost that should be incurred in making the unit.

6.1 Differences between actual and standard costs are called **variances**.

BPP PUBLISHING

6.2 The use of standard costs to simplify the keeping of cost accounting records should not be overlooked, but the CIMA's *Official Terminology* emphasises the control and variance analysis aspect of standard costing. Study the following definitions carefully, bearing in mind that subjective judgements go into establishing standards and standard costs.

> **KEY TERMS**
>
> - **Standard**: 'A benchmark measurement of resource usage, set in defined conditions.'
>
> - **Standard cost**: 'The planned unit cost of the products, components or services produced in a period ... The main uses of standard costs are in performance measurement, control, stock valuation and in the establishment of selling prices ... '
>
> - **Standard costing**: 'A control technique which compares standard costs and revenues with actual results to obtain variances which are used to stimulate improved performance.'

6.3 A **standard cost card** (or standard cost sheet) will be prepared for each product. The card will normally show the following.

- The quantity and price of each direct material to be consumed
- The time and rate of each grade of direct labour required
- The overhead recovery
- The full cost

The **standard selling price** and the **standard profit per unit** may also be shown.

Activity 9.4

The standard time allowed for product X is 2 hours and the standard labour rate is £5.00 per hour. Last month the output of product X was 1,000 units and the actual hours worked were 1,850. What was the value in standard hours of last month's production?

7 STANDARD COSTING AS A COST ACCOUNTING SYSTEM

7.1 You should be aware that standard costs make the task of recording costs in books of account a relatively simple matter.

7.2 EXAMPLE: STANDARD COSTS

Suppose that the standard cost card of product Y is as follows.

		£
Direct material	6 kg of material A at £3	18.00
Direct labour	3 hours at £2.50	7.50
Production overhead	3 hours at £3.50	10.50
		36.00

The standard cost per unit for administration, selling and distribution is £4.

During one month the following results were recorded.

Opening stocks of raw material, WIP and finished goods are nil. (Stocks in a manufacturing business comprise raw materials, work in progress (WIP) and finished goods. We return to these terms later in the text.)

Purchases	10,000 kg of material A
Used in production	8,000 kg of material A
Units of product Y made	1,500 units
Units of product Y sold	1,200 units

There was no closing stock of work in progress.

What costs would be entered in the books of account for:

(a) the value of closing stocks of raw materials;
(b) the value of closing stocks of finished goods;
(c) the cost of units produced;
(d) the cost of units sold?

7.3 SOLUTION

(a) Closing stocks of material A are valued at standard cost.

2,000 kg × £3 = £6,000

(b) Closing stocks of finished goods (product Y) are valued at standard production cost.

300 units × £36 = £10,800

(c) Units produced are valued at standard production cost.

1,500 units × £36 = £54,000

(d) Units sold are valued at the standard cost of sales.

1,200 units × £40 = £48,000

Any variance arising because actual costs are different from standard costs will be recorded in the cost accounts as a **variance**.

Variances will be included in the profit and loss account at the end of a period as an **adjusting item**.

In this example it may be seen that the materials actually used (8,000 kg) were less than expected to make 1,500 units of product Y (9,000 kg); therefore a favourable materials usage variance has occurred. The cost of this variance would be recorded in the books of account.

8 PRODUCTIVITY RATIOS

Production and productivity

8.1 It is important to distinguish between the terms '**production**' and '**productivity**'.

> ### KEY TERMS
>
> - **Production** is the quantity or volume of output produced. It is the number of units produced, or the actual number of units produced converted into an equivalent number of 'standard hours of production'.
>
> - **Productivity** is a measure of the efficiency with which output has been produced.

8.2 EXAMPLE: PRODUCTION AND PRODUCTIVITY

Suppose that an employee is expected to produce three units in every hour worked. The standard rate of productivity is three units per hour, and one unit is valued at 2 of a standard hour of output. If, during one week, the employee makes 126 units in 40 hours of work:

(a) production in the week is 126 units;

(b) productivity is a relative measure of the hours actually taken and the hours that should have been taken to make the output; either:

(i)	126 units should take	42 hours
	But did take	40 hours
	Productivity ratio = 42/40 × 100% =	105%
(ii)	or alternatively:	
	In 40 hours, production should be (× 3)	120 units
	But was	126 units
	Productivity ratio = 126/120 × 100% =	105%

A productivity ratio greater than 100% indicates that actual efficiency is better than the expected or 'standard' level of efficiency.

8.3 Management will wish to plan and control both production levels and labour productivity.

(a) **Production levels** can be raised as follows.

- Working overtime
- Hiring extra staff
- Sub-contracting some work to an outside firm
- Raising productivity – increase output in a given number of hours worked

Production levels can be reduced as follows.

- Cancelling overtime
- Laying off staff

If possible, managers will wish to avoid paying employees (in full) for doing nothing (ie idle time payments) and will also wish to avoid a drop in productivity.

(b) **Productivity**, if improved, will enable a company to achieve its production targets in fewer hours of work, and therefore at a lower cost.

Productivity and its effect on cost

8.4 Improved productivity is an important means of **reducing total unit costs**. In order to make this point clear, a simple example will be used.

8.5 EXAMPLE: PRODUCTIVITY AND ITS EFFECT ON COST

Clockwork Zombies Ltd has a production department in its factory consisting of a work team of just two men, Rob Ottley and Cy Burnett. Rob and Cy each work a 40 hour week and refuse to do any overtime. They are each paid £100 per week and production overheads of £400 per week are charged to their work.

(a) In week one, they produce 160 units of output between them. Productivity is measured in units of output per man hour.

Production	160 units
Productivity (80 man hours)	2 units per man hour
Total cost	£600 (labour plus overhead)
Cost per man hour	£7.50
Cost per unit	£3.75

(b) In week two, management pressure is exerted on Rob and Cy to increase output and they produce 200 units in normal time.

Production	200 units (up by 25%)
Productivity	2.5 units per man hour (up by 25%)
Total cost	£600
Cost per man hour	£7.50 (no change)
Cost per unit	£3.00 (a saving of 20% on the previous cost)

(c) In week three, Rob and Cy agree to work a total of 20 hours of overtime for an additional £50 wages. Output is again 200 units and overhead charges are increased by £100:

Production	200 units (up 25% on week one)
Productivity (100 man hours)	2 units per hour (no change on week one)
Total cost (£600 + £50 + £100)	£750
Cost per unit	£3.75

(d) **Conclusions**

   (i) An increase in production without an increase in productivity will not reduce unit costs (week one compared with week three).

   (ii) An increase in productivity will reduce unit costs (week one compared with week two).

8.6 Labour cost control is largely concerned with **productivity**. Rising wage rates, however, have accelerated the trend towards greater automation as the best means of improving productivity and reducing costs.

8.7 Where automation is introduced, productivity is often, but misleadingly, measured in terms of **output per man-hour**.

Suppose for example, that a work-team of six men (240 hours per week) is replaced by one machine (40 hours per week) and a team of four men (160 hours per week), and as a result output is increased from 1,200 units per week to 1,600 units.

	Production	**Man hours**	**Productivity**
Before the machine	1,200 units	240	5 units per man hour
After the machine	1,600 units	160	10 units per man hour

Labour productivity has doubled because of the machine, and employees would probably expect extra pay for this success. For control purposes, however, it is likely that a new measure of productivity is required, output per machine hour, which may then be measured against a standard output for performance reporting.

Measuring productivity in service industries

8.8 In a service industry, productivity measures need to be based on **measures of output appropriate to the service being provided**.

(a) For example, a supermarket chain's main activity is selling, and an appropriate productivity measure might be **sales per employee**.

(b) In a professional service organisation, such as a firm of accountants, the product may be best measured in terms of **hours of time chargeable to clients**. One appropriate productivity measure would be **chargeable hours per employee** in a particular period.

The examples of cost units we looked at earlier in this chapter provide further examples. (Look back now to the table in Section 4 of this chapter.)

DEVOLVED ASSESSMENT ALERT

Note that the guidance on element 6.1 emphasises that reports on performance are *not* restricted to financial measurements. This is clearly demonstrated in paragraph 8.8 (b) in which productivity is measured in terms of **chargeable hours per employee.**

Activity 9.5

What is the difference between 'production' and 'productivity'? (Answer in approximately 50 words.)

Activity 9.6

Lawry Ltd distributes its goods to a regional dealer using a single lorry. The dealer's premises are 40 kilometres away by road. The lorry has a capacity of 10½ tonnes, and makes the journey twice a day fully loaded on the outward journeys and empty on the return journeys. The following information is available for a 4-week budget control period, period 8, during 20X4.

Petrol consumption	8 kilometres per 5 litres petrol
Petrol cost	£0.36 per litre
Oil	£8 per week
Driver's wages and national insurance	£140 per week
Repairs	£72 per week
Garaging	£4 per day (based on a 7-day week)
Cost of lorry when new (excluding tyres)	£18,750
Life of the lorry	80,000 kilometres
Insurance	£650 per annum
Cost of a set of tyres	£1,250
Life of a set of tyres	25,000 kilometres
Estimated sale value of lorry at end of its life	£2,750
Vehicle licence cost	£234 per annum
Other overhead costs	£3,900 per annum

The lorry operates on a five-day week.

Task

You are asked to carry out the following tasks.

(a) Prepare a statement to show the total costs of operating the vehicle in period 8, 20X4 analysed into running costs and standing costs.

(b) Calculate the vehicle cost per kilometre, and the cost per tonne/kilometre in the period.

(c) Using the costs you have calculated, what would be the charge, to cover full costs, for a special delivery of 6 tonnes on each of an outward and a return journey (so the lorry is loaded both going out and returning) to a destination 120 kilometres away, if costs are estimated:

(i)   on a kilometres travelled basis;
(ii) on the basis of tonne/kilometres carried?

Key learning points

- **Cost accounting** is a management information system which analyses **past, present** and **future** data to provide a basis for managerial action - it is an internal reporting system for an organisation's own management. **Financial accounting** is primarily a method of reporting the results and financial position of a business.

- A **direct cost** is a cost that can be traced in full to a product or service. An **indirect cost** is a cost that is incurred in the course of making a product, providing a service or running a department, but which cannot be traced directly in full to the product, service or department.

- Functional costs include the following.

  - Production costs
  - Administration costs
  - Selling costs
  - Distribution costs
  - Research and development costs

- A **cost centre** is a location, person, or item of equipment for which costs may be ascertained and related to unit cost units for control purposes.

- Charging costs to a cost centre involves identifying the relevant **cost centre** and **allocating** the cost to the cost centre (usually by means of a code).

- The main types of coding method are as follows.

  - Sequence (or progressive) codes
  - Group classification codes
  - Faceted codes
  - Significant digit codes
  - Hierarchical codes

- A **standard cost** is an estimated unit cost which is planned and which represents the cost that should be incurred in making the unit. **Variances** are the differences between actual and standard costs.

- A **standard cost card** shows the following.

  - Quantity and price of each direct material to be consumed
  - The time and rate of each grade of labour required
  - The overhead recovery
  - The full cost
  - The standard selling price
  - The standard profit per unit

- A **budget** is a financial and/or quantitative plan of operations for a forthcoming accounting period. Its **purposes** are as follows.

  - Co-ordination of all the different departments of an organisation
  - Communication of an organisation's policies or targets
  - Control (comparison of plan and actual results)
  - To compel planning

- **Reporting by exception.** This means that variances should only be reported where the difference between actual and standard is significant.

- **Production** is the quantity or volume of output produced. **Productivity** is a measure of the efficiency with which output has been produced.

Quick quiz

1. What do the total costs of a product consist of?

2. Give five examples of functional costs.

3. What are the two steps involved in charging costs to a cost centre?

4. What is the name given to differences between actual and standard costs?

183

5   How often are standard costs usually revised?

6   When setting standards, what two requirements must managers be aware of?

7   How does productivity differ from production?

Answers to quick quiz

1   •   Cost of materials consumed in making the product
        •   Cost of the wages and salaries of employees directly involved in producing the product
        •   Cost of other expenses

2   •   Production costs
        •   Administration costs
        •   Selling/marketing costs
        •   Distribution costs
        •   Research and development costs

3   **Identifying** the relevant cost centre and **allocating** the cost to the cost centre.

4   Variances.

5   Once a year.

6   •   The need to establish a useful control measure.
        •   The need to set a standard that will have the desired motivational effect.

7   **Production** is the quantity or volume of output produced whereas **productivity** is a measure of the efficiency with which that volume of output has been produced.

Answers to activities

Answer 9.1

Items (a) and (b) are direct labour costs of the items produced in the 42 hours worked in week 5.

Overtime premium, item (c), is usually regarded as an overhead expense, because it is 'unfair' to charge the items produced in overtime hours with the premium. Why should an item made in overtime be more costly just because, by chance, it was made after the employee normally clocks off for the day?

Group bonus scheme payments (d) are usually overhead costs, because they cannot normally be traced directly to individual products or jobs.

In this example, the direct labour employee costs were £168 in direct costs and £36 in indirect costs, and these costs would be coded differently, to allocate them to different cost units or overhead cost centres.

Answer 9.2

(a)   The reference numbers for each expense can be classified as follows.

	Reference numbers
Production overhead	1, 3, 8, 9, 14, 16
Selling and distribution overhead	2, 5, 7, 10, 11
Administration overhead	6, 13, 15
Research and development overhead	4, 12

(b)   Direct production labour cost might be regarded as a fixed cost rather than as a variable cost for the following reasons.

        (i)   Direct labour may be paid a guaranteed salary, regardless of output.

        (ii)   Production methods may be highly mechanised, with the result that direct labour cost is insignificant and may be approximated to a fixed cost.

        (iii)   A no-redundancy policy may result in labour costs remaining fixed regardless of output.

        (iv)   Union agreements featuring guaranteed manning levels can result in fixed production labour costs.

        (*Tutorial note:* you need only give *three* reasons, as requested.)

Answer 9.3

(a)   Any one of the following is an acceptable answer.

(i)   Bed occupied
(ii)   Patient
(iii)   Bed-day

(b)   Possible cost units:

(i)   Enrolled student
(ii)   Successful student
(iii)   Course-week

Possible cost centres:

(i)   An academic department, such as the Accounting and Finance Department
(ii)   Administration Department
(iii)   Catering Section

Answer 9.4

Standard hours	=	standard time allowed × output
	=	2 hours × 1,000 units
	=	2,000 standard hours

Answer 9.5

Production is the quantity or volume of output produced. It is the number of units produced, or the actual number of units produced converted into an equivalent number of standard hours of production. 'Standard hours of production' is a concept used in standard costing.

Productivity is a measure of the efficiency with which output has been produced, for example production per employee.

Answer 9.6

(a)   Distance travelled per day   40 × 2 × 2 = 160 km
        Distance travelled in the period   160 × 5 days × 4 weeks = 3,200 km
        Distance travelled in the period fully loaded
              (½ of 3,200)   1,600 km
        Tonnes carried, per trip   10½ tonnes
        Tonnes/kilometres in the period   16,800 tonne/kilometres

STATEMENTS OF COSTS PERIOD 8 20X4

(i)   Running costs:

	£
Petrol (3,200 km ÷ 8 km per 5 litres × £0.36 per litre)	720
Oil (£8 × 4 weeks)	32
Repairs (£72 × 4 weeks)	288
Wages (£140 × 4 weeks)	560
Tyres cost (£1,250 ÷ 25,000 km × 3,200 km)	160
Depreciation ((£18,750 − 2,750) ÷ 80,000 km × 3,200 km)	640
Running costs	2,400

Depreciation is assumed to be a running cost, charged on distance travelled, rather than a fixed charge per period.

(ii)   Standing costs:

	£
Garaging (£4 per day × 7 days × 4 weeks)	112
Insurance (£650 ÷ 13)	50
Licence cost (£234 ÷ 13)	18
Other overheads (£3,900 ÷ 13)	300
	480

(iii)   Total costs:

	£
Running costs	2,400
Standing costs	480
Total costs, period 8	2,880

(b)   Cost per km travelled $\dfrac{£2,880}{3,200\,\text{km}}$ = £0.90 per km

Cost per tonne/km $\dfrac{£2,880}{16,800\,\text{tonne/km}}$ = £0.171 per tonne/km

(c)   To deliver six tonnes to a destination 120 km away, and to return loaded with a further six tonnes, 240 km would be travelled and the tonne/kilometres would be:

$240 \times 6 = 1,440$ tonne/kilometres

Charge:

(i)   on a kilometre basis of costs: 240 kilometres × £0.9 =   £216
(ii)   on a tonne/kilometre basis of costs: 1,440 tonne/kilometres × £0.171 = £246

Chapter 10   Reporting performance. Analysing results

Chapter topic list

1   Management accounts

2   Accounting for separate organisational units

3   Profit centres

4   Reporting non-financial results

5   Analysis of results

Learning objectives

On completion of this chapter you will be able to:

	Performance criteria	Range statement
• account for transactions between separate units of the organisation in accordance with the organisation's procedures	7.1.4	7.1.1, 2 - 4

1 MANAGEMENT ACCOUNTS

1.1 Most financial accounts have as their aim **the provision of summarised information about the progress or state of a business as a whole**. Such information is generally of limited use for those who manage the business, because it is retrospective and does not distinguish between different sections of the same business.

1.2 Most large businesses also produce **internal accounts** periodically for the purposes of management control. Such accounts are generally referred to as **management accounts** and are an important practical aspect of accounting, especially in larger organisations where managers tend to need more **formal regular reports** to learn what is happening in business operations.

1.3 There is no obligation to produce management accounts and no set layout; they are solely for **internal consumption** and are produced in whatever format is convenient. The main reasons for producing such accounts are as follows.

(a) To generate **up-to-date information** for management purposes (because if a business is making a loss action must be taken soon, not six months after the end of the accounting period, when the profit and loss account is published)

(b) To provide **analysis of results** from various sections of the business (because some sections might be profitable and others not)

1.4 Because management accounts are primarily concerned with the analysis of costs they are also known as **cost accounts** and the person who produces them is sometimes referred to as a **cost accountant**.

1.5 Management accounts might be presented in the format below.

June management accounts

	Month (a) £'000	Budget (b) £'000	YTD (c) £'000	Budget for year Year (d) £'000	Plan (e) £'000
Sales	95	100	1,000	2,400	2,800
Cost of sales	48	45	460	1,000	1,000
Gross profit	47	55	540	1,400	1,800
Sales overheads	18	18	175	430	500
Administrative overheads	11	12	101	245	260
Net profit	18	25	264	725	1,040

1.6 The following notes explain the purpose of each column.

(a) **Month**. These are the actual figures for the month of June.

(b) **Budget**. The budgeted figures for the month may have been seasonally adjusted or they may be just the total figure for the year, divided by twelve.

(c) **Year to date**. These are the actual figures for the year up to the end of June.

(d) **Budget for year**. This is, say, the budgeted figure for the year adjusted for the actual figures to date.

(e) **Year plan**. This is the original budget for the year.

1.7 The breakdown of costs and expenses shown in management accounts is at the **discretion of the management**. The way the figures are presented will depend on what kind of information the managers require to **control the business**. The allocation of costs to the various profit and loss account categories in a **published profit and loss account,** as all companies are required to produce, will be much more restricted.

1.8   It is common for management accounting reports to be issued **monthly.** For certain types of report, **weekly** or **quarterly** reporting may be more appropriate.

> ## DEVOLVED ASSESSMENT ALERT
>
> Remember that before completed reports are despatched, authorisation must be sought from the appropriate person.

1.9   It may be helpful to include **running annual totals**, adding the last month or quarter and dropping the equivalent month or quarter from the previous year each time. This can be particularly worthwhile if there are **seasonal patterns** and can help to indicate whether a **longer-term trend** is developing.

Degrees of details

1.10   Internal management reports often include **too much detail.** In particular, it is common for too many digits to be included, even in reports prepared for public record. For example, up to 1975, the largest manufacturing company in the world, General Motors Corporation, showed the figures in its annual report to the nearest dollar. Having said that, there may be certain figures (such as the emoluments of the highest paid director) which need to be reported to the nearest pound (or dollar!) in order to meet the relevant disclosure requirements.

1.11   Why should too high a level of detail be avoided?

(a)   Too many figures may make it **difficult for the reader to understand** the main messages conveyed by the report.

(b)   Too much detail may convey a **spurious impression of accuracy**. General Motors' accounts could certainly not have been claimed to be accurate to the nearest $1.

1.12   In general, the first **two significant digits** of a number are those which matter. For example, for most reporting purposes, the important part of the figure £29,120 are the figures 2 and 9: the figure might as well be rounded to £29,000. A third digit may be included to avoid too much rounding: for example, the figure might be presented as 29.1 in a £'000 column. However, additional digits are probably excessive for effective appraisal of the figures.

1.13   Where information on costs and revenues from different units of the organisation is aggregated (or 'consolidated') together, it will be necessary to make sure that the resulting consolidated figures are compiled in a **consistent way**. This may involve ensuring that costs are **categorised** in a reasonable way and adopting the methods which have been used in past management reports. Note in particular that VAT should be excluded from sales turnover. The current VAT position is reflected in the accounts by showing in the balance sheet net amounts due to or repayable by HM Customs and Excise.

Manufacturing accounts

1.14   A **manufacturing account** might be prepared by a manufacturing company, in order to establish the cost of the work it has produced during a period of time. When a manufacturing account is prepared, it precedes the trading, profit and loss account, so that there are the following accounts.

- A **manufacturing** account, to establish the cost of goods produced
- A **trading** account, to establish the cost of goods sold and gross profit
- A **profit and loss** account, to establish the net profit

1.15 Manufacturing accounts are **not obligatory** for manufacturing companies, because they can prepare a trading, profit and loss account without a manufacturing account if they wish to do so. However, a manufacturing account is needed if management want to know what the cost of producing goods has been, for **internal information**.

Component elements in the manufacturing process

1.16 A manufacturing account is basically a list of the costs of producing the work in a factory, or in several factories, during a period. These costs consist of the following.

(a) The cost of **raw materials and components** that are used to make up the products (**direct materials**).

(b) The cost of the **labour** that makes the products. As this is labour that is directly involved in producing an item of output, it is called **direct labour**.

(c) **Other** costs incurred in the factory, which cannot be attributed to the production of any specific output but which are incurred to keep the factory running. These **indirect costs**, or **overheads**, include the salaries of supervisors, factory rent, depreciation of the factory building, depreciation of plant and machinery, factory rates, cleaning materials and other general expenses relating to the factory.

1.17 The total direct costs of production are often known as **prime cost**, and the total of direct costs plus overheads is known as **factory cost** (or **works cost**).

1.18 A further distinction is often made between variable costs and fixed costs.

KEY TERMS

- **Variable costs** are costs that **vary** with the number of goods produced, or the number of hours worked.

- **Fixed costs** are the costs which are the **same** total amount for a period of time, regardless of the number of units produced or the number of hours worked.

For example, if a unit of production has a variable cost of £10, the total variable cost of 10 such units would be £100, and the total variable cost of 20 such units would be £200.

Factory rent and rates, and depreciation of factory premises are examples of fixed costs.

Some kinds of cost have **both fixed and variable elements**. For example, utility charges (gas, electricity and so on) often include a **basic fixed charge** as well as a **variable charge** based on usage. In general, direct costs are variable costs. Most overhead costs, or even all overhead costs, are regarded as fixed costs, although there are often some variable overhead costs too.

2   ACCOUNTING FOR SEPARATE ORGANISATIONAL UNITS

Departmental and branch accounts

2.1   A large proportion of organisations are large enough for a certain degree of **divisionalisation** to make sense. Organisations and businesses of different kinds may be divided into the following.

- Departments
- Sales areas
- Divisions
- Branches

2.2   Where an organisation is increasing in size and/or is intending to diversify its activities, it may find it necessary or advantageous to control operations more precisely by instituting a system of **departmental or branch accounting**. As each department or branch is established as a **separate cost and/or accounting centre**, the net profit per branch can be found and accumulated to arrive at the profit for the whole business.

2.3   A **profit target** can be set for each unit of the organisation. These targets will form part of a larger plan: the company's **long-term profit target**. The profit earned by separate parts of the enterprise can each be compared with its own target.

2.4   Various types of organisation may operate through branches; examples include the following.

- Banks
- Building societies
- Estate agents
- Accountants
- Travel agents
- Retailing businesses such as department stores or chain stores

2.5   **Divisional** or **branch accounts** may be considered to fall into three main categories.

(a)   **Departmental accounts** are prepared where a large retail store is divided into various departments.

(b)   **Branch accounts** may be prepared to show the performance of both a main trading centre (the head office) and subsidiary trading centres (the branches), but with all accounting records being maintained by the head office.

(c)   **'Separate entity' branch accounts** are prepared where branches maintain their own records, which must therefore be combined with head office records in order to prepare accounts for the whole business.

Departmental accounts

2.6   In **retail store accounting**, although all departments may be in the same building, it is useful to control operations by finding the **net profit per department** as well as for the total business. Usually, trading and profit and loss accounts are prepared in columnar form for each department and the business as a whole.

2.7   An important aspect of departmental accounting is the **allocation** and **apportionment of expenses** to the various departments. Direct department expenses are easily allocated as separate records are usually kept for each department. However, where a number of departments share in the use of facilities, such as a canteen service, or administration for processing invoices and other documents, some method must be found to **apportion** the expenses (overheads) on the most equitable basis to the departments. In practice, several bases of apportionment are used depending upon some relationship of the expense to the benefit derived by the respective departments.

Typical overheads	Usual bases of apportionment
Supervisor's salary	Time spent in respective departments, or production output
Power, heating and lighting	Measured units of electricity or floor area
Rent and rates	Floor area
Insurance	Average book value of assets insured
Canteen services	Number of employees
Advertising and selling expenses	Sales value
General administration expenses	Number of employees, or the sum of expenses purchases and costs/sales values (linked to the volume of paperwork involved)

2.8 EXAMPLE: APPORTIONMENT OF OVERHEADS

Bracedep Ltd has two production departments, which both do work on three products, sirks, varks, and zooks.

(a) Wages costs in each department for the year to 31 December 20X7 were as follows.

	£
Assembly department	70,000
Finishing department	30,000
	100,000

(b) Manufacturing overheads in total for the year were £150,000. These are to be apportioned between departments in proportion to wages costs incurred during the year.

(c) Departmental overhead costs are to be apportioned between products as follows:

	Assembly dept	*Finishing dept*
Sirks	30%	50%
Varks	40%	10%
Zooks	30%	40%

Calculate the overhead cost attributable to each product during the year.

2.9 SOLUTION

	Assembly Dept		*Finishing Dept*		*Total*
		£		£	£
Manufacturing overhead	(70%)	105,000	(30%)	45,000	150,000
Apportioned as follows:					
Sirks	(30%)	31,500	(50%)	22,500	54,000
Varks	(40%)	42,000	(10%)	4,500	46,500
Zooks	(30%)	31,500	(40%)	18,000	49,500
		105,000		45,000	150,000

2.10 EXAMPLE: DEPARTMENTAL ACCOUNTS

Departmental trading and profit and loss accounts for a retailer could be presented in the following format.

ALLSALES LIMITED
DEPARTMENTAL TRADING AND PROFIT AND LOSS ACCOUNTS
FOR THE YEAR ENDED 31 DECEMBER 20X0

	Furniture dept		*Electrical goods dept*		*Total*	
	£	£	£	£	£	£
Sales		180,000		270,000		450,000
Cost of sales:						
Opening stock	36,000		45,000		81,000	
Purchases	105,000		162,000		267,000	
	141,000		207,000		348,000	
Less closing stock	39,000		54,000		93,000	
		102,000		153,000		255,000
Gross profit		78,000		117,000		195,000
Less expenses:						
Selling & distribution (in sales ratio 2:3)	22,800		34,200		57,000	
Administration (in employee ratio)	17,450		26,450		43,900	
Lighting & heating (as measured)	1,000		4,800		5,800	
Rent & rates (in floor area ratio of 2:1)	19,000		9,500		28,500	
		60,250		74,950		135,200
Net profit		17,750		42,050		59,800

2.11 The normal problems of preparing accounts (such as calculating provisions for bad debts, accruals and prepayments) have to be dealt with. Indeed, records may be incomplete and 'unknowns' may have to be calculated before the accounts can be fully prepared.

2.12 Note the different **bases of apportioning costs** used in the above example. These bases are essentially **arbitrary**, and different methods are possible. What is important is that within one business, the methods applied are **consistent**, unless there is good reason to change the basis of apportionment at some stage.

DEVOLVED ASSESSMENT ALERT

One of the tasks in the AAT's sample simulation for Unit 7 required you to consolidate the results of two different companies. The steps involved are exactly the same as those demonstrated in the example in Paragraph 2.10.

Accounting for branches

2.13 When a branch is established, considerable trust is placed in its manager, where stocks are despatched to his sole control. One way in which Head Office can check the manager's honesty and performance and deter him from fraud and outright theft is to establish an **internal audit department**, whose staff, amongst other duties, will visit branches to **check**

the records and to **count the stock,** ensuring that all material differences from the expected value are accounted for.

2.14 It is the responsibility of a business's managers to establish an adequate system of **internal control** so that the business is carried on efficiently and the assets are safeguarded. One way of doing this is for Head Office to keep records of stock and other assets sent to the branch and for the branch manager to record sales proceeds in **memorandum only,** forwarding his sales and stock returns daily, weekly or monthly and banking the sales proceeds intact (probably daily). Expenses will probably be paid centrally from Head Office (except for petty cash items, like staff refreshments). Head office staff can see from the branch returns whether the branch is meeting its sales targets and whether there has been any unusual stock wastage. Internal and external audit procedures should confirm the accuracy of the branch returns.

2.15 You do not need to learn the specific techniques involved in **branch accounting** for the purposes of Unit 7. You should however have a general awareness of branch accounting as one means of accounting for transactions between **separate units of an organisation.**

Preparation of final accounts

2.16 Where a complete and independent set of records is maintained by the branch (or branches) trading and profit and loss accounts and balance sheets can be prepared for each branch and the head office. Accounts for the business as a whole can then be produced by **combining the individual accounts.**

2.17 At the end of an accounting period trial balances are extracted from the head office and branch ledgers. Using the trial balances accounts may be prepared for the following.

- The head office
- The branch
- The combined firm or company

2.18 Generally, the trading and profit and loss accounts and balance sheets are produced in columnar form, the head office and branch being treated almost as if they were **separate legal entities.** The organisation is only regarded as a **single concern** in the 'combined' **columns** which are arrived at by totalling appropriate items in the head office and branch columns. In the **combined balance sheet** the branch current account is replaced by the underlying assets and liabilities.

3 PROFIT CENTRES

3.1 In some businesses, management establishes **profit centres** of operations, with each centre held accountable for making a profit, and the manager of the centre made responsible for its good or bad results.

3.2 Where there are transfers of goods or services between divisions of a **divisionalised organisation,** the transfers could be made 'free' or 'as a favour' to the division receiving the benefit. For example, if a garage and car showroom has two divisions, one for car repairs and servicing and the other for car sales, the servicing division will be required to service cars before they are sold and delivered to customers. There is no requirement for this service work to be charged for: the servicing division could do its work for the car sales division without making any record of the work done. However, unless the cost or value of such work is recorded, management cannot keep a proper check on the amount of resources (like labour time) being used up on new car servicing. It is necessary for control purposes that **some record of the inter-divisional services should be kept,** and one way of doing this is through the accounting system. Inter-divisional work can be given a cost or charge: a **transfer price.**

3.3 It is particularly important in the case of transferred goods that a transfer price should be charged. A proper system of accounting demands that goods should be costed as they progress through work in progress to finished goods and so the need for a transfer cost or transfer price should be clear.

> ### KEY TERM
>
> A **transfer price** is 'The price at which goods or services are transferred from one process or department to another or from one member of a group to another.'
> CIMA *Official Terminology*

The bases on which transfer prices might be set

3.4 A transfer price may be based upon the following.

- Marginal cost (at marginal cost or with a gross profit margin on top)
- Full cost (at full cost, or at a full cost plus)
- Market price
- At a discount to the market price
- Negotiated price, which could be based on any of the above

3.5 A transfer based on cost might be at **marginal cost** or **full cost** only but in a profit centre system of divisionalisation, is more likely to be a price based on **marginal cost** or **full cost plus a margin for contribution or profit**. This is to allow profit centres to make a profit on work they do for other profit centres, and so earn a reward for their effort and use of resources on the work.

> ### DEVOLVED ASSESSMENT ALERT
>
> Remember that you will need to make adjustments for any inter-company or inter-departmental sales and purchases when preparing consolidated accounts.

4 REPORTING NON-FINANCIAL RESULTS

4.1 In addition to reporting financial information, some organisations may find it useful to report **non-financial results** where these might give more meaningful information.

4.2 Examples of organisations which might find it useful to report non-financial results are as follows.

- Hospitals
- Railways
- Hotels
- Educational establishments (colleges and schools)

We shall now have a look at how some of these organisations might report non-financial information.

Hospitals

4.3 The financial management departments of most hospitals will be concerned with financial results such as monthly management accounts and year-end published accounts. Cost accountants will also be involved with costing the services provided by the hospital, for example, the cost of a hip replacement operation and so on.

4.4 In addition to the large volume of financial information passing through this department, there will also be a large amount of **relevant non-financial data**.

Examples of such information are as follows.

- The number of inpatients
- The number of outpatient attendances
- The number of daycases
- The number of beds available
- The average stay per inpatient (days)
- The average number of beds occupied

4.5 Organisations such as those listed in Paragraph 4.2 are usually required to complete returns (to the Area Health Authority, for example) that summarise both financial and non-financial data for a certain period.

4.6 EXAMPLE: REPORTING NON-FINANCIAL INFORMATION

The following data relates to two hospitals, the Trent South Hospital and the Brigden Royal Hospital.

	Trent South		Brigden Royal	
	Inpatients	*Outpatients*	*Inpatients*	*Outpatients*
	£	£	£	£
Cost of services				
Direct patient care	23,400,000	3,600,000	15,000,000	650,000
Medical support services				
X Ray	1,400,000	1,100,000	395,000	165,000
Pathology	2,500,000	1,700,000	650,000	295,000
Pharmacy	4,700,000	1,950,000	4,040,000	72,000
Non-medical support services				
Laundry	415,000	42,500	35,400	19,700
Catering	725,000	17,500	525,000	4,950
Administration	6,540,000	1,890,000	5,980,000	1,250,000

Other data	Trent South	Brigden Royal
Number of inpatients	31,900	1,620
Average stay per inpatient	16 days	179 days
Number of beds available	1,250	750
Average number of beds occupied	890	690
Number of outpatient attendances	329,500	26,400

Number of inpatient days

Number of inpatients × average stay per inpatient = number of inpatient days

Trent South = 31,900 × 16 = 510,400 inpatient days

Brigden Royal   = $1,620 \times 179 = 289,980$ inpatient days

Bed occupancy rates

$$\text{Bed occupancy rate} = \frac{\text{Average number of beds occupied}}{\text{Number of beds available}} \times 100\%$$

Trent South $= \dfrac{890}{1,250} \times 100\%$ $= 71.2\%$

Brigden Royal $= \dfrac{690}{750} \times 100\%$ $= 92\%$

Armed with information such as the number of inpatient days for each hospital, it is possible to produce more meaningful financial information. For example, the hospitals might wish to compare the costs of their X Ray departments per inpatient day.

For Trent South, the cost per inpatient day for the X Ray department $= \dfrac{\pounds1,400,000}{510,400} =$ £2.70.

For the Brigden Royal, the cost per inpatient day for the X Ray department $= \dfrac{\pounds395,000}{289,980} =$ £1.40.

4.7 The data in the example above shows bed occupancy rates of 71.2% and 92% for the hospitals under consideration. Such information is very useful, since if bed occupancy rates in any hospital were below a certain level then the Area Health Authority might wish to investigate the reasons for this.

4.8 Railway companies are also likely to be interested in reporting non-financial information. For example, they might be interested in the number of passengers using their trains in a given period, the number of train services running or the average capacity (number of seats per train). Such data might provide more meaningful information, such as follows.

- The number of passengers per train service
- The percentage of seats filled per train service

4.9 In order to compare the performances of different hotels, information such as the number of rooms let and room occupancy rates might prove useful.

DEVOLVED ASSESSMENT ALERT

In an assessment, be prepared to report *and* comment upon non-financial data as well as financial data. Always draw on any experience that you have gained in the work place when tackling devolved assessments - you are much more likely to impress the assessor if you do so!

Activity 10.1

The Grand Garden Bench Company manufactures high quality garden benches. Wyn Lotkins is manager of the main factory based in Hay-on-Wye in Wales. There is a second factory in Tonbridge in Kent. The production department is made up of the following sections.

1   Moulding
2   Assembly
3   Finishing

Wyn Lotkins has collected performance data from her two factories which is given below.

	Quarter 1	Quarter 2	Quarter 3	Quarter 4
Benches completed				
Hay-on-Wye	4,800	5,400	5,600	5,200
Kent	4,000	4,200	4,600	4,400
Budgeted labour hours per bench				
Moulding	13.6			
Assembly	17.2			
Finishing	25.6			
Actual hours worked				
Hay-on-Wye				
Moulding	16,800	17,280	19,040	19,760
Assembly	19,800	23,180	23,980	22,896
Finishing	29,728	34,980	37,260	34,248
Kent				
Moulding	14,400	14,280	16,100	15,240
Assembly	16,852	18,120	20,480	19,500
Finishing	25,828	28,084	31,060	27,648

Task

Wyn Lotkins is concerned about the performance of the factory in Hay-on-Wye, compared to that of the factory in Kent, and would like you (her accounting assistant) to calculate the following for her.

- The total actual hours worked in each factory.
- The actual hours per bench manufactured (to two decimal places).

---

5 ANALYSIS OF RESULTS

5.1 The accounting records maintained for departments and branches provide managers with much useful information. Appropriate management action may need to be taken if certain departments and branches are performing badly. If a branch is unprofitable, for example, it may be necessary to consider **cost-cutting measures** if there is little prospect of raising the branch revenues significantly. Ultimately, unsuccessful branches may need to be **closed**.

5.2 Managers may also make use of information on the results of different parts or areas of the organisation analysed in other ways. Two examples which we look at below are the **analysis of results by sales areas** and the **analysis of results by product**. It should not be difficult for you to see that broadly similar principles can be applied to the analysis of results in other ways. In all cases, a suitable set of methods for performing the analysis must be agreed and followed.

5.3 EXAMPLE: ANALYSIS OF RESULTS BY SALES AREA

(a) Most sales and marketing activities are organised on a **territorial basis**. The purpose of making an analysis of the profitability of **sales areas** or **territories** is to identify areas in which there are **weaknesses** or **problems**. Action taken to correct a weakness might be to increase the number of sales people operating in the area, for example.

- **Direct costs** will be those incurred in respect of particular sales areas.

- **Indirect costs** are those incurred for all of the sales areas together. Some kind of apportionment of indirect costs between the various sales areas must be made (see Chapter 9).

(b) An analysis of results by sales area might look like the table below.

SIERRA LIMITED: ANALYSIS OF RESULTS BY SALES AREA

	Area 1 £'000	*Area 2* £'000	*Area 3* £'000	*Total* £'000
Sales (A)	600	500	150	1,250
Direct costs by areas:				
Cost of goods sold	320	250	60	630
Transport & outside warehousing	60	35	15	110
Regional office expenses	40	45	28	113
Salespeople's expenses	30	25	11	66
Other regional expenses	20	15	8	43
Total direct cost by areas (B)	470	370	122	962
Contribution to head office overheads and profit (A – B)	130	130	28	288
Indirect costs:				
Central administration	44	52	12	108
Central warehousing	16	18	3	37
Advertising	30	30	8	68
Total indirect costs (C)	90	100	23	213
Net profit (A – B – C)	40	30	5	75
Percentage of net profit	53%	40%	7%	100%
Percentage of sales	48%	40%	12%	100%
Contribution/sales %(A – B) ÷ A	22%	26%	19%	23%

(c) Performance indicators which can be used to compare the results of the different sales areas include the following.

- Percentage of net profit
- Percentage of sales
- Contribution/sales percentage

Can you see how they have been calculated?

(d) Calculating these performance indicators for different areas, divisions or departments may also help to disclose whether costs are being misclassified between different parts of the organisation, as this could lead to unusual or unexpected changes in the indicators.

5.4 EXAMPLE: ANALYSIS OF RESULTS BY PRODUCT AND COST CENTRE

Analysing results of an enterprise by **product,** or **product type,** not only indicates the relative profitability of different products or types of product, but also highlights **strengths** or **weaknesses** which should be taken into account in future **decision-making**.

5.5 **Profitability is not the only basis on which a product should be judged**: a major reason for this is that indirect costs must be **spread** or **apportioned** across the product range somehow, and this apportionment must be **arbitrary** to some extent. The analysis below follows the previous analysis in looking at the **contribution** of each product.

PIPER LIMITED: ANALYSIS OF RESULTS BY PRODUCT

	Product A £'000	Product B £'000	Product C £'000	Total £'000
Sales	200	350	250	800
Variable costs of goods sold	95	175	90	360
Gross contribution	105	175	160	440
Variable marketing costs:				
Transport and warehousing	5	26	37	68
Office expenses	8	20	7	35
Sales salaries	15	44	25	84
Other expenses	2	7	6	15
Total variable marketing costs	30	97	75	202
Contribution to fixed costs and profit	75	78	85	238
Fixed costs:				
Manufacturing	15	20	20	55
Administration	25	35	25	85
Marketing	20	30	20	70
Total fixed costs	60	85	65	210
Net profit (loss)	15	(7)	20	28
Contribution/sales %	37%	22%	34%	30%

Variable costs by cost centre

	Cost centre 1 £'000	Cost centre 2 £'000	Cost centre 3 £'000
Product A	50	45	30
Product B	115	60	97
Product C	40	50	75
Total	205	155	202

Variable costs by product

	Product A £'000	Product B £'000	Product C £'000	Total £'000
Cost centre 1	50	115	40	205
Cost centre 2	45	60	50	155
Cost centre 3	30	97	75	202
	125	272	165	562

5.6 A graphical presentation of some of the key information in this analysis might take the following form.

£'000

Variable costs by cost centre

Variable costs by product

Contribution for Product A

Net profit

5.7 A product may be making a loss after fixed expenses and still be worth producing. Piper Limited's product B above, for example, is shown as making a net loss although it still makes a **contribution** to fixed expenses. Product B should continue in production, although steps ought to be taken to improve its profitability in future.

5.8 In these analyses, we have made use of some **performance indicators**, a topic which is covered further in the next chapter.

Activity 10.2

Allmain Ltd is a retailer of electrical goods. It operates from a single retail outlet in which 50% of the floor space is occupied by the white goods department which employs three members of staff, with the remaining floor space being split equally between the TV department and the audio department, which employ one and two members of staff respectively.

VAT of 17½% is chargeable on all sales, which were as follows together with cost of sales figures in the quarter ending 31 March 20X3. (The figures exclude VAT.)

Department	Sales (net of VAT)	Cost of sales
	£	£
White goods	44,500	28,500
TV	25,850	16,200
Audio	20,900	13,850

Expenses were as follows.

	£
Selling and distribution	10,250*
Administration	9,480
Heating and lighting	2,211
Rent and rates	5,200

*Of which £5,362 related to white goods, £2,252 to TV and £2,636 to audio.

Administration costs are allocated in the ratio 3:2:2 between white goods, TV and audio departments. Heating and lighting, and rent and rates, are allocated in proportion to the floor space occupied by each department.

Tasks

(a) Prepare the figures to be included in the departmental management accounts for the quarter ending 31 March 20X3, showing the following for each department and overall.

Sales
Gross profit
Expenses
Selling and distribution
Administration
Heating and lighting
Rent and rates
Net profit before interest and taxation

(b) Calculate the gross profit percentage and the net profit percentage for each department and overall.

Note on methods

$$\text{Gross profit percentage} = \frac{\text{Gross profit}}{\text{Sales}} \times 100$$

$$\text{Net profit percentage} = \frac{\text{Net profit before interest and taxation}}{\text{Sales}} \times 100$$

(c) Indicate what figures might be shown in the management accounts alongside the figures you have calculated for the purposes of comparison.

Activity 10.3

The company for whom you work as an accounting trainee is a distributor of office equipment and operates through three departments, namely, Communications Equipment, Data Processing Equipment and Office Furniture. The directors have decided to publish a house magazine for distribution to staff and you have been asked by the chief accountant to suggest appropriate forms of diagrammatic presentation for conveying financial information in a meaningful but non-technical manner. Selected for inclusion in the first issue of the magazine is information concerning:

(a) total sales income for each of the past five years;

(b) the value of sales by each department for each of the past five years;

(c) the proportions of total sales contributed by the various geographical areas, namely United Kingdom (Southern, Midlands and Northern Regions), and Export (Europe and Other countries), for the year recently ended.

Task

Submit sketches of appropriate types of diagram for each of the above and add brief comments explaining your choices.

Information for Activities 10.4 to 10.7

You are employed by Delicious Confectionery Ltd, a company whose chocolate department sells six different types of chocolate bar. These bars are referred to in management information using the abbreviations WIZ, PER, MRL, WLD, BKR and CRK. Value added tax at 17½% is charged on all sales.

Your manager presents you with costing statements for the department for the year as set out below.

	WIZ	PER	MRL	WLD	BKR	CRK
	£	£	£	£	£	£
Direct labour	20,248	7,567	14,521	4,499	39,661	22,079
Direct materials	14,210	6,991	11,100	5,217	19,147	12,269
Variable overheads	9,410	7,292	9,622	6,414	15,003	12,241
	43,868	21,850	35,243	16,130	73,811	46,589
Fixed costs	16,320	8,160	10,200	8,160	20,400	12,240
Total costs	60,188	30,010	45,443	24,290	94,211	58,829
Sales (excluding VAT)	72,421	31,229	41,522	27,611	101,019	52,722
Profit/(loss)	12,233	1,219	(3,921)	3,321	6,808	(6,107)

She is concerned that production of MRL and CRK should cease.

Activity 10.4

Present the data shown above in an alternative format, to show the contribution which each product type makes to fixed costs, and the contribution/sales percentage. Round figures to the nearest tenth of one thousand. Also show the total figures for the whole company.

Activity 10.5

(a) Use graphical presentation techniques (charts) to show how the relative sizes of sales and contribution for Delicious Confectionery Ltd's products compare and the direct labour, direct materials and variable overheads for each product. This can be done by showing for each product how:

Contribution = sales – (direct labour + direct materials + variable overheads)

(b) Show on another chart the total net profit of the company. This can be done by showing on the chart how:

Net profit = total of each product's contributions - total fixed costs

Activity 10.6

Prepare a revised statement in the same format as that used in Activity 10.5 showing what would have been the position if there had been no production of MRL and CRK during the year. Assume that all direct and variable costs for MRL and CRK are now eliminated, and that the total of fixed costs is unchanged and is to be allocated to the remaining product lines in the same proportions as it is now.

Activity 10.7

(a) Prepare a chart like that prepared in Activity 10.6 (part (b)) showing total net profit or loss if production of MRL and CRK ceases.

(b) Comment briefly on your findings about what happens if production of MRL and CRK is stopped.

Key learning points

* **Management accounts** are internal accounts which can be produced in whatever format is most convenient. They are produced to generate **up-to-date information** for management purposes and to provide an **analysis of results** from various sections of the business.

* The following columns are usually found in management accounts.

    ° Actual month figures
    ° Budgeted figures for the month
    ° Actual year to date figures
    ° Budget for year
    ° Year plan (original budget for the year)

* **Variable costs** are costs that vary with the number of goods produced, or the number of hours worked. **Fixed costs** are the costs which are the same total amount for a period of time, regardless of the number of units produced or the number of hours worked.

* Some organisations are large enough for **divisionalisation** to make sense. **Divisional** or **branch accounts** fall into three main categories.

    ° Departmental accounts
    ° Branch accounts
    ° 'Separate entity' branch accounts

* **Profit centres** are established in some businesses where each centre is held accountable for making a profit, and the manager is held responsible for its good or bad results.

* Examples of organisations which might find it useful to report non-financial results are as follows.

    ° Hospitals
    ° Railways
    ° Hotels
    ° Educational establishments

* **Performance indicators** are used to compare results between different areas, divisions or departments.

* **Contribution** is the amount which remains after paying direct or variable costs, or the amount available for **contributing** towards indirect costs.

Quick quiz

1 What is the difference between prime cost and factory cost?

2 What might be the usual bases of apportionment for the following overheads?

(a) Power, heating and lighting
(b) Canteen services

3   What is contribution?

Answer to quick quiz

1   Prime cost is the total direct costs of production, whereas the factory cost is the total of direct costs *plus* overheads.

2   (a)   Measured units of electricity or floor area
        (b)   Number of employees

3   The amount which remains once direct or variable costs have been paid.

Answers to activities

Answer 10.1

	Quarter 1	Quarter 2	Quarter 3	Quarter 4
Total actual hours				
Hay-on-Wye	66,328	75,440	80,280	76,904
Kent	57,080	60,484	67,640	62,388
Benches completed				
Hay-on-Wye	4,800	5,400	5,600	5,200
Kent	4,000	4,200	4,600	4,400
Hours per bench				
Hay-on-Wye	13.82	13.97	14.34	14.79
Kent	14.27	14.40	14.70	14.18

Note how the non-financial results reported here enable an easy comparison to be made between the performances of the two factories.

Answer 10.2

(a)   *Allmain Limited*

    Departmental management accounts

	White goods £	TV £	Audio £	Total £
Sales	44,500	25,850	20,900	91,250
Cost of sales	(28,500)	(16,200)	(13,850)	(58,550)
Gross profit	16,000	9,650	7,050	32,700
Expenses				
Selling and distribution	5,362	2,252	2,636	10,250
Administration	4,062	2,709	2,709	9,480
Heating and lighting	1,105	553	553	2,211
Rent and rates	2,600	1,300	1,300	5,200
Total expenses	13,129	6,814	7,198	27,141
Net profit before interest and taxation	2,871	2,836	−148	5,559

(b)

	White goods	TV	Audio	Total
Gross profit percentage	36.0	37.3	33.7	35.8
Net profit percentage	6.5	11.0	− 0.7	6.1

Workings

	White goods	TV	Audio
Selling and distribution	£5,362	£2,252	£2,636
Administration			
£9,480 ×	$^3/_7$	$^2/_7$	$^2/_7$
=	£4,062	£2,709	£2,709
Heating and lighting, rent and rates			
£2,211/£5,200 ×	½	¼	¼
Heating and lighting	£1,105	£553	£553
Rent and rates	£2,600	£1,300	£1,300

(c)   Comparative figures might include budgeted (forecast) figures, year to date figures, last year's figures and annual moving average figures.

Answer 10.3

Tutorial note. You should have ensured that your sketches reflected the facts given in the question. Thus the right departments and the right geographical areas should have been shown.

(a)   *Total sales income for each of the past five years*

A simple bar chart, with one bar for each year, is appropriate. The bars will make the trend of total sales immediately apparent, and sales for any one year can be easily read from the vertical axis.

(b)   *Sales by department for each of the last five years*

A multiple bar chart is appropriate. The trend of sales in each department will then be clearly visible. Total sales will not be obvious, but this does not matter if the simple bar chart described in part (a) is also supplied.

(c)   *The proportions of sales for one year contributed by various geographical areas*

A pie chart is a good way of showing proportions rather than absolute values. Exact proportions cannot be easily read from such a chart, but a good general impression can easily be gained.

Here are sketches of all the above types of graph.

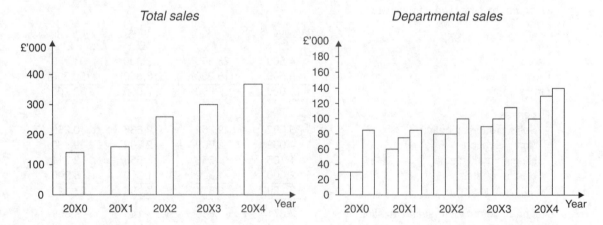

*Geographical distribution
of sales in 20X4*

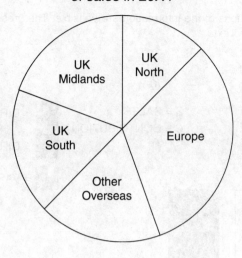

Answer 10.4

	WIZ	*PER*	*MRL*	*WLD*	*BKR*	*CRK*	*Total*
	£'000	*£'000*	*£'000*	*£'000*	*£'000*	*£'000*	*£'000*
Sales	72.4	31.2	41.5	27.6	101.0	52.7	326.4
Direct labour	20.2	7.6	14.5	4.5	39.7	22.1	108.6
Direct materials	14.2	7.0	11.1	5.2	19.1	12.3	68.9
Variable overheads	9.4	7.3	9.6	6.4	15.0	12.2	59.9
	43.8	21.9	35.2	16.1	73.8	46.6	237.4
Contribution	28.6	9.3	6.3	11.5	27.2	6.1	89.0
Fixed costs	16.3	8.2	10.2	8.2	20.4	12.2	75.5
Profit/(loss)	12.3	1.1	(3.9)	3.3	6.8	(6.1)	13.5
Contribution/sales	39.5%	29.8%	15.2%	41.7%	26.9%	11.6%	27.3%

Answer 10.5

Tutorial note. Different presentations of the information are possible. The presentation below is similar to one suggested in the BPP Interactive Text.

(a)

(b)

Contribution

Answer 10.6

	WIZ £'000	PER £'000	WLD £'000	BKR £'000	Total £'000
Sales	72.4	31.2	27.6	101.0	232.2
Direct labour	20.2	7.6	4.5	39.7	72.0
Direct materials	14.2	7.0	5.2	19.1	45.5
Variable overheads	9.4	7.3	6.4	15.0	38.1
	43.8	21.9	16.1	73.8	155.6
Contribution	28.6	9.3	11.5	27.2	76.6
Fixed costs	23.2	11.6	11.6	29.0	75.4
Profit/(loss)	5.4	(2.3)	(0.1)	(1.8)	1.2
Contribution/sales	39.5%	29.8%	41.7%	26.9%	33.0%

Working

Fixed overheads

	Proportions		£
WIZ	16,320	4/13	23,225
PER	8,160	2/13	11,612
WLD	8,160	2/13	11,612
BKR	20,400	5/13	29,031
			75,480

Answer 10.7

(a)

(b) Even though the statement in Activity 10.4 shows MRL and CRK as giving an overall loss, eliminating their production reduces the total profit from £13,500 to £1,200. This is because both MRL and CRK made a positive contribution to fixed costs. Fixed overheads now have to be spread over a smaller range of products.

Chapter 11 Measuring performance

Chapter topic list

1   Ratio analysis

2   Measuring divisional performance: profit or contribution?

3   Performance measurement in the public sector

Learning objectives

On completion of this chapter you will be able to:

	Performance criteria	Range statement
• calculate ratios and performance indicators accurately and in accordance with the organisation's procedures	7.1.5	7.1.1, 2 - 4
• *be aware of relevant performance and quality measures*	n/a	n/a
• *calculate the following ratios: gross profit margin; net profit margin; return on capital employed*	n/a	n/a
• *calculate the following performance indicators: productivity; cost per unit; resource utilisation; profitability*	n/a	n/a

Italicised objectives are areas of knowledge and understanding underlying the elements of competence for Unit 7.

1   RATIO ANALYSIS

1.1   For Unit 7: *Preparing Reports and Returns* you are expected to have an awareness of relevant **performance and quality measures**. You are also expected to be able to calculate accurately ratios and performance indicators in accordance with the organisation's procedures. We looked at productivity ratios in Chapter 9. We also looked earlier at the cost per unit as a performance indicator.

1.2   The profit and loss account, the balance sheet and forms of divisional income statement used by management of business enterprises are all sources of useful information about the condition of the business. The analysis and interpretation of these statements can be done by **calculating certain ratios**, between one item and another, and then using the ratios for **comparison**, either:

(a)   **between one year and the next** for a particular business or division, in order to identify any trends, or significantly better or worse results than before; or

(b)   **between one business or division and another**, to establish which has performed better, and in what ways.

Some of the most important ratios concerning performance measurement in business enterprises are described below.

1.3   When ratio analysis is used to assess the relative strength of a particular business, by comparing its profitability and financial stability with another business, the two businesses should be broadly similar:

- in size; and
- in their line of activities.

1.4   Suppose for example, that we compared the results of a manufacturing company with the results of a company which operates a chain of hairdressing salons and beauty parlours.

(a)   The manufacturing company might specialise in undertaking large-scale contracts for major customers (eg shipbuilding, building telephone exchange equipment or defence contracts with the Ministry of Defence). These companies might operates so as to make a small profit percentage on a very large turnover - eg a profit of £1 million on a contract with a sales value of £20 million, say. In contrast, a service industry such as hairdressing and beautician service, might be more likely to derive a higher profit percentage, but on a relatively lower total sales turnover.

(b)   The assets of the two companies would differ. Both might own freehold property, but the manufacturing company would have much larger amounts of fixed assets (plant and machinery, for example) and also much more stock-in-trade and debtors - since much shop business is paid for in cash.

1.5   Comparing the accounting ratios of the two businesses would be pointless, since the ratios would merely serve to inform us that the businesses are different, not that either business is less profitable or less financially stable than it should be. We do not need ratios to tell us that one business is larger, or that two businesses operate in entirely different industries!

Indicators of profitability

1.6   There are **three principal ratios** which can be used to measure how well the operations of a business are doing. These are as follows.

- Profit margin
- Asset turnover
- Return on capital employed

1.7 For example, if a company makes a net profit of £20,000 on sales of £100,000 its profit percentage or profit margin is 20%. This also means that its costs are 80% of sales. A high profit margin indicates that either:

(a) **costs are being kept well under control** because if the ratio of costs to sales goes down, the profit margin will automatically go up. For example, if the cost:sales ratio changes from 80% to 75%, the profit margin will go up from 20% to 25%; or

(b) **sales prices are high**. For example, if a company sells goods for £100,000 and makes a profit of £16,000, costs would be £84,000 and the profit margin 16%. Now if the company can raise selling prices by 20% to £120,000 without affecting the volume of goods sold or their costs, profits would rise by the amount of revenue increase (£20,000) to £36,000 and the profit margin would also rise (from 16% to 30%).

1.8 **A gross profit percentage** - (sales less cost of sales) ÷ sales - is also often calculated, for example as below.

	£	£	
Sales		140,000	
Cost of sales			
Purchases	62,000		
Less closing stock	6,000		
		56,000	
Gross profit		84,000	60%
Selling and distribution expenses	30,000		
Administrative expenses	24,000		
		54,000	
Net profit		30,000	21%

1.9 For example, if a company has sales in 20X4 of £720,000 and has assets of £360,000, the asset turnover will be:

$$\frac{£720,000}{£360,000} = 2 \text{ times}$$

This means that for every £1 of assets employed, the company can generate sales turnover of £2 per annum. **To utilise assets more efficiently, managers should try to create a higher volume of sales and a higher asset turnover ratio**. For example, suppose that our firm with assets of £360,000 can increase its sales turnover from £720,000 to £900,000 per annum. The asset turnover would improve to:

$$\frac{£900,000}{£360,000} = 2.5 \text{ times}$$

The significance of this improvement is that if a business can create more sales turnover from the same amount of assets it should make larger profits (because of the increase in sales) without having to increase the size of its investment.

> **KEY TERM**
>
> **Return on capital employed (ROCE)** is the amount of net profit as a percentage of capital employed.

1.10 If a company makes a profit of £30,000, we do not know how good or bad the result is until we look at the amount of capital which has been invested to achieve the profit. £30,000 might be a good sized profit for a small firm, but it would not be good enough for a 'giant' firm such as Marks and Spencer, say. For this reason, it is helpful to measure performance by **relating profits to capital employed**, and because this seems to be the only satisfactory ratio or percentage which judges profits in relation to the size of business, it is sometimes called the **primary ratio in financial analysis**.

1.11 Capital employed can be taken as **capital plus reserves** (which is usually simply the balance sheet total), which is normally equal to the net book value of **fixed assets plus net current assets**. We discuss the calculation of ROCE further below.

1.12 You may already have realised that there is a mathematical connection between return on capital employed, profit margin and asset turnover:

$$\frac{\text{Profit}}{\text{Capital employed}} = \frac{\text{Profit}}{\text{Sales}} \times \frac{\text{Sales}}{\text{Capital employed}}$$

ROCE = Profit margin × Asset turnover

This is important. If we accept that **ROCE is the single most important measure of business performance**, comparing profit with the amount of capital invested, we can go on to say that business performance is dependent on two separate 'subsidiary' factors, each of which contributes to ROCE:

- profit margin;
- asset turnover.

For this reason, just as ROCE is sometimes called the **primary ratio**, the profit margin and asset turnover ratios are sometimes called the **secondary ratios**.

1.13 The implications of this relationship must be understood. Suppose that a return on capital employed of 20% is thought to be a good level of business performance in the retail trade for electrical goods.

(a) *Company A* might decide to sell its products at a fairly high price and make a profit margin on sales of 10%. It would then need only an asset turnover of 2.0 times to achieve a ROCE of 20%.

(b) *Company B* might decide to cut its prices so that its profit margin is only 2½%. Provided that it can achieve an asset turnover of 8 times a year, attracting more customers with its lower prices, it will still make a ROCE of 2½% × 8 = 20%.

1.14 Company A might be a department store and company B a discount warehouse. Each will have a **different selling price policy,** but each, in its own way, can be effective in achieving a **target ROCE.** In this example, if we supposed that both companies had capital employed of £100,000 and a target return of 20% or £20,000:

(a) company A would need annual sales of £200,000 to give a profit margin of 10% and an asset turnover of 2 times;

(b) company B would need annual sales of £800,000 to give a profit margin of only 2½% but an asset turnover of 8 times.

The inter-relationship between profit margin and asset turnover

1.15 Consider the following.

(a) A higher return on capital employed can be obtained by increasing the profit margin or the asset turnover ratio.

(b) The profit margin can be increased by reducing costs or by raising selling prices.

However, if selling prices are raised, it is likely that sales demand will fall, with the possible consequences that the asset turnover will also decline. If higher prices mean lower sales turnover, the increase in profit margin might be offset by the fall in asset turnover, so that total return on capital employed might not improve.

1.16 EXAMPLE: INTER-RELATIONSHIP BETWEEN PROFIT MARGIN AND ASSET TURNOVER

Suppose that Swings and Roundabouts Ltd achieved the following results in 20X6:

Sales	£100,000
Net profit	£5,000
Capital employed	£20,000

The company's management wish to decide whether to raise its selling prices. They think that if they do so, they can raise the profit margin to 10% and by introducing extra capital of £55,000, sales turnover could be increased to £150,000.

Evaluate the decision in terms of the effect on ROCE, profit margin and asset turnover.

1.17 SOLUTION

At present, ratios are:

Profit margin	5%
Asset turnover	5 times
ROCE (5/20)	25%

With the proposed changes, the profit would be $10\% \times £150,000 = £15,000$, and the asset turnover would be:

$\dfrac{£150,000}{£75,000} = 2$ times, so that the ratios might be:

Profit margin	×	Asset turnover	=	ROCE
10%	×	2 times	=	20% $\dfrac{£15,000}{£75,000}$

In spite of increasing the profit margin and raising the total volume of sales, the extra assets required (£55,000) only raise total profits by £(15,000 - 5,000) = £10,000.

The return on capital employed falls from 25% to 20% because of the sharp fall in asset turnover from 5 times to 2 times.

Whose return and whose capital employed?

1.18 Most of the providers of finance to a business expect some **return on their investment**.

(a) Trade creditors and other current liabilities merely expect to be paid what they are owed.

(b) A bank charges interest on overdrafts.

(c) Interest must be paid to the holders of loan stock and debentures.

(d) Preference shareholders expect a dividend at a fixed percentage rate of the nominal value of their shares.

(e) Ordinary shareholders also expect a dividend. However, any retained profits kept in the business also represent funds 'owned' or 'provided' by them.

1.19 So when we refer to '**return**' we must be clear in our mind about which providers of finance we are concerned with, and we should relate the return earned for those providers of finance to the amount of capital they are providing.

(a) If 'return' is **profit after tax**, it is return earned by ordinary and preference shareholders. The capital employed by these investors is as follows.

    (i) The nominal value of preference shares.

    (ii) The nominal value of ordinary shares.

    (iii) The amount in various reserves, because reserves are surpluses or profits retained in a business and 'owned' by the equity investors - ie the ordinary shareholders in a company.

(b) If 'return' is **profit after tax and preference dividend**, the left-over return is for ordinary shareholders, and is called **earnings**. The return on equity capital is:

$$\frac{\text{Earnings}}{\text{Ordinary share capital plus reserves}}$$

(c) If we prefer to consider the business as a whole, then the fixed assets and net current assets are financed by **long-term capital** which may include **loan creditors** as well as **shareholders**. The fund available to satisfy the claims of all these providers of finance is the profit before interest payments and taxation. In this case ROCE may be calculated as:

$$\frac{\text{Profit before interest and tax (PBIT)}}{\text{Loan capital plus share capital plus reserves}}$$

which equals

$$\frac{\text{PBIT}}{\text{Fixed assets plus net current assets}}$$

1.20 EXAMPLE: DIFFERENT WAYS OF CALCULATING ROCE

Suppose that Draught Ltd reports the following figures.

PROFIT AND LOSS ACCOUNT FOR 20X4 (EXTRACT)

	£
Profit before interest and tax	120,000
Interest	(20,000)
Profit before tax	100,000
Taxation	(40,000)
Profit after tax	60,000
Preference dividend	(1,000)
Profit available for ordinary shareholders (= earnings)	59,000
Ordinary dividend	(49,000)
Retained profits	10,000

BALANCE SHEET AT 31 DECEMBER 20X4

	£	£
Fixed assets: tangible assets		350,000
Current assets	400,000	
Less current liabilities	150,000	
Net current assets		250,000
Total assets less current liabilities		600,000
Creditors: amounts falling due after more than one year:		
10% debenture loans		200,000
		400,000
Capital and reserves:		
Called up share capital:		
5% preference shares		20,000
ordinary shares		80,000
		100,000
Profit and loss account		300,000
		400,000

1.21 Using the three alternatives described in paragraph 1.19, ROCE might be calculated in any of the following ways.

(a) **Return on shareholders' capital**

$$\frac{\text{Profit after tax}}{\text{Share capital plus reserves}} = \frac{£60,000}{£400,000} = 15\%$$

(b) **Return on equity capital**

$$\frac{\text{Profit after tax and preference dividend (earnings)}}{\text{Ordinary share capital plus reserves}} = \frac{£59,000}{£380,000} = 15.5\%$$

(c) **Return on total long-term capital**

$$\frac{\text{Profit before interest and tax}}{\text{Loan capital plus share capital plus reserves}} = \frac{£120,000}{£600,000} = 20\%$$

DEVOLVED ASSESSMENT ALERT

Remember that there is no single formula that is the correct one to use when calculating ratios. You *must* understand the concepts underlying the ratios. For example, when considering the return on capital employed, both the return and the capital employed might be measured in different ways. Different ratios for ROCE may therefore be used for different purposes at different times.

Turnover periods

> **KEY TERMS**
>
> A **turnover period** is an (average) length of time.
>
> - A **stock turnover period** is the length of time an item of stock is held in stores before it is used.
>
>   ° A **raw materials stock turnover period** is the length of time raw materials are held before being issued to the production department.
>
>   ° A **work in progress turnover period** is the length of time it takes to turn raw materials into finished goods in the factory.
>
>   ° A **finished goods stock turnover period** is the length of time that finished goods are held in a warehouse before they are sold.
>
>   ° When a firm buys goods and re-sells them at a profit, the stock turnover period is the time between their purchase and their resale.
>
> - The **debtors turnover period**, or debt collection period, is the length of the credit period taken by customers - ie it is the time between the sale of an item and the receipt of cash for the sale from the customer.
>
> - The **creditors turnover period**, or period of credit taken from suppliers, is the length of time between the purchase of materials and the payment to suppliers.

1.22 Turnover periods can be calculated from information in a firm's profit and loss account and balance sheet.

Stock turnover periods are calculated as follows.

(a) **Raw materials**:

$$\frac{\text{(Average) raw material stocks held}}{\text{Total raw materials consumed in one year}} \times 12 \text{ months}$$

(b) **Work in progress** (the length of the production period):

$$\frac{\text{(Average) finished goods stocks held}}{\text{Total cost of production in the year}} \times 12 \text{ months}$$

(c) **Finished goods**:

$$\frac{\text{(Average) stocks}}{\text{Total cost of goods sold in one year}} \times 12 \text{ months}$$

(d) **Stocks of items bought for re-sale**:

$$\frac{\text{(Average) stocks}}{\text{Total (materials) cost of goods bought and sold in one year}} \times 12 \text{ months}$$

The word 'average' is put in brackets because although it is strictly correct to use average values, it is more common to use the value of stocks shown in a balance sheet - ie at one point in time - **to estimate the turnover periods**.

1.23 For example, if a company buys goods costing £620,000 in one year but uses goods costing £600,000 in production (in regular monthly quantities) and the cost of material in stock at 1 January is £100,000, the stock turnover period could be calculated as:

$$\frac{£100,000}{£600,000} \times 12 \text{ months} = 2 \text{ months}$$

In other words, stocks are bought two months before they are eventually re-sold.

1.24 The debt collection period is calculated as:

$$\frac{\text{Average debtors}}{\text{Annual credit sales}} \times 12 \text{ months}$$

For example, if a company sells goods for £1,200,000 per annum in regular monthly quantities, and if debtors in the balance sheet are £150,000, the debt collection period is:

$$\frac{£150,000}{£1,200,000} \times 12 \text{ months} = 1.5 \text{ months}$$

In other words, debtors will pay for goods 1½ months on average after the time of sale.

1.25 The period of credit taken from suppliers is calculated as:

$$\frac{\text{Average trade creditors}}{\text{Total purchases in one year}} \times 12 \text{ months}$$

(Notice that the creditors are compared with materials bought whereas for raw material stock turnover, raw material stocks are compared with materials used in production. This is a small but significant difference.)

For example, if a company sells goods for £600,000 and makes a gross profit of 40% on sales, and if the amount of trade creditors in the balance sheet is £30,000, the period of credit taken from the suppliers is:

$$\frac{£30,000}{(60\% \text{ of } £600,000)} \times 12 \text{ months} = 1 \text{ month}$$

In other words, suppliers are paid in the month following the purchase of goods.

1.26 Stocks, debtors and cash, less creditors, make up what is called the **working capital** of the business, and the turnover periods for these items are known as **working capital ratios**.

Information for activities 11.1 and 11.2

The following (fictitious) figures relate to a public sector rail passenger service operation.

	20X1	20X2	20X3	20X4	20X5
Profit/(loss) as a percentage of receipts	−16.0	−12.4	+7.9	+6.0	+4.6
Receipts per train mile (£)	12.18	13.41	14.26	15.42	16.49
Total operating expenses per train mile (£)	14.33	15.26	13.28	15.42	16.20
On-board services sales per £'000 of direct operating costs (£)	2,291	2,185	2,645	2,843	2,560

An index for general inflation over the period is as follows.

Year	Inflation index
20X1	97.8
20X2	101.9
20X3	106.9
20X4	115.2
20X5	126.1

Activity 11.1

A table of performance indicators is to be prepared adjusting the above figures *where appropriate* to real terms (based on 20X5 pounds).

Tasks

(a) Identify how any of the above figures should be adjusted and carry out any adjustment necessary, using the inflation index given.

(b) Comment briefly on your methods.

Activity 11.2

(a) Calculate receipts per £'000 of total operating expenses from the information shown above, showing your workings clearly.

(b) Answer briefly the following question from your colleague: 'Shouldn't the figures you've calculated [in (a)] be adjusted for the effect of inflation?'

Activity 11.3

The figures below relate to a retailing division of a diversified company at which you are employed.

	20X1 £'000	20X2 £'000	20X3 £'000	20X4 £'000
Sales	1,288	1,342	1,378	1,473
Cost of sales	729	792	859	928
Gross profit	559	550	519	545
Operating expenses	245	250	290	310
Net profit before interest and taxation	314	300	229	235
Number of employees				
Selling	18	19	20	20
Other	5	7	8	8
Retail Prices Index (RPI) average	202	207	214	217

It was remarked at a recent management meeting that the results for 20X4 continue an unbroken record of sales growth since 20X1. However, it was also questioned whether the record of sales volume growth per employee was so good. In particular, the performance of individual sales staff was questioned.

Tasks

You have been asked to produce a summary in tabular form showing:

(a) real sales growth;

(b) appropriate productivity measures (real sales per selling employee and real sales per employee);

(c) gross profit percentage;

(d) operating expenses, expressed in real terms;

(e) net profit percentage.

Comment briefly on the results.

2 MEASURING DIVISIONAL PERFORMANCE: PROFIT OR CONTRIBUTION?

2.1 A principle of what is known as 'responsibility accounting' is that **profit centre managers should only be held accountable for those revenues and costs that they are in a position to control** (or at least to explain). Short-term controllable costs are **mainly variable** (although there may be some fixed costs which are discretionary) and it is therefore arguable that a divisional manager's performance should perhaps be measured in terms of total contribution, an idea which we touched on earlier.

(a) The costs he is capable of reducing (by improvements in efficiency) are mainly variable costs.

(b) Increases in production volume, within the relevant range of output, will raise profit by the amount of increase in contribution.

2.2 A divisional performance statement based on contribution might appear as follows.

	Division A	*Division B*	*Total*
	£'000	£'000	£'000
Sales	80	100	180
Less variable costs	60	50	110
Contribution	20	50	70
Less fixed costs			50
Profit			20

(a) Divisional performance can be improved by increasing the sales price, or volume of sales, or reducing the unit variable costs.

(b) The relative profitability of divisions A and B could be compared by means of their contribution/sales ratio (in this example, 25% and 50% respectively).

Directly attributable fixed costs

2.3 One drawback to using contribution alone as a measure of divisional performance is that although it indicates the **short-term controllable results** of the division, it **gives no indication as to longer-term underlying profitability**. Suppose, for example, that a division is closed down. Apart from the 'one-off' effects of closure, such as redundancy payments and receipts from the sale of assets, there would be some **reduction of annual running costs**.

2.4 The variable costs of production would be avoided, but there would also be a **reduction in fixed costs**. All the fixed costs which are directly attributable to the division would be saved, so that even if a contribution towards profits is being earned, it might still be profitable to close the division because **directly attributable costs exceed the size of the contribution.**

2.5 In the following example, closure of division X might be justified, since there would be a net saving in annual running costs of £5,000.

	Division X	*Division Y*	*Total*
	£'000	£'000	£'000
Sales	70	120	190
Less variable costs	50	80	130
Contribution	20	40	60
Less directly attributable fixed costs	25	25	50
Profit of the division	(5)	15	10
Less fixed costs (general)			8
Company profit			2

2.6 The longer-term performance of divisions should therefore be measured **after deducting directly attributable fixed costs**, but contribution should also be shown, since this indicates **short-term controllable results.**

Information for activities 11.4 and 11.5

You have recently been appointed as Accounting Technician attached to the headquarters of the Alphabet Group plc, with special responsibility for monitoring the performances of the companies within the group. Each company is treated as an investment centre and every month produces an operating statement for the group headquarters. Summaries of the statements for companies X and Y, which make similar products selling at similar prices, for the last month showed a typical situation.

EXTRACT FROM COMPANY MONTHLY OPERATING STATEMENTS

		X	Y
		£'000	£'000
	Sales	600	370
less	Variable costs	229	208
	= Contribution	371	162
less	Controllable fixed overheads		
	(including depreciation on company assets)	65	28
	= Controllable profit	306	134
less	Apportioned group costs	226	119
	= Net profit	80	15
	Company assets	£6.4m	£0.9m
	Estimated return on capital employed (on annual basis)	15%	20%

Although both companies are earning more than the target return on capital of 12%, there is pressure on interest rates which means that this rate must be increased soon and the board is concerned at the relatively low return achieved by X.

Activity 11.4

Compare and discuss the relative performance of the two companies as shown in the summarised operating statements above.

Activity 11.5

(a)   Re-draft the summarised operating statements given above using residual income, an alternative performance measure to return on capital employed, and interpret them against a background of rising interest rates.

Notes on methods

Residual income = divisional profit less imputed interest cost.

The imputed interest cost is calculated as the cost of capital (12%) ÷ divisional investment (company assets).

(b)   Compare the use of return on capital employed and the residual income measure used in (a) to assess the performance of investment centres.

Activity 11.6

In the public sector, individual performance targets fall under the four headings of financial performance, volume of output, quality of service and efficiency.

Task

Identify the heading under which each of the following measures would fall.

(a)   Time taken to deal with applications in the Drivers and Vehicles Licensing Agency.

(b)   Revenue from ancillary services provided by a hospital (eg shops in hospitals, television rental services) to cover costs.

(c)   20% reduction in the cost of common services over a five year period.

(d)   95% of work completed to time and to standards (Military Survey)

(e) Target of 1,300,000 placings in the year for unemployed people into jobs of which 16% are to be long term claimants, 2.4% to be people with disabilities and 34% are to be unemployed people in inner cities. (Employment Service Agency)

Activity 11.7

Give one example each of a performance indicator which might measure:

(a) the productivity of a coal mine;
(b) the effectiveness of a newspaper advertisement for a staff vacancy.

3 PERFORMANCE MEASUREMENT IN THE PUBLIC SECTOR

3.1 In public sector organisations, an increasing volume of information on **performance** and **'value for money'** is produced for internal and external use. The ways in which performance can be measured depends very much upon which organisation is involved.

3.2 The first question which would need to be asked is **'what are the aims and objectives of the organisation**?' For example, the objective of Companies House is to maintain and make available records of company reports.

3.3 The next question to ask is **'How can we tell if the organisation is meeting the objectives**?' Quantified information - ie information in the form of numbers - will be useful, and this will consist mainly of output and performance measures and indicators. For these, targets can be set. Any individual organisational unit should have no more than a handful of **key targets**.

3.4 Individual targets are likely to fall under the following broad headings.

- Financial performance targets.
- Volume of output targets.
- Quality of service targets.
- Efficiency targets.

Performance measurement in central government

3.5 Over recent years, much of the work of central government has been reorganised into **semi-autonomous 'executive agencies'**.

3.6 Targets related to financial performance which you may become aware of, for example if you work for an executive agency, could include ones similar to the following.

(a) Full cost recovery (Civil Service College, Office for National Statistics and others), plus unit cost targets.

(b) Commercial revenue to offset costs (Met Office).

(c) Non-Exchequer income as a percentage of total income (National Engineering Laboratory).

3.7 Targets related to output can be difficult to set. While the output of the Vehicle Inspectorate can be measured on the number of tests performed, and the output of the Hydrographic Office consists of charts for navigators, in many other cases the output of executive agencies is less tangible. For example, the Historic Royal Palaces Agency not only deals with visitors, whose numbers can be counted, but is also responsible for maintaining the fabric of royal palaces - an output which is more difficult to measure. In such cases, performance will be best measured by appraising the progress of the 'project' as a whole (called 'project appraisal').

3.8   Examples of **quality targets** set for executive agencies include the following.

(a)   **Timeliness**

(i)   Time to handle applications (Passport Office, Vehicle Certification Agency and many others)

(ii)   Car driving tests to be reduced to 6 weeks nationally and 10 weeks in London (Driving Standards Agency)

(iii) All cheques to be banked within 35 hours (Accounts Services Agency)

(b)   **Quality of product**

(i)   Number of print orders delivered without fault (HMSO)

(ii)   Error rate in the value of benefit payments (Employment Service)

(iii) 95% business complaints handled within 5 days (Radio Communications Agency)

(iv)   85% overall customer satisfaction rating (Recruitment and Assessment Services Agency)

(v)   Hold meetings of creditors within 12 weeks in 90% of cases (Insolvency Service)

3.9   **Efficiency improvements may come through reducing the cost of inputs without reducing the quality of outputs**. Alternatively, areas of activity affecting total costs may be reduced. Targets related to efficiency include the following.

(a)   Percentage reduction in price paid for purchases of stationery and paper (HMSO).

(b)   Reduction in the ratio of cost of support services to total cost (Laboratory of the Government Chemist).

(c)   8.7% efficiency increase in the use of accommodation (Recruitment and Assessment Services Agency).

Performance measurement in local government

3.10   The performance measures chosen by local authorities usually consist of the following.

- Comparative statistics
- Unit costs

These measures do two things.

- They give details, statistics and unit costs of an authority's own activities.
- They show statistical and cost comparisons with other authorities.

3.11   Reporting on comparative statistics is recommended by the Department of the Environment in its code of practice *Local authority annual reports* (1982).

3.12 The following table illustrates the types of comparative statistic suggested in the code of practice.

Local government activity	Comparative statistics
For the authority's total expenditure and for each function	Net cost per 1,000 population Manpower per 1,000 population
Primary education, secondary education	Pupil/teacher ratio Cost per pupil
School meals	Revenue/cost ratio Pupils receiving free meals as a proportion of school roll
Children in care	As a proportion of total under-18 population Cost per child in care
Care of elderly	Residents of council homes as a proportion of total over-75 population Cost per resident week
Home helps	Contract hours per 1,000 population over 65
Police	Population per police officer Serious offences per 1,000 population
Fire	Proportion of area at high risk
Public transport	Passenger journeys per week per 1,000 population
Highways	Maintenance cost per kilometre
Housing	Rents as a proportion of total cost Management cost per dwelling per week Rent arrears as a percentage of year's rent income Construction cost per dwelling completed
Trading services	Revenue/gross cost ratio

Activity 11.8

The Testing Office is a (fictitious) executive agency in the public (government) sector which carries out tests required by law. Since 20X0 the agency has operated a unit cost target of £26.00 per test at 20X0 prices. The agency uses a general price deflator to convert from cash to real terms. Unit costs in cash terms and the value of the general price deflator for the years 20X0 to 20X5 are as follows.

	Unit costs (cash) £	General price deflator
20X0	25.78	1.00
20X1	24.57	1.05
20X2	27.58	1.11
20X3	29.97	1.18
20X4	32.06	1.22
20X5	32.13	1.24

In which of the years 20X0 to 20X5 did the agency beat its unit cost target?

Activity 11.9

The following figures are extracted from the accounts of Hockley plc.

	20X2		20X1	
	£m	£m	£m	£m
Fixed assets		25.4		17.8
Current assets	10.4		17.4	
Creditors: amounts falling due within one year	10.0		12.6	
Net current assets		0.4		4.8
		25.8		22.6
Creditors: amounts falling due after more than one year		(15.4)		(16.2)
Provisions for liabilities and charges		(1.6)		(1.0)
		8.8		5.4
Turnover		35.6		28.2
Operating profit		6.0		4.6
Profit on ordinary activities before tax		5.2		4.2
Profit on ordinary activities after tax		3.6		3.0
Extraordinary items		0.4		0.4
Profit for the financial year		4.0		3.4

The company calculates the following profitability ratios.

$$\text{Return on capital employed (ROCE)} = \frac{\text{Operating profit}}{\text{Shareholders' funds}}$$

$$\text{Profit margin} = \frac{\text{Operating profit}}{\text{Turnover}}$$

$$\text{Asset turnover} = \frac{\text{Turnover}}{\text{Shareholders' funds}}$$

Shareholders' funds are taken to be the average of the opening and closing balance sheet figures for fixed assets plus net current assets.

Tasks

(a)   Calculate the following figures for 20X2.

(i)   ROCE
(ii)   Profit margin
(iii)   Asset turnover

(b)   What is the mathematical relationship between the three ratios calculated above?

Key learning points

- Certain **ratios** can be used for analysing and interpreting profit and loss accounts, balance sheets and forms of divisional income statement, and then using the ratios for comparison between one year and the next or between one business division and another.

- The three principal ratios used to indicate profitability are **profit margin, asset turnover** and **return on capital employed (ROCE).**

  ° Profit margin is the ratio of net profit to sales, and is also called profit percentage or net profit percentage

  ° Asset turnover is the ratio of sales turnover in a year to the amount of capital employed

  ° Return on capital employed (ROCE) is the amount of net profit as a percentage of capital employed

- ROCE = Profit margin × Asset turnover

- A **turnover period** is an average length of time, and reflects the condition of the working capital of the business. The main turnover periods are **stock, debtors,** and **creditors**.

- The main principle of **responsibility accounting** is that profit centre managers should only be held accountable for those revenues and costs that they are in a position to control.

- **Divisional performance** may be better measured by contribution (which is within the manager's direct control) rather than by profit.

- **Performance measurement** is becoming increasingly important in the public sector, although there can be problems in deciding how the output of any particular organisational units is to be defined.

Quick quiz

1   When using ratio analysis to compare the profitability and financial stability of two different businesses, in what respects should the businesses be broadly similar?

2   If a company makes a net profit of £40,000 on sales of £200,000, what is its profit percentage or profit margin?

3   If a company has sales in 20X8 of £500,000 and has assets of £200,000, what will its asset turnover be?

4   What is the mathematical connection that exists between return on capital employed, profit margin and asset turnover?

5   What are the three main ways of calculating ROCE?

6   If a company buys goods costing £500,000 in one year but uses goods costing £450,000 in production (in regular monthly quantities) and the cost of material stock at the beginning of the year is £75,000, what is the stock turnover period.

7   Under what broad headings are the individual targets of public sector organisations likely to fall?

8   What two things do the performance measures chosen by local authorities usually consist of?

Answers to quick quiz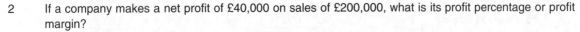

1   In size and in their line of activities.

2    $\dfrac{£40,000}{£200,000} = 20\%$

3    $\dfrac{£500,000}{£200,000} = 2\frac{1}{2}$ times

4   Return on capital employed = Profit margin × Asset turnover

227

5 (a) **Shareholders capital** $= \dfrac{\text{Profit after tax}}{\text{Share capital plus reserves}}$

(b) **Return on equity capital** $= \dfrac{\text{Profit after tax and preference dividend (earnings)}}{\text{Ordinary share capital plus reserves}}$

(c) **Return on total long term capital** $= \dfrac{\text{Profit before interest and tax}}{\text{Loan capital plus share capital plus reserves}}$

6 $\dfrac{£75,000}{£450,000} \times 12 \text{ months} = 2 \text{ months}$

7
- Financial performance targets
- Volume of output targets
- Quality of service targets
- Efficiency targets

8
- Comparative statistics
- Unit costs

Answers to activities

Answer 11.1

(a) *Performance indicators*

	20X1	20X2	20X3	20X4	20X5
Profit/(loss) as a percentage of receipts	−16.0	−12.4	+7.9	+6.0	+4.6
Receipts per train mile (20X5 £)*	15.70	16.59	16.82	16.88	16.49
Total operating expenses per train mile (20X5 £)*	18.48	18.88	15.67	16.88	16.20
On-board services sales per £'000 of direct operating costs (£)	2,291	2,185	2,645	2,843	2,560
Inflation index	97.8	101.9	106.9	115.2	126.1
*Conversion factor	$\dfrac{126.1}{97.8}$	$\dfrac{126.1}{101.9}$	$\dfrac{126.1}{106.9}$	$\dfrac{126.1}{115.2}$	1

(b) *Comments on methods*

Inflation will affect both costs and revenues. The profit/(loss) as a percentage of receipts does not require adjustment since it is expressed as a percentage. Similarly, as on-board services sales per £'000 of direct operating costs is a ratio of revenues to costs, no adjustment is necessary: inflation will affect both sales prices and operating costs.

The other indicators (receipts per train mile, and total operating costs per train mile) are each calculated using only one monetary term (receipts and total operating costs, respectively) and are adjusted by 126.1 ÷ inflation index for the relevant year, in order to express them in real terms (20X5 £s).

Answer 11.2

(a)

	20X1	20X2	20X3	20X4	20X5
Receipts per train mile × 1,000	12,180	13,410	14,260	15,420	16,490
Total operating expenses per train mile	14.33	15.26	13.28	15.42	16.20
= Receipts per £'000 of total operating expenses (£)	850	879	1,074	1,000	1,018

(b) No. Both 'sides' of the ratio, receipts and total operating expenses, will be affected by general inflation. Strictly speaking, it might be meaningful to adjust each factor by an appropriate specific price index. For example, receipts might be adjusted by an index of transport fares and total operating costs might be adjusted by an index of general industrial costs. However, such indices are not available here.

Answer 11.3

	20X1	*20X2*	*20X3*	*20X4*
Sales (20X4 £'000s)	1,384	1,407	1,397	1,473
Annual real sales growth	-	1.7%	-0.7%	5.4%
Selling employees	18	19	20	20
Total employees	23	26	28	28
Sales per selling employee (20X4 £'000s)	76.9	74.1	69.9	73.7
Sales per employee (20X4 £'000s)	60.2	54.1	49.9	52.6
Gross profit percentage	43.4%	41.0%	37.7%	37.0%
Operating expenses (20X4 £'000s)	263	262	294	310
Net profit percentage	24.4%	22.4%	16.6%	16.0%

Comments

Sales growth needs to be viewed in terms of real sales by adjusting for inflation. Real sales show little change in 20X2 and 20X3, followed by 5.4% growth in real sales (ie in volume terms) in 20X4.

Real sales per selling employee declined in 20X2 and 20X3 but showed some recovery in 20X4. However, real sales per employee overall has shown larger percentage falls, with only a small rise in 20X4.

Over the period 20X1 to 20X4, the gross profit percentage declined each year, standing at 37% in 20X4 against 43.4% in 20X1. Accompanying a rise in expenses in real terms, partly reflecting the increase in non-selling staff numbers, there has been a decline in the net profit percentage from 24.4% to 16.0% between 20X1 and 20X4.

It is unclear from the figures given why it should have been necessary to increase non-selling staff employed from five to eight over the period.

Answer 11.4

ROCE $\quad=\quad$ Asset turnover × profit percentage

$$= \quad \frac{\text{Sales}}{\text{Capital employed}} \times \frac{\text{Profit}}{\text{Sales}}$$

	X	*Y*
Profit (annual basis)	£960,000 (×12)	£180,000
Sales (annual basis)	£7,200,000 (×12)	£4,440,000

ROCE $\quad \dfrac{£7.2m}{£6.4m} \times \dfrac{£0.96m}{£7.2m} \qquad \dfrac{£4.44m}{£0.9m} \times \dfrac{£0.18m}{£4.44m}$

$\quad\quad = \quad 1.125 \text{ times} \times 13.3\% \qquad = \quad 4.933 \text{ times} \times 4.1\%$

$\quad\quad = \quad 15\% \qquad\qquad\qquad\quad = \quad 20\%$

	X	*Y*
	%	%
Sales	100	100
Variable costs	38	56
	62	44
Controllable fixed costs	11	8
Controllable profit	51	36
Apportioned group costs	38	32
Net profit	13	4

Controllable annual ROCE $\qquad\qquad \dfrac{306 \times 12}{6,400} \qquad\qquad \dfrac{134 \times 12}{900}$

$\qquad\qquad\qquad\qquad\qquad\qquad = 57.4\% \qquad\qquad = 178.7\%$

(a) Y achieves a higher return on capital employed (ROCE) than X, even when controllable profit is used in the calculation.

(b) Y achieves a higher asset turnover rate than X, which outweighs the effect of the lower profitability of sales, producing a higher ROCE.

(c) The higher contribution to sales ratio achieved by X suggests that its ROCE could be substantially improved if sales were increased at the same prices.

(d) The higher sales to capital employed ratio achieved by Y may indicate a different basis of operating compared with X (high sales, low profitability), but it may be due to the fact that Y is using older or fully depreciated fixed assets. It may therefore be misleading to draw firm conclusions from these ratios.

Answer 11.5

Residual income can be used as an alternative performance measure as follows.

		X		Y	
		£'000		£'000	
(a)	Sales	600		370	
	Variable costs	229		208	
	Contribution	371		162	
	Controllable fixed overhead	65		28	
	Controllable profit	306		134	
	Imputed interest	64	(W1)	9	(W2)
	Controllable residual income	242		125	
	Apportioned group costs	226		119	
	Net residual income	16		6	

Workings

1. £6.4m × 12% × $^{1}/_{12}$ = £64,000 per month
2. £0.9m × 12% × $^{1}/_{12}$ = £9,000 per month

Both companies have a positive residual income, indicating that they earn returns in excess of the target return on capital. X has a greater investment in company assets, therefore the imputed interest charge is greater.

The apparent relative performance of the two companies is now reversed - X achieves a higher residual income than Y. This is because, although X has a ROCE of only 15%, it is returning 15% on a much larger asset base and therefore the absolute profit in excess of cost of capital is greater.

(b) (i) ROCE can discourage managers from undertaking new investments since the high balance sheet values of new assets tend to depress the ROCE initially.

(ii) Residual income uses absolute values and highlights those investments which return more than the cost of capital by showing a positive residual income.

(iii) ROCE tends to be used by external analysts in assessing company performance, therefore it is important to ensure that its level is maintained. However, it must not be applied too rigidly and it is probably better used in conjunction with other performance measures.

Answer 11.6

(a) Quality of service. (This target relates to timeliness; other quality targets relate to quality of product.)

(b) Financial performance

(c) Efficiency

(d) Quality

(e) Output

Answer 11.7

(a) Monthly tonnes of coal produced per mining worker.

(b) Number of applications made as a result of the advertisement.

Answer 11.8

The correct answer is: every year except 20X4.

	(1) Unit costs (cash) £	(2) General price deflator	(3) Unit costs (real) £
20X0	25.78	1.00	25.78
20X1	24.57	1.05	23.40
20X2	27.58	1.11	24.85
20X3	29.97	1.18	25.40
20X4	32.06	1.22	26.28
20X5	32.13	1.24	25.91

(3) = (1) ÷ (2)

Answer 11.9

(a) (i) $\dfrac{6.0}{(25.8 + 22.6) \div 2} = \dfrac{6.0}{24.2} = 24.8\%$

(ii) $\dfrac{6.0}{35.6} = 16.9\%$

(iii) $\dfrac{35.6}{24.2} = 1.5 \text{ times}$

(b) $\dfrac{\text{Operating profit}}{\text{Turnover}} \times \dfrac{\text{Turnover}}{\text{Shareholders' funds}} = \dfrac{\text{Operating profit}}{\text{Shareholders' funds}}$

   Profit margin × Asset turnover = Return on capital employed

Part B
Preparing VAT returns

Chapter 12   The VAT charge and VAT records

Chapter topic list

1   Basic principles of VAT

2   The scope of VAT

3   Invoices and records

4   Registration for VAT

Learning objectives

On completion of this chapter you will be able to:

	Performance criteria	Range statement
• calculate the VAT due on a supply	7.3.2	
• account for VAT	7.3.1	7.3.1
• complete a VAT return	7.3.1	
• recognise and complete appropriate VAT documentation and accounts	7.3.1	7.3.1
• identify when a business can and should register for VAT	7.3.2	
• deal with pre-registration input VAT	7.3.2	

1   BASIC PRINCIPLES OF VAT

1.1   In Element 7.3, you will study value added tax (VAT). VAT applies to a great many business transactions, and you will often see it mentioned on invoices and in price lists and advertisements. In your work as an accounting technician, you will not be able to deal with sales, purchases, receipts and payments correctly unless you understand how VAT works.

1.2   You will find that the style of this part of the Interactive Text is very different from the style of Part A. This is because VAT, like all taxes, was created by law, and the law has to be very precise and detailed to prevent people from avoiding the tax. If any loopholes are left in the law, someone will use them in order to pay less tax than they should.

1.3   Because there are a lot of hard and fast rules to learn (instead of recommended approaches), you may find it helpful to try new approaches to study. Here are some suggestions.

(a)   Start by quickly reading through the whole of this section of the Interactive Text twice. Do not spend time puzzling out the meaning of a paragraph which is not clear to you, but move on so that you get an overall view.

(b)   Then read through the section much more carefully, making sure that you do understand everything as you go. Work through each activity as you reach it during the chapter. When you come to a rule, try to see the point of it. For example, what could taxpayers get away with if the rule did not exist? (However, not all rules are aimed at the deliberate tax dodger.)

(c)   Finally, try the activities and the end of Chapter quizzes again. Note that you can have a copy of the Customs & Excise Notice 700, the VAT Guide, with you during your devolved assessment. The VAT Guide gives quite a lot of detailed information, and is a useful memory-jogger.

Computing VAT due

1.4   **VAT is a tax on sales, not on income or profit. Whenever goods or services are sold, VAT (usually at a rate of 17.5%) may be due. The VAT is added to the price, so the money is collected by the seller. The seller then pays over the VAT collected by him to HM Customs & Excise,** who administer VAT.

1.5   The system is arranged so that all the VAT on the full value of the item sold is borne by the final consumer, however many stages there are before him. Everybody except the final consumer goes through the following procedure.

(a)   Work out the VAT on sales (the **output VAT**).

(b)   Work out the VAT on purchases (the **input VAT**).

(c)   **Pay to HM Customs & Excise the output VAT minus the input VAT, or claim from HM Customs & Excise the input VAT minus the output VAT.**

KEY TERM

Output VAT is the VAT charged on sales of goods or provision of services.

Input VAT is the VAT suffered when goods or services are purchased by a business.

1.6 EXAMPLE: THE VAT CHARGE

Anne makes a table from some wood she has grown herself. She sells it to Bob for £100, who sells it to Christine for £150. Christine sells it to David for £280. All these prices exclude VAT, and David is the final consumer.

Tasks

(a) Show the profits made by Anne, Bob and Christine, ignoring VAT.

(b) Show the effect of imposing VAT at 17.5%.

1.7 SOLUTION

(a)

	Selling price £	Purchase price £	Profit £
Anne	100	0	100
Bob	150	100	50
Christine	280	150	130

(b) In the following table, the selling and purchase prices have all been increased by 17.5%, to take account of the VAT. The VAT payable is the output VAT minus the input VAT. The profit is the selling price minus the purchase price minus the VAT payable.

	Selling price £	Purchase price £	Output VAT £	Input VAT £	VAT payable £	Profit £
Anne	117.50	0	17.50	0	17.50	100
Bob	176.25	117.50	26.25	17.50	8.75	50
Christine	329.00	176.25	49.00	26.25	22.75	130
					49.00	

The imposition of VAT has made no difference to any of Anne, Bob and Christine. Each of them makes the same profit as before. The two parties who are affected are:

(i) David, who pays £329 for the table instead of £280, so he is £49 worse off;

(ii) HM Customs & Excise, who collect £49 in VAT. They collect £17.50 from Anne, £8.75 from Bob and £22.75 from Christine.

Accounting for VAT

1.8 **A trader does not in practice pay over to Customs the VAT due every time he sells something. Instead he works out the total VAT due for a VAT period** (usually three months). **He fills in a VAT return (form VAT 100) for the period, showing the total output VAT, the total input VAT and the total VAT due or repayable.** He then sends this return to HM Customs & Excise, together with any VAT due. HM Customs & Excise then send him a return for the next period. Every VAT return shows a trader's name, address and VAT registration number pre-printed on the return.

1.9 EXAMPLE: VAT FOR A VAT PERIOD

In a VAT period, Susan sold goods for £10,000 (excluding VAT). She bought goods for £7,050 (including VAT). Show the VAT figures for her VAT return for the period.

1.10 SOLUTION

The output VAT is £10,000 × 17.5% = £1,750.

The input VAT is 17.5% of the purchases excluding VAT, so it is 17.5/117.5 = 7/47 of the purchases including VAT. This fraction of 7/47, the VAT in an amount including VAT, is called the **VAT fraction**.

The input VAT is £7,050 × 7/47 = £1,050.

The VAT payable is £(1,750 - 1,050) = £700.

1.11 **Most VAT periods last for one quarter (three months).** They may end on the last day of June, September, December and March; July, October, January and April; or August, November, February and May. A trader is allocated to one of these groups (called Stagger Groups) depending on the type of trade carried on, but may ask to be put into the stagger group which will fit in with his own accounting year.

1.12 **Some traders regularly get refunds of VAT** (see the next chapter). **Such traders can elect to have monthly VAT periods, so that they get their refunds more quickly.**

1.13 Some traders can have annual VAT periods. This **annual accounting scheme** is dealt with in the next chapter.

Paying VAT

1.14 **The return is due within one month after the end of the VAT period.** Any VAT due must be paid within the same time limit.

1.15 If a repayment to the trader is due, the trader may receive it through the post or, if he prefers, by credit transfer directly to his bank account.

Substantial traders

1.16 **If a trader does not make monthly returns, and the total VAT liability over 12 months to the end of a VAT period exceeds £2,000,000, he must thereafter make payments on account of each quarter's VAT liability during the quarter.** Payments are due a month before the end of the quarter and at the end of the quarter, with the final payment due at the usual time, a month after the end of the quarter. Payments must be made electronically, not by a cheque through the post.

1.17 **Each payment on account is 1/24 of the total annual VAT liability.** Thus if a trader had, last year, a VAT liability of £3,000,000, each payment would be £3,000,000/24 = £125,000. If, in the quarter to 30 June, the VAT liability was £400,000, the trader would pay £125,000 on 31 May, £125,000 on 30 June and the balance of £150,000 on 31 July.

1.18 The payments on account are recomputed annually, using the latest annual VAT liability. They are also recomputed in between annual reviews if the total liability for the past 12 months changes by more than 20% (up or down).

1.19 Traders can choose to switch from making quarterly returns to monthly returns instead of making the payments on account calculated by Customs. For example, the actual return and liability due for January would be due at the end of February.

1.20 Traders can also choose to pay their actual monthly liability without having to make monthly returns. Customs can refuse to allow a trader to continue to do this if they find he has abused the facility by not paying enough. The trader will then either have to make payments on account or switch to making monthly returns.

1.21 A trader has the right to appeal to a VAT tribunal if Customs refuse to allow him to make monthly returns of his VAT liability.

Activity 12.1

In January 20X3, Roger paints a picture using materials which he acquired at negligible cost. In March 20X3, he sells it to Susan for £400 excluding VAT.

Susan immediately buys materials to frame the picture from Thomas for £70.50 including VAT, and frames it. She sells it to Victor in May 20X3 for £700 excluding VAT. Victor keeps the picture.

Roger, Susan and Thomas are all registered for VAT and account for VAT quarterly. Roger and Thomas have tax periods ending at the end of June, September, December and March and Susan's tax periods end at the end of August, November, February and May.

Task

Show all payments to HM Customs & Excise arising from these transactions, and the due dates.

The boxes on a VAT return

1.22 The boxes on a VAT return which a trader must fill in are as follows.

- **Box 1**: the VAT due in the period on sales and other outputs

- **Box 2**: the VAT due on acquisitions from other EC member states

- **Box 3**: the total of boxes 1 and 2

- **Box 4**: the VAT reclaimed in the period on purchases and other inputs

- **Box 5**: the net VAT to be paid or reclaimed: the difference between boxes 3 and 4

- **Box 6**: the total value (before cash discounts) of sales and all other outputs in the period, excluding VAT but including the total in box 8

- **Box 7**: the total value (before cash discounts) of purchases and all other inputs in the period, excluding VAT but including the total in box 9

- **Box 8**: the total value of all sales and related services to other EC member states

- **Box 9**: the total value of all purchases and related services from other EC member states

Amounts in boxes 1 to 5 are given in pounds and pence. All other amounts are given to the nearest pound below.

Value Added Tax Return

For the period

01 06 X6 to 31 08 X6

For Official Use

Registration number

483 8611 98

Period

08 X6

You could be liable to a financial penalty if your completed return and all the VAT payable are not received by the due date.

MS S SMITH
32 CASE STREET
ZEDTOWN
ZY4 3JN

Due date: 30 09 X6

For
Official
Use

Your VAT Office telephone number is 0123-4567

Before you fill in this form please read the notes on the back and the VAT Leaflet *"Filling in your VAT return"*.
Fill in all boxes clearly in ink, and write 'none' where necessary. Don't put a dash or leave any box blank. If there are no pence write "00" in the pence column. Do not enter more than one amount in any box.

For official use			£	p
	VAT due in this period on sales and other outputs	1		
	VAT due in this period on acquisitions from other EC Member States	2		
	Total VAT due (the sum of boxes 1 and 2)	3		
	VAT reclaimed in this period on purchases and other inputs (including acquisitions from the EC)	4		
	Net VAT to be paid to Customs or reclaimed by you (Difference between boxes 3 and 4)	5		
	Total value of sales and all other outputs excluding any VAT. Include your box 8 figure	6		00
	Total value of purchases and all other inputs excluding any VAT. Include your box 9 figure	7		00
	Total value of all supplies of goods and related services, excluding any VAT, to other EC Member States	8		00
	Total value of all acquisitions of goods and related services, excluding any VAT, from other EC Member States	9		00

Retail schemes. If you have used any of the schemes in the period covered by this return, enter the relevant letter(s) in this box.

If you are enclosing a payment please tick this box.	DECLARATION: You, or someone on your behalf, must sign below.
	I, _____ declare that the (Full name of signatory in BLOCK LETTERS) information given above is true and complete.
	Signature_____ Date 20

A false declaration can result in prosecution.

1.23 The introduction of revised retail schemes in 1 August 1997 has made it impractical for retailers to indicate on each VAT return which retail scheme they are using. However, VAT returns currently in use have a box in which to show this information. Customs have announced that future versions of the VAT return will not include this box and have asked traders in the meantime to ignore this part of the VAT return.

The notes on the back of a return (which are referred to on the front) are reminders of what goes in which box, of how to correct errors and of how to pay VAT.

DEVOLVED ASSESSMENT ALERT

You might be asked to complete a VAT return in a devolved assessment. **It is essential that you are familiar with the VAT return** and understand which numbers are entered into each box. Try to get hold of a real VAT return and read the notes on the back.

Errors in previous periods

1.24 **Where errors have been made in previous periods and the net error** (error in VAT payable net of error in VAT allowable) **is £2,000 or less, the error may be corrected on the next VAT return** by changing the figures in boxes 1, 2 and 4 as appropriate. If an amount was overstated, the figure must be reduced. If a figure becomes negative because of this, it should be shown in brackets.

1.25 **Larger errors must be separately notified to the local VAT office, either on form VAT 652 or by letter.**

The time of a supply

KEY TERM

Because sales and purchases (supplies by and to a business) are grouped together in VAT periods, rules are needed to fix the time of a supply. It can then be decided which VAT period a supply falls into. This time of supply is the **tax point.**

1.26 **The basic tax point is the date on which goods are removed or made available to the customer, or the date on which services are completed.**

1.27 **If a VAT invoice** (an invoice meeting the conditions set out in Section 3 of this chapter) **is issued or payment is received before the basic tax point, the earlier of these dates automatically becomes the tax point. If the VAT invoice is issued within 14 days after the basic tax point (and the earlier tax point mentioned previously does not apply), the invoice date becomes the tax point** (although the trader can elect to use the basic tax point for all his supplies if he wishes). This 14 day period may be extended to accommodate, for example, monthly invoicing; the tax point is then the VAT invoice date or the end of the month, whichever is applied consistently.

1.28 Goods supplied on sale or return are treated as supplied on the **earlier of adoption by the customer** or **12 months after despatch**. Continuous supplies of services paid for periodically normally have tax points on the earlier of the receipt of each payment and the issue of each VAT invoice. However, if one invoice covering several payments is issued in advance for up to a year, the tax point becomes the earlier of each due date or date of actual payment.

Activity 12.2

Bernini plc has made sales and purchases as indicated by the following documents.

BERNINI PLC

Jacob Ltd   1 Long Lane
45 Broad Street   Anytown
Newtown   AN4 5QP
NE7 2LH   VAT reg no GB 212 7924 36

Invoice no. 324
Date: 4 July 20X5
Tax point: 4 July 20X5

	VAT rate	
	%	£
Sale of 300 pens	17.5	600.00
Sale of 400 calculators	17.5	2,500.00
Total excluding VAT		3,100.00
Total VAT at 17.5%		542.50
Total payable within 30 days		3,642.50

BERNINI PLC

Brahms GmbH   1 Long Lane
Peterstr 39   Anytown
Hamburg   AN4 5QP
Germany   VAT reg no GB 212 7924 36

VAT reg no DE 99369326 5
Invoice no. 325
Date: 5 July 20X5
Tax point: 5 July 20X5

	VAT rate	
	%	£
Sale of 500 rulers	0.0	50.00
Sale of 2,000 calculators	0.0	12,500.00
Total excluding VAT		12,550.00
Total VAT at 0.0%		0.00
Total payable within 30 days		12,550.00

BERNINI PLC

Michael plc   1 Long Lane
12 Narrow Road   Anytown
Oldtown   AN4 5QP
OL4 7TC   VAT reg no GB 212 7924 36

Invoice no. 326
Date: 24 August 20X5
Tax point: 24 August 20X5

	VAT rate	
	%	£
Sale of 700 staplers	17.5	756.00
Sale of 3,000 rulers	17.5	300.00
Total excluding VAT		1,056.00
Total VAT at 17.5%		184.80
Total payable within 30 days		1,240.80

BERNINI PLC

Jacob Ltd   1 Long Lane
45 Broad Street   Anytown
Newtown   AN4 5QP
NE7 2LH   VAT reg no GB 212 7924 36
Credit note no. 28
Date: 18 September 20X5

                                    VAT rate
                                        %   £

Return of defective goods: 30 calculators
(invoice no. 324, date 4 June 20X5)   17.5   187.50
Total credited excluding VAT   187.50
Total VAT credited at 17.5%   32.81
Total credited including VAT   220.31

ANGELO PLC

78 Madras Road, London NW14 2JL
VAT registration number 187 2392 49

                                    Invoice to: Bernini plc
                                                       1 Long Lane
                                                          Anytown
                                                          AN4 5QP

Date: 3 August 20X5
Tax point: 3 August 20X5
Invoice no. 873
                                                              £
Sale of 10,000 pens   4,200.00
VAT at 17.5%   735.00
Amount payable   4,935.00
Terms: strictly net 30 days

INVOICE
QUANTUM LTD

                                             To: Bernini plc
472 Staple Street   1 Long Lane
London   Anytown
SE4 2QB   AN4 5QP

VAT reg no 162 4327 56
Date: 7 September 20X5
Tax point: 7 September 20X5
Invoice no. 634

	VAT rate %	Net £	VAT £	Gross £
Sale of 600 calculators	17.5	2,700.00	472.50	3,172.50
Sale of 1,000 rulers	17.5	80.00	14.00	94.00
		2,780.00	486.50	3,266.50

£3,266.50 is payable by 7 October 20X5. Interest will be charged thereafter at 1.5% per month.

Input VAT for the VAT period ended 30 June 20X5 was overstated by £800.

Task

Complete the following VAT return for Bernini plc.

Value Added Tax Return

For the period
01 07 X5 to 30 09 X5

For Official Use

Registration number	Period
212 7924 36	09 X5

You could be liable to a financial penalty if your completed return and all the VAT payable are not received by the due date.

Due date: 31 10 X5

For Official Use	

BERNINI PLC
1 LONG LANE
ANYTOWN
AN4 5QP

Your VAT Office telephone number is 0123-4567

Before you fill in this form please read the notes on the back and the VAT Leaflet *"Filling in your VAT return"*.
Fill in all boxes clearly in ink, and write 'none' where necessary. Don't put a dash or leave any box blank. If there are no pence write "00" in the pence column. Do not enter more than one amount in any box.

For official use			£	p
	VAT due in this period on sales and other outputs	1		
	VAT due in this period on acquisitions from other EC Member States	2		
	Total VAT due (the sum of boxes 1 and 2)	3		
	VAT reclaimed in this period on purchases and other inputs (including acquisitions from the EC)	4		
	Net VAT to be paid to Customs or reclaimed by you (Difference between boxes 3 and 4)	5		
	Total value of sales and all other outputs excluding any VAT. Include your box 8 figure	6		00
	Total value of purchases and all other inputs excluding any VAT. Include your box 9 figure	7		00
	Total value of all supplies of goods and related services, excluding any VAT, to other EC Member States	8		00
	Total value of all acquisitions of goods and related services, excluding any VAT, from other EC Member States	9		00
	Retail schemes. If you have used any ot the schemes in the period covered by this return, enter the relevant letter(s) in this box.			

If you are enclosing a payment please tick this box.

DECLARATION: You, or someone on your behalf, must sign below.

I, ... declare that the
(Full name of signatory in BLOCK LETTERS)
information given above is true and complete.

Signature .... Date 20

A false declaration can result in prosecution.

2   THE SCOPE OF VAT

2.1   (a)   VAT is charged on supplies of goods and services, provided that the following conditions are met.

        (i)   Taxable supplies

        (ii)   Made in the UK

        (iii)   Made by a taxable person

        (iv)   Made in the course or furtherance of any business carried on by that taxable person

    (b)   VAT is charged on imports of goods into the UK, whether or not made by a taxable person or for business purposes.

    (c)   VAT may also be charged on certain types of services received from abroad. This is called the **reverse charge**.

Special rules, covered in the next chapter, apply to trade with other European Community (EC) countries and overseas countries in general.

2.2   Supplies may be **taxable** or **exempt**.

> ### KEY TERMS
>
> - **Exempt supplies** are not subject to VAT.
> - **Taxable supplies** may be **standard rated** or **zero rated**.
>   - Standard rated supplies are subject to VAT at 17.5%
>   - Zero rated supplies are subject to VAT at 0%.

Some supplies have a lower standard rate applying, for example, domestic fuel at a rate of 5%.

Examples of standard rated, zero rated and exempt supplies are given in the next chapter.

2.3   There is a difference between exempt and zero rated supplies. A trader making exempt supplies cannot recover the VAT paid to purchase goods and services for use in his business (known as input VAT) but a trader making zero rated supplies can.

> ### KEY TERM
>
> A **taxable person** is someone who is or ought to be registered for VAT. Such a person may be an individual, a partnership, a company, a club, an association or a charity.

3   INVOICES AND RECORDS

VAT invoices

3.1   **A taxable person making a taxable supply to another person registered for VAT must supply a VAT invoice within 30 days of the time of supply, and must keep a copy. The recipient of a supply can only claim the VAT he paid on the supply as input VAT if he**

holds a valid VAT invoice. VAT invoices need not be issued for zero rated supplies except for supplies to other EC member states.

3.2 There is no set form for a VAT invoice, but it must show the following.

(a) The supplier's name, address and registration number. A trader who makes supplies to other EC member states will normally show his country code (for example GB) before his registration number.

(b) The date of issue, the tax point and an invoice number.

(c) The name and address of the customer.

(d) The type of supply (sale, hire purchase, loan, exchange, hire, goods made from the customer's materials, sale on commission, sale or return etc).

(e) A description of the goods or services supplied, giving for each description the quantity, the rate of VAT and the VAT exclusive amount.

(f) The rate of any cash discount.

(g) The total invoice price excluding VAT (with separate totals for zero rated and exempt supplies).

(h) Each VAT rate applicable, the amount of VAT at each rate and the total amount of VAT.

Credit notes must give the reason for the credit (such as 'returned goods'), **and the number and date of the original VAT invoice.** If a credit note makes no VAT adjustment, it should state this.

3.3 For supplies to other EC member states, the type of supply may be omitted but the supplier's VAT registration number must be prefixed by 'GB' and the customer's registration number (including the state code, such as DE for Germany) must be shown.

3.4 **A less detailed VAT invoice may be issued by a retailer where the invoice is for a total including VAT of up to £100 and the supply is not to another EC member state.** Such an invoice must show the following.

- The supplier's name, address and registration number.
- The date of the supply.
- A description of the goods or services supplied.
- The rate of VAT chargeable.
- The total amount chargeable including VAT.

Zero rated and exempt supplies must not be included in less detailed invoices.

3.5 **VAT invoices are not required for payments of up to £25 including VAT which are for telephone calls or car park fees or are made through cash operated machines. In such cases, input VAT can be claimed without a VAT invoice.**

DEVOLVED ASSESSMENT ALERT

Input VAT cannot be recovered unless a valid VAT invoice is held to support the claim. **You must be able to review a batch of invoices and decide if the criteria for 'valid VAT invoice' have been satisfied.** This is a typical devolved assessment task.

Activity 12.3

Klopstock Ltd holds the following invoices from suppliers.

(a)

ALTONA plc

VAT reg no 337 4849 26

Klopstock Ltd
32 Verse Street
Greentown
GN4 8PJ

Invoice no. 3629
Date: 6 May 20X7
Tax point: 6 May 20X7

	£
Sale of 12,500 tea services	50,000
VAT at 17.5%	8,750
Total	58,750

Terms: strictly net 14 days

(b)

HEINE LTD

1 Market Square
Bluetown
BL1 8VA

Klopstock Ltd
32 Verse Street
Greentown
GN4 8PJ

Invoice no.
Date: 12 June 20X7
Tax point: 12 June 20X7

	Net	VAT	Total
	£	£	£
4,000 cups	2,000.00	350.00	2,350.00
8,000 saucers	2,500.00	437.50	2,937.50
3,500 cookery books	5,880.00	0.00	5,880.00
	10,380.00	787.50	11,167.50

(c)

MANN & CO
36 Lubeck Street, Gatestown. GN2 SY4

VAT reg no 499 3493 27

Date: 15 June 20X7

30 wine glasses sold for £35.25 including VAT at 17.5%.

(d)

VAT reg no 446 9989 57			KLEIST PLC
Date: 16 June 20X7			254 Metric Street
Tax point: 16 June 20X7			Ruletown
Invoice no. 328			RL3 7CM

Klopstock Ltd
32 Verse Street
Greentown
GN4 8PJ

Sales of goods

Type	Quantity	VAT rate %	Net £
Plates	700	17.5	700.00
Mats	800	17.5	240.00
Leaflets	4,000	0.0	200.00
Booklets	1,200	0.0	120.00
			1,260.00
VAT at 17.5%			156.28
Payable within 60 days			1,416.28
Less 5% discount if paid within 14 days			63.00
			1,353.28

Task

For each of the above invoices, state whether it is a valid VAT invoice. Give your reasons.

Records

3.6   **Every VAT registered trader must keep records for six years,** although HM Customs & Excise may sometimes grant permission for their earlier destruction. They may be kept on paper, on microfilm or microfiche or on computer. However, there must be adequate facilities for HM Customs & Excise to inspect records.

3.7   All records must be kept up to date and in a way which allows the following.

- The calculation of VAT due.
- Officers of HM Customs & Excise to check the figures on VAT returns.

3.8   The following records are needed.

(a)   Copies of VAT invoices, credit notes and debit notes issued

(b)   VAT invoices, credit notes and debit notes received

(c)   Records of goods received from and sent to other EC member states

(d)   Documents relating to imports from and exports to countries outside the EC

(e)   A VAT account (see Paragraph 3.12 below)

(f)   Order and delivery notes, correspondence, appointment books, job books, purchases and sales books, cash books, account books, records of takings (such as till rolls), bank paying-in slips, bank statements and annual accounts

(g)   Records of zero rated and exempt supplies, gifts or loans of goods, taxable self-supplies (see Paragraphs 3.28 to 3.30 of the following Chapter) and any goods taken for non-business use

3.9 **A summary of supplies made must be kept,** in the same order as the copies of VAT invoices retained. It must enable the trader to work out the following totals for each VAT period.

(a) The VAT chargeable on supplies

(b) The values of standard rated and zero rated supplies excluding VAT

(c) The value of exempt supplies

(d) The value of all supplies, excluding VAT

(e) The VAT due on goods imported by post and on services received from abroad to which the reverse charge applies

Under (b), (c) and (d), credits allowed should be deducted but cash discounts should not be deducted.

3.10 **A summary of supplies received must be kept,** in the same order as the VAT invoices received. It must enable the trader to work out the following totals for each VAT period.

(a) The VAT charged on goods and services received

(b) The VAT due on goods imported by post and on services received from abroad to which the reverse charge applies

(c) The value excluding VAT of all supplies received, deducting credits received from suppliers but not deducting cash discounts

DEVOLVED ASSESSMENT ALERT

The summaries described in Paragraphs 3.9 and 3.10 above could be obtained by adding appropriate columns to sales and purchases day books. The cash book can alternatively be used for the summary of supplies received, if the trader normally claims a deduction for input VAT when the supplier is paid.

3.11 When credits are given or received, the **VAT should be adjusted**. Thus if goods are sold for £10,000 plus £1,750 VAT, and goods worth £1,000 plus £175 VAT are returned, the VAT to be accounted for should be shown as £(1,750 - 175) = £1,575. However, no adjustment need be made if both parties agree and the buyer makes no exempt supplies.

3.12 **A VAT account must be kept, made up for each VAT period.**

(a) The **VAT payable portion (the credit side)** shows the following.

(i) The output VAT due for the period (excluding VAT under (ii))

(ii) The output VAT due on acquisitions from other EC member states for the period

(iii) Any corrections to VAT payable for previous periods, provided that the net error (error in VAT payable net of error in VAT allowable) is not more than £2,000. Each error must be separately recorded

(iv) Any adjustments to the VAT on supplies made in previous periods which are evidenced by credit notes or debit notes

(v) Any other adjustment to the VAT payable for the period

(b) The **VAT allowable portion (the debit side)** shows the following.

(i) The input VAT allowable for the period (excluding VAT under (ii))

(ii)   The input VAT allowable on acquisitions from other EC member states for the period

(iii) Any corrections to VAT allowable for previous periods, provided that the net error (error in VAT payable net of error in VAT allowable) is not more than £2,000. Each error must be separately recorded

(iv)   Any adjustments to the VAT on supplies received in previous periods which are evidenced by credit notes or debit notes

(v)   Any other adjustment to the VAT allowable for the period

3.13 EXAMPLE: A VAT ACCOUNT

Jane has the following transactions in the VAT period from January to March 2000.

	Net	*VAT*	*Gross*
	£	£	£
Sales	15,000	2,625	17,625
Purchases	8,000	1,400	9,400
Credits allowed (current period's sales)	400	70	470
Credits allowed (previous periods' sales)	200	35	235
Credits received (current period's purchases)	800	140	940
Credits received (previous periods' purchases)	600	105	705

Jane discovered in March 2000 that she had under-declared the VAT payable for the VAT period from October to December 1999 by £74.

Task

Show Jane's VAT account for the period from January to March 2000.

3.14 SOLUTION

VAT ACCOUNT FOR THE PERIOD FROM JANUARY TO MARCH 2000

VAT allowable	£	*VAT payable*	£
Input VAT allowable		Output VAT due	
£(1,400 - 140)	1,260	£(2,625 - 70)	2,555
Adjustment for credits		Correction of error	74
received	(105)	Adjustment for credits	
		allowed	(35)
	1,155		2,594
Cash (payment to			
HM Customs & Excise)	1,439		
	2,594		2,594

Activity 12.4

Marc runs a hardware shop supplying both tradespeople and the general public, and is registered for VAT. He does not use the cash accounting scheme or any retail scheme. All his purchases and sales are standard rated.

Marc's transactions within a single VAT period included the following.

(a)   A retail cash sale for £56.40 including VAT, made using a till. The customer was registered for VAT.

(b) A retail sale on credit for £39.95 including VAT. The debtor paid by cheque two weeks later. The customer was not registered for VAT.

(c) A purchase for £270 plus VAT, paid for by cheque immediately.

Task

State what records should be kept reflecting the impact of these transactions, and what they should show.

Activity 12.5

Grove Ltd had the following transactions in the quarter ended 31 July 20X7.

Date	Type	Net amount £	VAT rate %
2 May	Purchase	4,200	17.5
7 May	Purchase	6,700	17.5
12 May	Sale	10,000	0.0
12 May	Sale	3,900	17.5
22 May	Sale	12,800	17.5
29 May	Sale	1,400	0.0
7 June	Purchase	20,000	0.0
8 June	Purchases returned	500	17.5
20 June	Sale	2,300	0.0
23 June	Sale	5,500	17.5
4 July	Sales returned	800	0.0
8 July	Purchase	730	17.5
14 July	Purchases returned	120	0.0
22 July	Sale	1,700	0.0
31 July	Sales returned	340	17.5

All returns of goods are evidenced by credit notes for both the net price and (where applicable) the VAT. All returns related to current period transactions, except for the return on 8 June.

On the previous period's VAT return, output VAT was overstated by £1,450 and input VAT was understated by £520. These errors are to be corrected through the VAT account for this quarter.

Task

Prepare Grove Ltd's VAT account for the quarter.

4 REGISTRATION FOR VAT

4.1 **Once a trader is registered for VAT, he must charge VAT on sales and may reclaim VAT on purchases. A registered trader has a VAT registration number, which must be shown on all VAT invoices issued and quoted in all correspondence with HM Customs & Excise.**

4.2 **A trader has one registration covering all his business activities.** The turnovers of all such activities are added together (no matter how different the business activities are) to determine whether the trader must register.

Compulsory registration

4.3 **A trader making taxable supplies becomes liable to register for VAT if, in any period of 12 consecutive calendar months or for a new business a shorter period, the value of his taxable supplies (excluding VAT) exceeds the registration limit of £52,000 from 1 April 2000.** The trader must notify HM Customs & Excise within 30 days of the end of the month period. HM Customs & Excise will then register the trader with effect from the end of the month following that period, or from an earlier date if they and the trader agree. **When looking at turnover only taxable (standard and zero rated) supplies are considered.**

Registration under this rule is not required if HM Customs & Excise are satisfied that the value of the trader's taxable supplies (excluding VAT) in the year starting at the end of the period will not exceed £52,000 from 1 April 2000.

> ### KEY TERM
>
> The **registration limit** from 1 April 2000 is £52,000. If the value of standard rated taxable turnover in a specified period exceeds this value the trader must become VAT registered.

4.4 **A trader is also liable to register at any time if there are reasonable grounds for believing that his taxable supplies (excluding VAT) in the following 30 days will exceed the registration limit.** HM Customs & Excise must be notified by the end of the 30 day period, and registration will be with effect from the beginning of that period.

4.5 EXAMPLE: COMPULSORY REGISTRATION

A trader had the following monthly turnovers of taxable supplies (excluding VAT) from the start of trade on 1 April 1999.

Period	Monthly turnover
	£
1 April - 31 December 1999	3,350
1 January - 30 September 2000	6,450
1 October 2000 onwards	7,250

By what date must the trader notify his liability to register for VAT?

4.6 SOLUTION

$9 \times £3,350 = £30,150$, so the registration limit is clearly not exceeded in 1999.

12 months to end of	Working	Turnover
		£
January 2000	$(9 \times 3,350) + 6,450$	36,600
February 2000	$(9 \times 3,350) + (2 \times 6,450)$	43,050
March 2000	$(9 \times 3,350) + (3 \times 6,450)$	49,500
April 2000	$(8 \times 3,350) + (4 \times 6,450)$	52,600

The registration limit is exceeded in the 12 months to 30 April 2000, so the trader must notify his liability to register by 30 May 2000. Customs will register the trader from 1 June 2000.

4.7 When we work out the value of a trader's taxable supplies for the purposes of the £52,000 tests, we ignore supplies of goods and services that are capital assets of the business, except for non-zero-rated supplies of interests in land.

4.8 When a trader should have registered in the past, it is his responsibility to pay any VAT due. If he is unable to collect it from those to whom he made taxable supplies, the VAT burden will fall on him. A trader must start keeping VAT records and charging VAT to customers as soon as he is required to register. However, VAT should not be shown separately on any invoices until the registration number is known. The invoice should show the VAT inclusive price and customers should be informed that a VAT invoice will be forwarded once the registration number is known. Formal VAT invoices should then be sent to such customers within 30 days of receipt of the registration number.

4.9 **Notification of liability to register must be made on form VAT 1.** Simply writing to, or telephoning, a local VAT office is not enough.

Voluntary registration

4.10 **A trader may decide to become VAT registered even though his taxable turnover falls below the registration threshold.** Unless a trader is registered he cannot recover the input VAT he pays on supplies to him.

4.11 **Voluntary registration is advantageous where a person wishes to recover input VAT on supplies to him.** For example, consider a trader who has one input during the year which cost £1,000 plus £175 VAT; he works on the input which becomes his sole output for the year and he decides to make a profit of £1,000.

(a) If he is not registered for VAT he will charge £2,175 and his customer will obtain no relief for any VAT (since none was charged).

(b) If he is registered for VAT he will charge £2,000 plus VAT of £350. His customer will have input VAT of £350 which he will be able to recover if he, too, is registered for VAT.

If the customer is not registered he will prefer (a) as the cost to him is £2,175 instead of £2,350. If he is registered he will prefer (b) as the net cost is £2,000 instead of £2,175. Thus, a decision whether or not to register may also depend upon the status of customers.

4.12 **Provided that a trader satisfies HM Customs & Excise that he is carrying on a business, and intends to make taxable supplies, he is entitled to be registered for VAT if he chooses. This is called intending trader registration.** But, once registered, he is obliged to notify HM Customs & Excise within 30 days if he no longer intends to make taxable supplies.

Exemption from registration

4.13 **If a trader makes zero rated supplies but no standard rated supplies, he may request exemption from registration.** The trader must notify any material change in the nature of his supplies.

HM Customs & Excise may also allow exemption from registration if only a small proportion of supplies are standard rated, provided that the trader would normally receive repayments of VAT if registered.

Group registration

> **KEY TERM**
>
> U.K. Companies under common control may apply for **group registration**. This allows two or more group companies who would normally register separately for VAT to register jointly for VAT.

4.14 Broadly, the effects of group registration are as follows.

(a) Each VAT group must appoint a representative member which must account for the group's output VAT and input VAT. However, all members of the group are liable for any VAT due from the representative member.

(b) Any supply of goods or services by a member of the group to another member of the group is disregarded for VAT purposes.

(c) Any other supply of goods or services by or to a group member is treated as a supply by or to the representative member.

(d) Any VAT payable on the import of goods by a group member is payable by the representative member.

4.15 **A group registration is not compulsory - it is voluntary**. Customs just require written notification to establish or amend a VAT group registration. Such a registration can be cancelled at any time.

Divisional registration

4.16 **A company which is divided into several units which each prepare accounts can apply for divisional registration**. Divisional registration is for administrative convenience; the separate divisions do not become separate taxable persons and the company is itself still liable for the VAT.

4.17 Broadly, the conditions for divisional registration are as follows.

(a) Each division must be registered even where that division's turnover is beneath the registration limit.

(b) The divisions must be independent, self-accounting units, carrying on different activities or operating in separate locations.

(c) Input VAT attributable to exempt supplies (see the partial exemption rules in the next chapter) by the company as a whole must be so low that it can all be recovered (apart from VAT which can never be recovered because of the type of expenditure).

(d) Each division must make VAT returns for the same VAT periods.

(e) VAT invoices must not be issued for supplies between the divisions of the same company as they are not supplies for VAT purposes.

Deregistration

4.18 **A trader is eligible for voluntary deregistration if HM Customs & Excise are satisfied that the value of his taxable supplies (net of VAT and excluding supplies of capital assets) in the following 12 month period will not exceed £50,000** (from 1 April 2000). However, deregistration will not be allowed if the reason for the expected fall in value of taxable supplies is the cessation of trading or the suspension of taxable supplies for a period of 30 days or more in that following year. Thus a trader cannot deregister just because he will soon retire.

4.19 HM Customs & Excise will cancel a trader's registration from the date the request is made or from an agreed later date.

4.20 Traders may suffer **compulsory deregistration**. Failure to notify a requirement to deregister may lead to a penalty. Compulsory deregistration may also lead to HM Customs

& Excise reclaiming input VAT which has been wrongly recovered by the trader since the date on which he should have deregistered.

4.21 If HM Customs & Excise are misled into granting registration then the registration is treated as void from the start.

A person may be **compulsorily deregistered** if he is no longer making nor intending to make taxable supplies.

Changes in legal status also require **cancellation of registration**. Examples include the following.

- A sole trader becoming a partnership
- A partnership reverting to a sole trader
- A business being incorporated
- A company being replaced by an unincorporated business

4.22 **On deregistration, a special final VAT return (form VAT 193) is completed.** The form has the same boxes 1 to 9 as an ordinary return. **VAT is chargeable on all stocks and capital assets in a business on which input VAT was claimed, because the registered trader is in effect making a taxable supply to himself as a newly unregistered trader. If the VAT chargeable does not exceed £1,000 (from 1 April 2000, prior to this date the limit was £250), it need not be paid.**

4.23 This special VAT charge does not apply if the business (or a separately viable part of it) is sold as a **going concern to another taxable person** (or a person who immediately becomes a taxable person as a result of the transfer). Such transfers are generally outside the scope of VAT. If the original owner ceases to be taxable, the new owner of the business may also take over the existing VAT number. If he does so, he takes over the rights and liabilities of the transferor as at the date of transfer.

Pre-registration input VAT

> **KEY TERM**
>
> VAT incurred before registration known as **pre-registration input VAT** can be treated as input VAT and recovered from HM Customs & Excise (on the trader's first VAT return) subject to certain conditions.

4.24 If the claim is for **input VAT paid on goods** bought prior to registration then the following conditions must be satisfied.

(a) The goods were acquired for the purposes of a business which either was carried on or was to be carried on at the time of supply.

(b) The goods have not been supplied onwards or consumed before the date of registration (although they may have been used to make other goods which are still held).

(c) **The VAT must have been incurred in the three years prior to registration.**

4.25 If the claim is for **input VAT paid on a supply of services** prior to registration then both of the following conditions must be satisfied.

(a) The services were supplied for the purposes of a business which either was carried on or was to be carried on at the time of supply.

(b) **The services were supplied within the six months prior to the date of registration.**

Activity 12.6

Valley Ltd has incurred the following expenses. Only the documentation noted is held. All amounts are shown including VAT.

Ref	Item	Documentation	Amount £
(a)	Purchase of goods	Full VAT invoice (Valley Ltd's registration number not shown)	82.25
(b)	Purchase of goods	Less detailed VAT invoice	105.75
(c)	Car park charge	None	10.00
(d)	Purchase of goods	Full VAT invoice (Valley Ltd's address not shown)	869.50
(e)	Purchase of goods	Less detailed VAT invoice	98.70
(f)	Computer repair services	Full VAT invoice (total price excluding VAT not shown)	383.05

Task

Compute the amount of VAT which Valley Ltd may recover as input VAT.

Key points in this chapter

- VAT is collected in stages along the production chain, but is effectively a burden on the final consumer.

- VAT is accounted for one VAT period at a time. The trader completes a VAT return.

- The tax point for a supply is in practice usually the invoice date.

- Supplies may be standard rated (usually 17.5% VAT), zero rated or exempt.

- VAT invoices must show specified information.

- Traders must keep full records, including a VAT account.

- Registration for VAT is compulsory if annual taxable turnover exceeds the registration threshold, unless exemption is granted.

- The registration threshold is £52,000 from 1 April 2000.

- Voluntary registration, group registration and divisional registration are also possible.

- Pre-registration input VAT can be reclaimed if certain conditions are satisfied.

Quick quiz

1 Peter is a VAT registered trader. In the quarter to 31 March 2000 Peter sold goods for £40,000 (excluding VAT) and bought stock to sell for £17,900 (including VAT). Show the VAT figures for his VAT return for this quarter.

2 When will the VAT return to 30 June 2000 be due for submission to Customs?

3 What is the tax point of a supply?

4 John delivers 6 boxes of chocolates to Mrs Smith on Monday 4 May 2000. On Friday 8 May John issues an invoice to Mrs Smith for the goods. Mrs Smith pays John on 18 May 2000. What is the tax point of the sale for John?

5 How do you notify Customs you need to be registered for VAT?

6 Zoe started in business last June but registered for VAT in May 2000. Can she claim any of the VAT she incurred on purchases made before her business was VAT registered?

Answers to quick quiz

1

		£
Output VAT (£40,000 × 17.5%)		7,000
Input VAT (£17,900 × 7/47)		(2,666)
Net VAT payable		4,334

2   A VAT return is usually due within one month after the end of the VAT period. The return to 30 June 2000 will be due to be received by Customs by 31 July 2000 at the latest. (see 1.14).

3   See 1.26.

4   Basic tax point is Monday 4 May but John raises an invoice within the next 14 days so the invoice date 8 May 2000 is the real tax point for this supply.

5   By completing and submitting form VAT 1 (see 4.9).

6   Yes. See 4.24 and 4.25.

Answers to activities

Answer 12.1

Tutorial note. The total collected by HM Customs & Excise is £700 × 17.5% = £122.50, the VAT on the final sale to Victor.

Trader	Working	Amount £	Due date
Roger	£400 × 0.175	70.00	30.4.X3
Susan	£700 × 0.175 - £70 - £10.50	42.00	30.6.X3
Thomas	£70.50 × 7/47	10.50	30.4.X3
		122.50	

Answer 12.2

Tutorial note. All the documents calculate the correct amount of VAT, but you should have checked that this was so. If an invoice issued by Bernini plc had shown too little VAT, the shortfall would have had to be accounted for.

The total VAT on sales and other outputs (Box 1) is as follows.

	£
Sale to Jacob Ltd	542.50
Sale to Brahms GmbH	0.00
Sale to Michael plc	184.80
	727.30
Less credit to Jacob Ltd	32.81
	694.49

The Box 2 figure is 'None' so the Box 3 figure is the same as the Box 1 figure.

The total input VAT (Box 4) is as follows.

	£
Purchase from Angelo plc	735.00
Purchase from Quantum Ltd	486.50
	1,221.50
Less overstatement in previous period	800.00
	421.50

The Box 5 figure is £(694.49 - 421.50) = £272.99. Because a payment will be made, the box to the left of the declaration must be ticked.

The Box 6 figure is £(3,100.00 + 12,550.00 + 1,056.00 - 187.50) = £16,518.50, to be rounded down to £16,518.

The Box 7 figure is £(4,200 + 2,780) = £6,980.

The Box 8 figure is £12,550.

The Box 9 figure is 'None'.

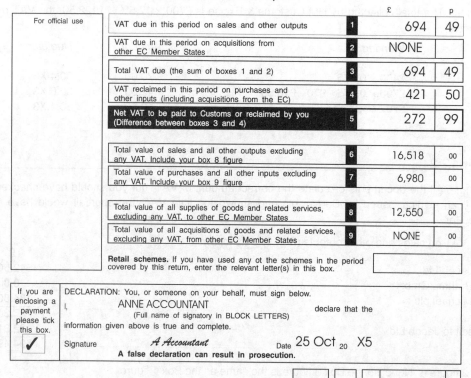

Value Added Tax Return
For the period
01 07 X5 ^{to} 30 09 X5

		£	p
VAT due in this period on sales and other outputs	**1**	694	49
VAT due in this period on acquisitions from other EC Member States	**2**	NONE	
Total VAT due (the sum of boxes 1 and 2)	**3**	694	49
VAT reclaimed in this period on purchases and other inputs (including acquisitions from the EC)	**4**	421	50
Net VAT to be paid to Customs or reclaimed by you (Difference between boxes 3 and 4)	**5**	272	99
Total value of sales and all other outputs excluding any VAT. Include your box 8 figure	**6**	16,518	00
Total value of purchases and all other inputs excluding any VAT. Include your box 9 figure	**7**	6,980	00
Total value of all supplies of goods and related services, excluding any VAT, to other EC Member States	**8**	12,550	00
Total value of all acquisitions of goods and related services, excluding any VAT, from other EC Member States	**9**	NONE	00

Answer 12.3

Tutorial note. All the invoices except (c) look superficially plausible, but in fact (c) is the only valid invoice. This shows the importance of attention to detail in applying VAT law.

(a)   The invoice from Altona plc is invalid because it does not show the supplier's address. In all other respects it meets the requirements for a valid VAT invoice.

(b)   The invoice from Heine Ltd is invalid because the invoice number has been omitted, because the supplier's VAT registration number is not shown and because the type of supply (presumably a sale) is not shown.

Finally, the invoice is invalid because the applicable rates of VAT (17.5% and 0%) are not shown.

(c)   The total value of the supply by Mann & Co, including VAT, does not exceed £100, so a less detailed invoice is permissible.

The invoice is valid, because it includes all the information which must be shown on a less detailed invoice.

(d) The invoice from Kleist plc is invalid because the total value of zero rated supplies is not shown.

Answer 12.4

Tutorial note. Extensive records must be kept for VAT purposes. In general, these records are no more than a trader would probably keep anyway, but even if a trader could manage without some of the required records, he must still keep them.

(a) *The retail cash sale*

   (i) The till roll, showing the gross sale of £56.40, must be kept.

   (ii) A cash book showing the sale (or the total of the day's cash sales) must be kept.

   (iii) A VAT invoice (possibly a less detailed invoice) will be issued, and a copy must be kept.

   (iv) A summary of supplies must be kept, showing this sale, in such a way as to allow the trader to work out, for each VAT period:

      (1) the VAT-exclusive values of standard rated supplies, zero rated supplies, exempt supplies and all supplies;

      (2) the VAT chargeable on supplies.

   (v) A VAT account must be kept. The VAT on the sale, £56.40 × 7/47 = £8.40, will appear on the credit (VAT payable) side of the account, probably as part of a total of VAT on several sales.

(b) *The retail credit sale*

   (i) The sale must appear in the summary of supplies described in (a)(iv) above, and the VAT on the sale (£39.95 × 7/47 = £5.95) in the VAT account mentioned in (a)(v) above.

   (ii) A sales day book showing the sale must be kept, and a cash book to record the eventual receipt. Records showing the debt must also be kept.

   (iii) Because the customer is not registered for VAT, no VAT invoice need be issued. If one is issued (possibly a less detailed invoice), a copy must be kept.

(c) *The cash purchase*

   (i) The VAT invoice received must be kept.

   (ii) A cash book showing the purchase must be kept.

   (iii) Any other documents relating to the purchase, such as a copy of the order or a delivery note, must be kept.

   (iv) A summary of purchases must be kept, showing this purchase, in such a way as to allow the trader to work out, for each VAT period, the VAT-exclusive value of all supplies received and the VAT charged on them.

   (v) The VAT on the purchase (£270 × 17.5% = £47.25) must appear (probably as part of a larger total) on the debit (VAT allowable) side of the VAT account mentioned in (a)(v) above.

Answer 12.5

Tutorial note. The errors in the previous period may be corrected through the VAT account (and on the VAT return), because the net error is £(1,450 + 520) = £1,970, which does not exceed £2,000. (For more details on this see the next chapter.)

Standard rated purchases total £(4,200 + 6,700 + 730) = £11,630.

Standard rated sales total £(3,900 + 12,800 + 5,500) = £22,200.

GROVE LTD
VAT ACCOUNT FOR THE VAT PERIOD FROM MAY TO JULY 20X7

VAT allowable	£	*VAT payable*	£
Input VAT allowable		Output VAT due	
£11,630 x 17.5%	2,035.25	£22,200 x 17.5%	
Adjustment for credits received		− £340 x 17.5%	3,825.50
£500 x 17.5%	(87.50)	Correction of error	(1,450.00)
Correction of error	520.00		
	2,467.75		2,375.50
		Cash (receipt from	
		HM Customs & Excise)	92.25
	2,467.75		2,467.75

Answer 12.6

Tutorial note. VAT suffered may only be reclaimed if the correct documentation is held. This rule plays an important role in enforcing the payment of VAT: VAT registered buyers will insist that VAT registered sellers prepare proper documentation.

Ref	Comment	Recoverable VAT Gross x 7/47 £
(a)	Buyer's registration number not required	12.25
(b)	Amount including VAT exceeds £100	0.00
(c)	Amount including VAT does not exceed £25	1.49
(d)	Buyer's address required	0.00
(e)	Amount including VAT does not exceed £100	14.70
(f)	Total price excluding VAT required	0.00
		28.44

Chapter 13 The computation and administration of VAT

Chapter topic list

1   Finding the VAT on a supply
2   Standard rated, zero rated and exempt supplies
3   The deduction of input VAT
4   Imports and exports and EC Trade
5   Special schemes
6   Administration
7   Penalties

Learning objectives

On completion of this chapter you will be able to:

	Performance criteria	Range statement
• identify VAT on a supply	7.3.2	7.3.2
• recognise the different types of supply; standard rated, zero rated and exempt	7.3.2	7.3.2
• be able to identify and recover input VAT	7.3.2	7.3.2
• understand the various schemes available for accounting for VAT	7.3.2	7.3.1
• understand how VAT is administered by Customs and Excise	7.3.3	
• be able to seek guidance from Customs and Excise in a professional manner	7.3.4	
• be aware of the penalties and problems that arise if the VAT accounting is not accurate or timely	7.3.3	

1 FINDING THE VAT ON A SUPPLY

1.1 **The VAT on a standard rated supply is 17.5% of the price excluding VAT, or 17.5/117.5 = 7/47 of the price including VAT.**

1.2 **If a discount is offered for prompt payment, VAT is computed on the amount after deducting the discount** (at the highest rate offered), **even if the discount is not taken.** (However, for imports from outside the EC, VAT is computed on the full price unless the discount is actually taken up.) If goods are sold to staff at a discount, VAT is charged on the reduced price.

1.3 If a trader charges different prices to customers paying with credit cards and those paying by other means, the VAT due on each standard rated sale is the full amount paid by the customer × 7/47.

1.4 The rules on the rounding of amounts of VAT are as follows.

(a) If amounts of VAT are calculated for individual lines on an invoice, they must be:

   (i) rounded down to the nearest 0.1p, so 86.76p would be shown as 86.7p; or

   (ii) rounded to the nearest 0.5p, so 86.7p would be shown as 87p and 86.3p would be shown as 86.5p.

(b) If amounts of VAT are calculated from an amount of VAT per unit or article, the amount of VAT should be:

   (i) calculated to the nearest 0.01p and then rounded to the nearest 0.1p, so 0.24p would be rounded to 0.2p; or

   (ii) rounded to the nearest 0.5p, but with a minimum of 0.5p for any standard rated item, so 0.2p would be rounded to 0.5p rather than to 0p.

(c) The total VAT shown on an invoice should be rounded down to the nearest 1p, so £32.439 would be shown as £32.43.

1.5 EXAMPLE: THE VAT ON SUPPLIES

Find the VAT on each of the following supplies.

(a) Goods with a normal retail price of £10,000 excluding VAT are sold net of a trade discount of 20% and a cash discount of 5% (for payment within ten days) or 3% (for payment within 21 days). The customer takes 30 days to pay.

(b) Goods which would be sold for £109 including VAT to a customer paying by cash or cheque, are sold to a customer paying by credit card subject to a 4% surcharge.

1.6 SOLUTION

(a)

	£
Normal retail price	10,000
Less trade discount £10,000 × 20%	2,000
	8,000
Less cash discount £8,000 × 5%	400
Amount on which VAT is calculated	7,600

VAT = £7,600 × 17.5% = £1,330

(b) Price including VAT = £109 × 1.04 = £113.36

VAT = £113.36 × 7/47 = £16.88

1.7 **When goods are permanently taken from a business for non-business purposes, VAT must be accounted for on their market value.** If services bought for business purposes are used for non-business purposes (without charge), then VAT must be accounted for on their cost, but the VAT to be accounted for is not allowed to exceed the input VAT deductible on the purchase of the services.

1.8 **Different goods and services are sometimes invoiced together at an inclusive price (a mixed supply).** Some items may be chargeable at the standard rate and some at the zero rate. In such cases the supplier must account for VAT separately on the standard rated and zero rated elements by splitting the total amount payable in a fair proportion between the different elements and charging VAT on each at the appropriate rate. There is no single way of doing this: one method is to split the amount according to the cost to the supplier of each element, and another is to use the open market value of each element.

An example of a mixed supply which may be sold at an inclusive price is a pack of audio-visual materials containing slides (standard rated) and books (zero rated).

1.9 **Where a supply cannot be split into components, there is a composite supply and one VAT rate applies to the whole supply.** The rate depends on the nature of the supply as a whole. A supply of air transport including an in-flight meal has been held to be a single, composite supply of transport (zero rated) rather than a supply of transport (zero rated) and a supply of a meal (standard rated).

1.10 **Gifts of goods must normally be treated as sales at cost (so VAT is due). However, business gifts are not supplies (so VAT need not be accounted for) if:**

(a) **the cost to the donor is £15 or less and the gift is not part of a series of gifts** made to the same person; or

(b) **the gift is a sample.** However, if two or more identical samples are given to the same person, all but one of them are treated as supplies.

Errors on invoices

1.11 **If an invoice shows too much VAT, the full amount shown must be accounted for unless the error is corrected by issuing a credit note to the customer.**

1.12 **If an invoice shows too little VAT and a supplementary invoice is issued to the customer to collect the extra VAT, the full correct amount of VAT must be accounted for.**

1.13 **If an invoice shows too little VAT but the extra VAT is not collected from the customer, the VAT which must be accounted for is the gross amount shown** $\times 7/47$.

2 STANDARD RATED, ZERO RATED AND EXEMPT SUPPLIES

2.1 A supply is a standard rated supply unless it is a zero rated supply or an exempt supply. This is not a helpful definition but unfortunately it is an accurate description of a standard rated supply. So the approach to take is as follows.

Step 1. Is the supply on the list of zero rated supplies (see 2.5 below). If yes, the supply is zero rated. If no move to step 2.

Step 2. Is the supply on the list of exempt supplies (see 2.6 below). If yes the supply is an exempt supply. If not the supply is standard rated.

There is no 'list' of standard rated supplies. If the supply is not zero-rated or exempt then it is standard rated. There are some standard rated supplies which are taxable at 5% rather than the usual 17.5%.

Such reduced VAT rate supplies are listed in the VAT legislation and include the following.

(a) Domestic fuel and power (for use in homes and for charity use).

(b) The installation of energy saving materials (including solar panels) in homes.

(c) The installation, maintenance and repair of central heating systems and home security goods in the homes of less well-off and the installation of heating measures in the homes of the less well-off where funded by Government grants.

(d) From 1 January 2001 women's sanitary products.

2.2 Zero rated supplies are taxable at 0%. A registered trader whose outputs are zero rated but whose inputs are standard rated will obtain VAT repayments. Here is an example.

	Net	*VAT*	*Gross*
	£	£	£
Sales	160	0.00	160.00
Less purchases	100	17.50	117.50
	60	17.50	42.50

The trader gets a repayment of the £17.50 of VAT he paid on his purchases, so that his own profit after this repayment is £160 (takings) - £117.50 (paid to supplier) + £17.50 (VAT repayment) = £60.

2.3 Exempt supplies are not so advantageous. In exactly the same way as for a non-registered trader, a trader making exempt supplies is unable to recover VAT on inputs. The exempt trader thus has to shoulder the burden of VAT.

Of course, he may increase his prices to pass on the charge, but he cannot issue a VAT invoice which would enable a registered customer to obtain a credit for VAT, because no VAT is chargeable on exempt supplies.

2.4 EXAMPLE: STANDARD RATED, ZERO RATED AND EXEMPT SUPPLIES

Here are figures for three traders, the first with standard rated outputs, the second with zero rated outputs and the third with exempt outputs. All their inputs are standard rated. All have purchases of £20,000 excluding VAT and sales of £30,000 excluding VAT.

	Standard rated	*Zero rated*	*Exempt*
	£	£	£
Inputs	20,000	20,000	20,000
VAT	3,500	3,500	3,500
	23,500	23,500	23,500
Outputs	30,000	30,000	30,000
VAT	5,250	0	0
	35,250	30,000	30,000
Pay/(reclaim)	1,750	(3,500)	0
Net profit	10,000	10,000	6,500

Zero rated supplies

2.5 The following goods and services are zero rated.

(a) Human and animal **food**, although pet food and certain luxury items, such as confectionery are standard rated. **Food supplied in the course of catering (which includes all hot takeaways) is standard rated**. Most beverages are standard rated, but milk, tea (excluding iced tea), coffee and cocoa are zero rated unless supplied in the course of catering.

(b) **Sewerage services and water** (other than such services supplied for industrial activities and supplies of heated water, which are standard rated).

(c) Periodicals, **books** and leaflets. In general this does not include stationery although certain supplies made in connection with charitable fundraising events are zero rated.

(d) **New construction work or the sale of new buildings** by builders, where the buildings are to be used for residential or non-business charitable purposes.

(e) **Passenger transport**, but pleasure transport and transport in vehicles seating fewer than 12 passengers (such as taxis) are standard rated.

(f) Large residential **caravans and houseboats**.

(g) **Drugs and medicines on prescription** or provided in private hospitals. Prostheses fixed by surgical intervention and certain aids, building alterations, special motor vehicles, boats and so on for the handicapped. Incontinence products supplied directly to the disabled or to a charity.

(h) **Exports of goods to outside the EC**, and supplies to VAT registered traders in other EC states where the purchaser's VAT registration number is shown on the invoice.

(i) **Clothing and footwear for young children** and certain protective clothing.

Exempt supplies

2.6 The following supplies are exempt.

(a) **Sales of freeholds** (unless the building is less than three years old) **and leaseholds of land and buildings** by someone other than the builder (although the seller may have an option to charge VAT at the standard rate except in the case of dwellings and charity buildings other than offices).

(b) **Financial services**, including credit card services to retailers, the arrangements for, and underwriting of, capital issues, and securities dealing services. Investment advice is standard rated.

(c) **Insurance**.

(d) **Postal services provided by the Post Office**.

(e) **Betting and gaming**, except admission charges and subscriptions.

(f) **Educational and vocational training** supplied by a school, a university or an independent private tutor, and tuition in English as a foreign language.

(g) **Health services**, including medical, nursing, dental and ophthalmic treatment and hospital accommodation. Medical products are exempt if supplied in connection with the provision of care or medical or surgical treatment in any hospital or other institution which is either registered or exempt from registration.

(h) **Burial and cremation** services.

DEVOLVED ASSESSMENT ALERT

It is crucial that you are able to recognise the three types of supply

- standard rated (17.5% VAT or very occasionally 5% VAT)
- zero rated (0% VAT)
- exempt (no VAT)

Getting the type of supply right is the first step towards calculating the correct amount of VAT.

Activity 13.1

Pippa Ltd supplied the following goods and services to Gold Ltd on 12 May 20X2. All amounts exclude any VAT. All amounts are totals, not unit costs.

	Quantity	£
Personal computer	1	980
Microscopes	3	360
Books	20	200
Periodicals	500	450
Insurance		1,200
Medical treatment services		400

Task

Complete the following invoice for all these supplies, giving only the figures which must be shown on VAT invoices and the overall totals with and without the cash discount.

PIPPA LIMITED
32 Hurst Road,
London NE20 4LJ
VAT reg no 730 4148 37

To: Gold Ltd   Date: 12 May 20X2
        75 Link Road   Tax point: 12 May 20X2
        London NE25 3PQ   Invoice no. 2794

Item	Quantity	VAT rate %	Net £	VAT £

Sales of goods

Terms: 30 days, 4% discount if paid within 10 days.

---

3 THE DEDUCTION OF INPUT VAT

3.1 **For input VAT to be deductible, the payer must be registered for VAT, with the supply being to him in the course of his business. In addition a VAT invoice must be held** (except for payments of up to £25 including VAT which are for telephone calls or car park fees or which are made through cash operated machines).

3.2 **There are a few special cases where the input VAT is not deductible.** These are as follows.

(a) **VAT on motor cars not used wholly for business purposes,** which is never reclaimable unless a car is acquired new for resale or is acquired for use in or leasing to a taxi business, a self drive car hire business or a driving school. Private use by a proprietor **or an employee** is non-business use unless the user pays a full commercial hire charge (not just a reimbursement of costs). However, VAT on accessories such as car radios is deductible if ordered on a separate purchase order and fitted after delivery of the car. The VAT charged when a car is hired for business purposes is reclaimable, but if there is some non-business use and the hire company has reclaimed VAT on the original purchase of the car now being hired out, only 50% of the VAT on hire charges can be reclaimed by the hirer. A hiring for five days or less is assumed to be for business use.

(b) VAT on **business entertaining**, except entertaining staff.

(c) VAT on expenses incurred on **domestic accommodation for directors**.

(d) VAT on **non-business items passed through the business accounts**. However, when goods are bought partly for business use, the buyer may:

(i) deduct all the input VAT, and account for output VAT in respect of the private use; or

(ii) deduct only the business proportion of the input VAT.

Where services are bought partly for business use, only method (ii) may be used. If services are initially bought for business use but the use then changes, a fair proportion of the input tax (relating to the private use) is reclaimed by HM Customs & Excise by making the trader account for output VAT;

(e) **VAT which does not relate to the making of supplies by the buyer in the course of a business.**

Where non-deductible input VAT arises the VAT inclusive amount will be included in the trader's accounts.

Partial exemption

> **KEY TERM**
>
> A taxable person may only recover the VAT he has paid on supplies to him so far as it is attributable to taxable supplies made by him. Where a trader makes a mixture of taxable and exempt supplies, his business falls within the concept of **partial exemption** and he is partially exempt, and not all his input VAT is recoverable because some of it is attributable to exempt supplies made by him. A person able to recover all input VAT (except as in Paragraph 3.2 above) is a **fully taxable person**.

3.3 **A partially exempt business has the problem of trying to analyse the input tax suffered into two categories.**

(a) **Attributable to making taxable supplies** (fully recoverable)

(b) **Attributable to making exempt supplies** (not recoverable unless very small – see **de minimis** limit in key term box below)

Customs may agree various methods with a trader to allow this apportionment to be calculated but the most popular method used is called the **standard method.**

3.4 The **standard method** of attributing input VAT involves the following steps.

Step 1. Calculate the amount of input VAT suffered on supplies made to the taxable person in the period.

Step 2. Calculate how much of the input VAT suffered relates to supplies which are wholly used or to be used by him in making taxable supplies: this input VAT is deductible in full.

Step 3. Calculate how much of the input VAT suffered relates to supplies which are wholly used or to be used by him in making exempt supplies: this input VAT is not deductible.

Step 4. Calculate how much of any remaining input VAT is deductible by taking the percentage (taxable turnover excluding VAT/total turnover excluding VAT) × 100%, rounded to the nearest whole percentage above.

3.5 EXAMPLE: THE STANDARD METHOD OF ATTRIBUTING INPUT VAT

In a three month VAT period, Mr A makes both exempt and taxable supplies: £100,000 exempt and £320,000 taxable. Most of the goods purchased are used for both types of supply which means that much of the input VAT cannot be directly attributed to either type of supply. After directly attributing as much input VAT as possible the following position arises.

	£
Attributed to taxable supplies	1,200
Attributed to exempt supplies	600
Unattributed VAT	8,200
	10,000

How much input VAT can Mr A recover?

3.6 SOLUTION

The amount of unattributed VAT which is attributable to the making of taxable supplies is

$$£\frac{320,000}{420,000} = £76.19047\% \text{ ie rounded up is } 77\%$$

$$77\% \times £8,200 = £6,314$$

Mr A can therefore recover £1,200 + £6,314 = £7,514 of input VAT.

3.7 Alternative bases of attributing input VAT may be agreed with HM Customs & Excise.

KEY TERM

Where the input VAT wholly attributable to exempt supplies plus the VAT apportioned to exempt supplies is no more than £625 a month on average and is also no more than 50% of all input VAT, all VAT is treated as being attributable to taxable supplies and therefore fully recoverable. This limit is known as the **de minimis limit**.

3.8 **An annual adjustment is made, covering the year to 31 March, 30 April or 31 May** (depending on when the return periods end). A computation of recoverable input VAT is made for the whole year, using the same method as for individual returns. The '£625 a month on average and 50%' test is also applied to the year as a whole, and if it is passed then all input VAT for the year is recoverable.

3.9 **The result for the whole year is compared with the total of results for the individual return periods.**

(a) If the result for the whole year shows that less input VAT is recoverable than has been recovered period by period, **the difference is accounted for** as output VAT **on the return for the next period after the end of the year.**

(b) If the result for the whole year shows that more input VAT is recoverable than has been recovered period by period, the difference is claimed as input VAT on the return for the next period after the end of the year.

3.10 **If the '£625 a month on average and 50%' de minimis test is passed for every return period in the year, no annual adjustment is made.**

3.11 If there was no exempt input VAT (that is, input VAT attributable to exempt supplies) for the preceding year, the 'year' for the purposes of the annual adjustment starts at the beginning of the first return period in which there was exempt input VAT.

In the year of registration, the 'year' starts on the day when exempt input VAT was first incurred.

If a trader ceases to be taxable, the 'year' ends when he ceases to be taxable.

Activity 13.2

Worth plc had the following sales and purchases in the three months ended 31 December 20X2. All amounts exclude any VAT, and all transactions were with United Kingdom traders.

	£
Sales	
Standard rated	450,000
Zero rated	237,000
Exempt	168,000
Purchases	
Standard rated	
Attributable to taxable supplies	300,000
Attributable to exempt supplies	75,000
Unattributable	240,000
Zero rated	4,200
Exempt	7,900

Task

Compute the figures which would be entered in boxes 1 to 5 of Worth plc's VAT return for the period.

Motoring expenses

3.12 **The VAT incurred on the purchase of a car not used wholly for business purposes is not recoverable** (except as in Paragraph 3.2 above). If accessories are fitted at a later date to the original purchase and a separate invoice is raised then the VAT on the accessories can be treated as input VAT (and recovered) so long as the accessories are for business use.

3.13 **If a car is used wholly for business purposes** (including leasing, so long as the charges are at the open market rate), **the input VAT is recoverable but the buyer must account for VAT when he sells the car. If a car is leased, the lessor recovered the input VAT and the lessee makes some private use of the car** (for example private use by employees), **the lessee can only recover 50% of the input VAT on the lease charges.**

3.14 If a car is used for business purposes then any VAT charged on repair and maintenance costs can be treated as input VAT. No apportionment has to be made for private use.

3.15 If an employee accepts a reduced salary in exchange for being allowed to use his employer's car privately, there is no supply, so VAT is not due on the salary reduction. However, VAT is due on charges for running costs. VAT is also due on charges for employee use in the rare cases where the charge is a full commercial rate so that the employer has recovered input VAT on the cost or on leasing charges in full.

3.16 **The VAT incurred on fuel used for business purposes is fully deductible as input VAT.** If the fuel is bought by employees who are reimbursed for the actual cost or by a mileage allowance, the employer may deduct the input VAT.

3.17 **If fuel is supplied for private use at less than the cost of that fuel to the business, all input VAT on the fuel is allowed but the business must account for output VAT using set scale charges per quarter or per month, based on the cylinder capacity of the car's engine.**

3.18 The scale charges (from 6 April 2000) are as follows;

Cylinder capacity	Scale figure (deemed supply including VAT)		VAT due (scale figure ×7/47)	
	Quarter	*Month*	*Quarter*	*Month*
cc	£	£	£	£
Diesel engines				
Up to 2,000	232	77	34.55	11.46
Over 2,000	295	98	43.93	14.59
Non-diesel engines				
Up to 1,400	256	85	38.12	12.65
1,401 - 2,000	325	108	48.40	16.08
Over 2,000	478	159	71.19	23.68

Relief for bad debts

3.19 **If a trader supplies goods or services on credit, he may well account for the VAT on the sale before receiving payment.** For example, if a trader prepares a VAT return for January to March he will include VAT on sales invoiced in March and will pay that VAT at the end of April, even though the customer may not pay him until May.

3.20 VAT may therefore have to be paid to HM Customs & Excise before the trader knows that he is going to be paid at all. **The customer might never pay. Without a special relief, the trader might lose both the amount of the bad debt excluding VAT and the VAT on the sale.**

> **KEY TERM**
>
> Under **VAT bad debt relief,** the trader can reclaim VAT already accounted for on debts which have gone bad. The VAT is reclaimed on the creditor's VAT return, by adding it to the figure for VAT reclaimed on purchases. The amount must be debited to a 'refunds for bad debts' account and the debit is then transferred to the VAT allowable portion of the VAT account.

3.21 All of the following **conditions must be met for VAT bad debt relief to be available.**

 (a) **The debt is over six months old** (measured from the date payment was due).

 (b) The **debt has been written off** in the creditor's accounts.

 (c) The consideration was not in excess of the market value of the goods or services.

 (d) **The creditor has a copy of the VAT invoice,** and records to show that VAT on the supply has been accounted for and that the debt has been written off.

3.22 If the debtor has paid some, but not all, of what he owes, the most recent debts are treated as the ones still owed.

3.23 If the relief is claimed but some payment from the debtor is later received, a corresponding part of the VAT must be paid back to HM Customs & Excise.

3.24 **The supplier must notify the customer that the debt is being written off** for VAT purposes, **and retain a copy of the notification.** The information to be stated in the notification is as follows.

 • The date of the issue of the notification
 • The date of the claim
 • The date and number of the VAT invoice in relation to the supply
 • The amount of the consideration written off as a bad debt
 • The amount of the claim

3.25 **This notification must be made within seven days after the date of the claim.**

3.26 A claim for bad debt relief is made by including it in the input tax box (ie box 4) of a VAT return. The conditions for relief must have been met by the end of the period for which the return is made. Relief must be claimed within three years from the later of the date when the consideration became payable and the tax point for the supply concerned.

3.27 **If the supplier claims bad debt relief because of non-payment by the customer, the customer's right to input tax recovery is forfeited.** The customer must repay any input tax previously claimed by making a negative input tax entry on the return for the period which covers the date of the claim. If the customer subsequently makes payment, the input tax can be claimed again on the return covering the date of payment.

DEVOLVED ASSESSMENT ALERT

The debtors listing should periodically be reviewed and debts over six months old can be 'written off' to a VAT Bad Debts account to allow bad debt relief to be claimed. It is not also necessary to write off the debt as bad through the accounts for VAT bad debt relief to be available. Such relief is claimed on the next VAT return.

Self supply

3.28 As we have seen, a trader making exempt supplies cannot reclaim input VAT charged on goods and services bought to make those supplies. This could lead to distortion of competition, as some traders with exempt outputs could obtain a VAT advantage by producing their own goods or making use of their own services rather than buying them. The Treasury has power to deal with such distortion by making regulations taxing self supplies. Regulations have been made covering the following.

 (a) Stationery in excess of £52,000 (from 1 April 2000) a year. The stationery regulation does not apply to fully taxable persons

 (b) Cars

KEY TERM

The effect of a **self supply** is that the trader is treated as supplying the goods or services to himself (in general, at market value). Output VAT is due to HM Customs & Excise, but if the trader is wholly or partly exempt (or the cars have some non-business use) all or some of that VAT cannot be recovered as input VAT. Thus the business suffers a VAT cost.

3.29 Regulations prevent the input VAT being fully recovered by the trader saying that it is attributable to the (taxable) supply of the goods or services concerned to himself. However, the VAT on materials bought to make self supplies is fully recoverable.

3.30 The amount of the self supply is excluded from both the numerator and the denominator of the fraction used in the partial exemption calculation.

4 IMPORTS AND EXPORTS AND EC TRADE

4.1 **Imports and exports are purchases from and sales to countries other than EC members. Imports are chargeable to VAT when the same goods supplied in the home market by a registered trader would be chargeable to VAT, and at the same rate.**

4.2 **An importer of goods from outside the EC must calculate VAT on the value of the goods imported and account for it at the point of entry into the UK. He can then deduct the VAT payable as input VAT** on his next VAT return. HM Customs & Excise issue monthly certificates to importers showing the VAT paid on imports. VAT is chargeable on the sale of the goods in the UK in the normal way. If security can be provided, the deferred payment system can be used whereby VAT and customs duty are automatically debited to the importer's bank account each month rather than payment being made for each import when the goods arrive in the UK.

4.3   All incidental expenses incurred up to the first destination of the goods in the UK should be included in the value of imported goods. Additionally, if a further destination in the UK or another member State is known at the time the goods are imported, any costs incurred in transporting the goods to that further place must also be included in the value.

4.4   **Exports of goods are zero rated (even if a sale of the same goods in the UK would be standard rated or exempt), but the exporter should retain evidence of export** (such as commercial documents).

4.5   **There is also a system of paying VAT on imports of services** (from inside or outside the EC), **known as the reverse charge.** A registered trader belonging in the UK who obtains certain services from abroad for business purposes is treated as supplying the services, so that VAT must be paid on them to Customs.

Trade in goods within the EC

4.6   **The general approach for trade in goods within the EC is as follows.**

(a)   **For goods sold between registered traders, the seller zero rates the supply. The buyer must pay VAT at his country's rate on the supply to him, and can treat it as input VAT.** Thus the buyer's country's VAT rate is substituted for the seller's country's VAT rate.

(b)   **On a sale to an unregistered buyer, the seller simply applies VAT** (at his own country's rate) in the same way as he would for a sale within his own country.

(c)   **However, if the seller makes substantial sales** (usually over £70,000 in total) **to unregistered buyers in one country, he may have to register in that country and apply its VAT rate.**

> ### KEY TERM
>
> VAT is charged on **taxable acquisitions** (the term 'imports' is not used) of goods from other EC member states.

4.7   An acquisition is taxable if it meets all of the following conditions.

(a)   The acquirer is a taxable person

(b)   (i)   The goods were acquired in the course or furtherance of a business, or of an activity of any corporate or unincorporated body

(ii)   The acquirer carries on the business or activity

(iii)   The supplier is taxable on the supply in another member state of the EC

(c)   The supply to the acquirer is not an exempt supply

4.8   No VAT is charged on an acquisition of zero rated goods.

4.9   If goods are supplied to someone acquiring them in another EC state, the supply is not zero rated or exempt unless:

(a)   a supply of the same goods in the UK would be zero rated or exempt; or

(b)   the acquirer is VAT registered and his registration number (preceded by a his state code) is shown on the invoice. The supply is then zero rated. If the number is not shown, but is later given to the supplier, a credit note can then be issued for the VAT charged and the supply can then be treated as zero rated.

4.10 **The time of any acquisition,** or supply to a trader in another EC state who is liable to VAT as acquirer, **is not determined by the usual tax point rules. It is the earlier of:**

- **the date of issue of a VAT invoice;**
- **the 15th of the month following removal of the goods.**

4.11 **When goods are acquired, the VAT due is accounted for as output VAT on the return form. If the goods are for business purposes, it may also be treated as input VAT so long as a VAT invoice issued by the supplier is held,** the invoice showing both the supplier's VAT registration number (prefixed by the state code) and the acquirer's VAT registration number (prefixed by GB). However, if the goods are for directors' domestic accommodation the VAT may not be treated as input VAT.

4.12 Certain advertising, banking, professional and freight transport services are, when supplied to people outside the EC or to VAT registered traders in other EC member states, outside the scope of VAT. No VAT is charged but the services are included in the Box 6 total on the VAT return.

4.13 **The EC Sales List (ESL) must be produced for each calendar quarter, and must be submitted to Customs within 42 days of the quarter end.**

The ESL is submitted on form VAT 101, and consists of a list of all customers elsewhere in the EC to whom supplies of goods have been made in the period, their VAT registration numbers (including country prefixes) and the value of supplies of goods to them during the period.

Traders whose total taxable supplies are low may apply to submit ESLs annually instead of quarterly.

4.14 **The Supplementary Statistical Declaration (SSD or INTRASTAT) is a monthly return detailing all movements of goods between the UK and other EC states.** It covers transfers between branches of the same business as well as purchases and sales of goods, and provides the information needed for the trade statistics.

The obligation to submit SSDs arises separately for acquisitions and despatches and depends on the value of the movements. The threshold is £233,000 pa from 1 January 2000.

The SSD must give details of each shipment, including such matters as the detailed trade classification of the goods, quantities, shipping costs, countries of departure and arrival etc.

The SSD must be submitted within ten days of the month end.

5 SPECIAL SCHEMES

The cash accounting scheme

KEY TERM

The **cash accounting scheme** enables businesses to account for VAT on the basis of cash paid and received. That is, the date of payment or receipt determines the return in which the transaction is dealt with.

5.1 **The scheme can only be used by a trader whose annual taxable turnover (excluding VAT) does not exceed £350,000.** A trader can join the scheme only if all returns and VAT payments are up to date (or arrangements have been made to pay outstanding VAT by instalments).

5.2 If the value of taxable supplies has exceeded £437,500 in the 12 months to the end of a VAT period and has also exceeded £350,000 in the following 12 months, the trader must leave the scheme and start using the normal method of accounting at the end of the second 12 months.

5.3 **A trader using the scheme should use his records of cash paid and received (for example his cash book) to prepare returns.**

5.4 Traders cannot use the cash accounting scheme

- For sales of goods and services invoiced in advance of the supply being made
- For sales where payment is not due for more than six months after the invoice date

DEVOLVED ASSESSMENT ALERT

If the cash accounting scheme is in operation you need only look at the entries in the cash book to determine the input VAT and output VAT to include in the VAT return. (However, do ensure that there are proper VAT invoices relating to the supplies to support your claim.) Thus the regular rule of 'tax point' is ignored.

Another plus point of the scheme is that it gives automatic bad debt relief – the output tax is only paid over to Customs when it is collected by the supplier from the customer.

Activity 13.3

Suzanne Smith is a trader who uses the cash accounting scheme. Some of her sales are standard rated, some are zero rated and some are exempt. Transactions for which the sale, the purchase or the receipt or payment of cash fell in the three months ended 31 August 20X4 are as follows. All amounts include any VAT. No input VAT is attributable to any particular type of supply. There are no transactions with anyone outside the United Kingdom.

Date of Transaction	Date cash received or paid	VAT rate %	Amount £
Sales			
14.5.X4	2.6.X4	17.5	270.35
29.5.X4	15.6.X4	17.5	420.00
2.6.X4	2.6.X4	17.5	620.74
4.6.X4	7.6.X4	0.0	540.40
10.6.X4	22.6.X4	0.0	680.18
14.6.X4	14.6.X4	17.5	200.37
27.6.X4	4.7.X4	Exempt	180.62
4.7.X4	12.7.X4	0.0	235.68
10.7.X4	12.7.X4	17.5	429.32
21.7.X4	21.7.X4	Exempt	460.37
31.7.X4	20.8.X4	Exempt	390.12
3.8.X4	3.8.X4	0.0	220.86
12.8.X4	2.9.X4	Exempt	800.28
20.8.X4	23.8.X4	17.5	350.38
25.8.X4	5.9.X4	17.5	380.07

Date of transaction	Date cash received or paid	VAT rate %	Amount £
Purchases			
20.5.X4	4.6.X4	17.5	521.44
3.6.X4	3.6.X4	17.5	516.13
22.6.X4	1.7.X4	0.0	737.48
1.7.X4	4.7.X4	17.5	414.68
12.7.X4	12.7.X4	Exempt	280.85
4.8.X4	1.9.X4	17.5	779.13
23.8.X4	7.9.X4	17.5	211.73

Suzanne also took fuel from the business (without payment) for use in her 1,700 cc petrol engined car, which she does not drive for business purposes. The scale charge is £325.

Task

Complete the following VAT return for Suzanne Smith.

Value Added Tax Return

For the period
01 06 X4 to 31 08 X4

For Official Use

Registration number | Period
483 8611 98 | 08 X4

You could be liable to a financial penalty if your completed return and all the VAT payable are not received by the due date.

MS S SMITH
32 CASE STREET
ZEDTOWN
ZY4 3JN

Due date: 30 09 X4

For Official Use

Your VAT Office telephone number is 0123-4567

Before you fill in this form please read the notes on the back and the VAT Leaflet *"Filling in your VAT return"*. Fill in all boxes clearly in ink, and write 'none' where necessary. Don't put a dash or leave any box blank. If there are no pence write "00" in the pence column. Do not enter more than one amount in any box.

For official use			£	p
	VAT due in this period on sales and other outputs	1		
	VAT due in this period on acquisitions from other EC Member States	2		
	Total VAT due (the sum of boxes 1 and 2)	3		
	VAT reclaimed in this period on purchases and other inputs (including acquisitions from the EC)	4		
	Net VAT to be paid to Customs or reclaimed by you (Difference between boxes 3 and 4)	5		
	Total value of sales and all other outputs excluding any VAT. Include your box 8 figure	6		00
	Total value of purchases and all other inputs excluding any VAT. Include your box 9 figure	7		00
	Total value of all supplies of goods and related services, excluding any VAT, to other EC Member States	8		00
	Total value of all acquisitions of goods and related services, excluding any VAT, from other EC Member States	9		00

Retail schemes. If you have used any ot the schemes in the period covered by this return, enter the relevant letter(s) in this box.

If you are enclosing a payment please tick this box.

DECLARATION: You, or someone on your behalf, must sign below.

I, _____ declare that the
(Full name of signatory in BLOCK LETTERS)
information given above is true and complete.

Signature_____ Date _____ 20

A false declaration can result in prosecution.

The annual accounting scheme

5.5 **The annual accounting scheme is only available to traders who regularly pay VAT to HM Customs & Excise,** not to traders who normally get repayments. It is available for traders **whose annual taxable turnover (excluding VAT) does not exceed £300,000** and have traded for at least 12 months. The year for which each return is made may end at the end of any calendar month.

> **KEY TERM**
>
> Traders opting for the **annual accounting scheme** make VAT returns only once a year. However, throughout the year they make payments on account of the ultimate liability.

5.6   **HM Customs & Excise estimate the annual liability based on the past performance of the business. The trader must pay 90% of this estimate during the year by means of nine monthly direct debit payments** starting in the fourth month of the year.

5.7   **Smaller payments are made for smaller businesses.** A business with turnover below £100,000 using the annual accounting scheme pays three quarterly payments on account, each equal to 20 per cent of the previous year's liability. However, if the previous year's liability was below £2,000, no interim payments are required. Interim payments may be made by credit transfer or direct debit, as the trader chooses.

5.8   **At the end of the year the trader completes an annual VAT return which must be submitted to HM Customs & Excise along with any payment due by two months after the end of the year.**

5.9   It is not possible to join the annual accounting scheme if input VAT exceeded output VAT in the year prior to application. In addition, all returns must have been made up to date.

5.10   If the expected value of a trader's taxable supplies exceeds £375,000 notice must be given to HM Customs & Excise within 30 days and the trader may then have to leave the scheme. If the £375,000 limit is in fact exceeded, the trader must leave the scheme.

        If a trader fails to make the regular payments required by the scheme or the final payment for a year, or has not paid all VAT shown on returns made before joining the scheme, he may be expelled from the scheme.

Retail schemes

5.11   **Retail schemes exist to facilitate VAT accounting by shops, particularly those making a mixture of standard rated, zero rated and exempt supplies.** Some schemes rely on separate totals being kept for different sorts of supply, and others make estimates of VAT due by reference to purchases. Customs may agree a bespoke scheme with an individual retailer or allow a retailer to operate one of a number of standard schemes.

The secondhand goods scheme

5.12   **The basic idea of the secondhand goods scheme is to restrict the amount of VAT due on goods sold under them to tax on the trader's margin, rather than on the entire amount charged on reselling the goods. The trader has to account for VAT at 7/47 of the difference between his buying price and his selling price.** The scheme applies to all secondhand goods, apart from precious metals and gemstones. It also applies to works of art, collectors' items and antiques. A trader does not have to apply the scheme: he can account for VAT in the normal way if he chooses.

5.13   No VAT invoice is issued, so a customer cannot reclaim the input VAT suffered.

5.14   **A dealer in large volumes of low value goods** (purchase price £500 or less per item) **can account for VAT of 7/47 of his total margin for a period (netting off profits and losses),** instead of working out each profitable margin individually and ignoring losses. **This global accounting cannot be used for motor vehicles, motorcycles, caravans, motor caravans, aircraft, boats, outboard motors, horses or ponies.** If the margin for a period is negative (because purchases have exceeded sales) the negative amount is carried forward and set against the margin for a future period.

5.15 **The scheme can only be applied where the goods have been purchased from a person who did not charge VAT on the supply or from one who was operating the secondhand goods scheme.** It can also be used by an agent who acts in his own name and is therefore treated as actually buying and selling goods himself.

5.16 The scheme cannot be used for goods which have been obtained VAT free as part of the transfer of a business as a going concern. However, goods remain eligible if they were obtained following a transfer as a going concern and were eligible for the scheme before transfer.

5.17 Goods sold under the scheme are not subject to the usual rules on trade with other EC member states. There is no VAT on their acquisition and sales to traders in other states are taxed just like sales in the UK. Exports to outside the EC are zero rated. Imports from outside the EC (apart from cars) cannot be included in the scheme.

5.18 In order to apply the second-hand goods scheme, the trader must keep certain records specified by Customs. The principal records required are a stock book and purchase and sale invoices.

6 ADMINISTRATION

Sources of information

6.1 The sources of law on VAT are as follows.

- The Value Added Tax Act 1994 (VATA 1994)
- Subsequent legislation contained in finance acts
- Statutory instruments
- Some sections of HM Customs & Excise Notice 700, The VAT guide

DEVOLVED ASSESSMENT ALERT

You are allowed to have **Notice 700** with you during your assessment so it is very worthwhile to obtain a copy now and become familiar with its contents.

6.2 Information on VAT is also available in notices and leaflets obtainable from local VAT offices. *VAT notes* is a newsletter sent with the VAT return.

Local VAT offices

6.3 **Customs has several head office divisions that deal with central administrative issues and policy matters.** There are 14 regional collections that are responsible for VAT matters within specified geographical areas. Each regional collection contains a number of local VAT offices.

6.4 **Local VAT offices are responsible for the local administration of VAT and for providing advice to registered persons whose principal place of business is in their area.** The local VAT office (LVO) deals with registration, deregistration, debt collection and visits to VAT-registered businesses. In some instances the functions of registration, deregistration and debt management are centralised within the region.

The head of the local VAT office is an Assistant Collector. The office comprises a number of sections, called districts. One surveyor is in charge of each district supervising Senior Officers, Officers and clerical staff within that district.

6.5 **Completed VAT returns should be sent to the VAT Central Unit at Southend, not to a local VAT office.**

6.6 Customs carry out VAT inspections periodically. As a rule, a Senior Officer or an Officer inspects a trader's VAT accounting records during such an inspection. The frequency and duration of the inspections depends on the size, complexity and VAT compliance record of the business.

Usually, the visiting officer makes an appointment for the inspection. Before the inspection a business should ensure that all the records are available (usually six years, or from the date of the last inspection). Key staff should be available on the day of the inspection.

It is also useful to review the periods covered by the inspection. Identify any unusual activities that might have caused VAT errors, for possible disclosure at the start of the inspection.

6.7 **Customs have many powers to assist them in the administration and control of VAT. These include the power to issue assessments for tax due if VAT returns have not been rendered or they consider that tax has been understated.** There is a time limit on Customs' powers to assess of three years from the end of the prescribed accounting period concerned. This is extended to 20 years in the case of fraud.

6.8 Immediately following a VAT inspection it is advisable to make a record of what took place, eg records inspected, points discussed, verbal agreements.

A point to remember is that **a VAT inspection is not an audit. The fact that an officer did not challenge a particular point on one VAT inspection does not necessarily preclude another officer raising the point on a subsequent inspection.** A record of each inspection will assist in any future dealings with Customs. It is also important to obtain any advice given by Customs during the visit or any Customs' rulings in writing. The full facts that might affect these rulings should be provided to the officer in writing.

Seeking guidance

6.9 **If there is any doubt in respect of any aspect of VAT it is advisable to seek guidance from the local VAT office. A letter should be sent outlining all the information necessary for the local office to be able to make an informed decision.** That decision should be requested in writing. If any telephone conversations are held records should be kept and again requests made for Customs to conclude their decisions in writing.

6.10 **It is essential that when the letter seeking guidance is sent to Customs all relevant information is disclosed. If this condition is complied with and it later turns out that Custom's ruling was incorrect the trader is protected from a retrospective claim for VAT under a concession known as the 'Sheldon Statement'.** However this concession only applies if full details were supplied to Customs and thus the local VAT office was not misled, or manipulated into giving a particular decision.

6.11 In the event of a dispute with Customs it is necessary for a trader to decide what action to take. Generally this will involve deciding whether to request the local VAT office to review the disputed decision or to formally appeal to a tribunal.

While a local VAT office can review any decision they make, not every decision can go to tribunal.

6.12 In some situations a local review will lead, relatively quickly, to a satisfactory solution. It also avoids the need for a more formal tribunal appeal.

The request for a local review should be made to the local VAT office within 30 days.

Appeals to VAT and duties tribunals

6.13 **VAT and duties tribunals, which are independent of HM Customs & Excise, provide an alternative method of dealing with disputes.** Provided that VAT returns and payments shown thereon have been made, appeals can be heard by a tribunal.

A tribunal can waive the requirement to pay all tax shown on returns before an appeal is heard in cases of hardship. It cannot allow an appeal against a purely administrative matter such as Customs refusal to apply an extra statutory concession.

6.14 An appeal must be lodged with the tribunal (not the local VAT office) **within 30 days of the date of any decision by HM Customs & Excise.** If the trader would also like the local VAT office to reconsider their decision he should apply within 30 days of the decision to the relevant VAT office. The local VAT office may either:

(a) confirm the original decision, in which case the taxpayer has a further 21 days from the date of that confirmation in which to lodge an appeal with a tribunal; or

(b) send a revised decision, in which case the taxpayer will have a further 30 days from the date of the revised decision in which to lodge an appeal with a tribunal.

6.15 A decision of Customs is appealable only if it concerns one of the matters listed below.

- Registration or cancellation of registration
- The tax chargeable on the supply of any goods
- The amount of any input tax allowable
- A claim for a refund because of a bad debt
- Any liability of Customs to pay interest
- A direction by Customs that the value of supplies shall be their open market value, eg supplies between connected persons
- Any requirements by Customs in respect of computer invoices
- An assessment to tax or the amount of an assessment
- Any liability to a penalty or surcharge under the Civil Penalty provisions
- The amount of any penalty, interest or surcharge under the Civil Penalty provisions
- A refusal to permit the use of the cash accounting provisions appeal to a tribunal

6.16 If one of the parties is dissatisfied with a decision on a point of law he may appeal to the courts. Tribunals may award costs.

Activity 13.4

You are employed by a business which owns a chain of shops selling Herbal goods and wholefoods to the public. The business is about to start selling a new product called Catha Edulis which is a herbal remedy. You are having difficulty in deciding whether the new product constitutes 'food' and will be a zero rated sale or rather is a non-food item and standard rated.

The product is imported by the business from Abyssinia where it is known locally as Khat and drunk as a tea.

Task

Draft a letter to your local VAT office requesting guidance on the correct treatment of the sale of this product.

7 PENALTIES

7.1 **There are many different penalties for failure to comply with VAT law.**

Late notification

7.2 **A trader who makes taxable supplies must tell HM Customs & Excise if supplies exceed the registration limit. A penalty can be levied for failure to notify a liability to register by the proper date.** In addition, the VAT which would have been accounted for had the trader registered on time, must be paid.

7.3 The penalty for late notification is based on the net tax due from the date when the trader should have been registered to the date when notification is made or, if earlier, the date on which HM Customs & Excise become aware of the trader's liability to be registered. The rate varies as follows.

Number of months *registration late by*	*Percentage* *of tax*
Up to 9	5%
Over 9, up to 18	10%
Over 18	15%

A minimum penalty of £50 applies. However Customs can waive the penalty if the trader has a 'reasonable excuse' for the late registration.

The unauthorised issue of invoices

7.4 This penalty applies where a person who is not registered for VAT nevertheless issues VAT invoices. The penalty is 15% of the VAT involved with a minimum penalty of £50.

The default surcharge

7.5 This penalty has the aim of encouraging tax payers to submit their VAT returns (and the VAT due) on time.

KEY TERM

A **default** occurs when a trader either submits his VAT return late, or submits the return on time but pays the VAT late. If a taxpayer defaults, HM Customs & Excise will serve a **surcharge liability notice** on the taxpayer. The notice specifies a **surcharge period** running from the date of the notice to the anniversary of the end of the period for which the taxpayer is in default.

7.6 **If a further default occurs during the surcharge period the original surcharge period will be extended to the anniversary of the end of the period to which the new default relates. In addition,** if the default involves a late payment of VAT (as opposed to simply a late return) **a surcharge is levied.**

7.7 **The surcharge depends on the number of defaults involving late payment of VAT which have occurred in the surcharge period,** as follows.

Default involving late payment of VAT in the surcharge period	Surcharge as a percentage of the VAT outstanding at the due date
First	2%
Second	5%
Third	10%
Fourth and over	15%

Any surcharge of less than £30 is increased to £30, but surcharges at the 2% and 5% rates are not normally demanded unless the amount would be at least £200. Customs have the power to waive the penalty if the trader has a 'reasonable excuse' for submitting the return late or paying the VAT late.

7.8 A trader must submit one year's returns and pay the VAT shown on them on time in order to break out of the surcharge liability period and the escalation of surcharge percentages.

Activity 13.5

Lazy Ltd often submits its VAT returns and payments late, as shown in the following schedule.

Quarter ended	VAT due	Return and payment
	£	
30.6.X2	4,000	On time
30.9.X2	2,500	Late
31.12.X2	5,000	On time
31.3.X3	4,000	On time
30.6.X3	5,000	Late
30.9.X3	4,500	Late
31.12.X3	7,000	On time
31.3.X4	3,500	Late
30.6.X4	4,500	Late
30.9.X4	500	Late
31.12.X4	3,600	On time

Task

Compute the default surcharges arising from the above.

The misdeclaration penalty: very large errors

7.9 The making of a return which understates a person's true liability or overstates the repayment due to him incurs a penalty of 15% of the VAT which would have been lost if the return had been accepted as correct. The same penalty applies when HM Customs & Excise issue an assessment of VAT due which is too low and the trader fails to notify the error within 30 days from the issue of the assessment.

7.10 These penalties apply only where the VAT which would have been lost equals or exceeds the lower of £1m or 30% of the sum of the true input VAT and the true output VAT. This sum is known as the gross amount of tax (GAT). (In the case of an incorrect assessment 30% of the true amount of tax, the VAT actually due from or to the trader, is used instead of 30% of the GAT.) The penalty may be mitigated.

7.11 **Errors on a VAT return of up to £2,000** (net: underdeclaration minus overdeclaration) **may be corrected on the next return without giving rise to a misdeclaration penalty or interest** (see 7.15 below). **Larger errors must be notified to Customs as a voluntary disclosure.** On such notified errors no penalty will arise although interest may be charged (see 7.15 below).

The misdeclaration penalty: repeated errors

7.12 **If a trader submits an inaccurate return, and the VAT which would have been lost if it had been accepted as accurate equals or exceeds the lower of £500,000 or 10% of the GAT, the inaccuracy is material.**

7.13 Before the end of the fourth tax period following the period of a material inaccuracy, HM Customs & Excise may issue a penalty liability notice, specifying a **penalty period**. The period is the eight VAT periods starting with the one in which the notice is issued.

7.14 **If there are material inaccuracies for two or more VAT periods falling within the penalty period, then each such inaccuracy apart from the first one leads to a penalty of 15% of the VAT which would have been lost.**

Interest

7.15 **Interest** (not deductible in computing taxable profits) **is charged on VAT which is the subject of an assessment (where returns were not made or were incorrect)**, or which could have been the subject of an assessment but was paid before the assessment was raised. **It runs from the reckonable date until the date of payment.**

7.16 **The reckonable date is when the VAT should have been paid** (one month from the end of the return period), or in the case of VAT repayments to traders which should not have been made, seven days from the issue of the repayment order. However, where VAT is charged by an assessment interest does not run from more than three years before the date of assessment; and where the VAT was paid before an assessment was raised, interest does not run for more than three years before the date of payment.

Repayment supplement

7.17 **Where a trader is entitled to a repayment of VAT and the original return was rendered on time but HM Customs & Excise do not issue a written instruction for the repayment to be made within 30 days of receiving the return, then the trader will receive a supplement of the greater of £50 and 5% of the amount due.**

7.18 If, however, the return states a refund due which differs from the correct refund by more than the greater of 5% of the correct refund and £250, no supplement is added.

7.19 Days spent in raising and answering reasonable enquiries in relation to the return do not count towards the 30 days allowed to HM Customs & Excise to issue an instruction to make the repayment.

Interest on overpayments due to official errors

7.20 **If VAT is overpaid or a credit for input VAT is not claimed because of an error by HM Customs & Excise, then the trader may claim interest on the amount eventually refunded, running from the date on which he paid the excessive VAT** (or from the date on which HM Customs & Excise might reasonably be expected to have authorised a VAT repayment owing to him) **to the date on which HM Customs & Excise authorise a repayment.**

7.21 Interest must be claimed within three years of the date on which the trader discovered the error or could with reasonable diligence have discovered it. Interest is not available where a repayment supplement is available. Interest does not run for periods relating to reasonable enquiries by HM Customs & Excise into the matter in question.

Activity 13.6

In the quarter ended 31 December 20X5, Roland plc made sales as follows. All amounts given exclude any VAT.

	£
Standard rated sales	3,100,000
Zero rated sales	670,000
Exempt sales	1,920,000

The VAT on purchases attributable to standard rated and zero rated sales was £400,000. The VAT on purchases attributable to exempt sales was £160,000. In addition, VAT on purchases not attributable to any particular type of sale was £37,000.

The company also supplied itself with standard rated stationery (not related to any particular type of supply) which would have cost £40,000 before VAT, a typical quarterly figure. Materials used to make those supplies cost £9,400 including VAT at the standard rate.

Task

Compute the amount payable to or recoverable from HM Customs & Excise in respect of the quarter.

Activity 13.7

In one VAT period, Heimat plc has the following transactions in goods which would be standard rated if supplied in the UK. All amounts exclude any VAT, and all goods sold are sent to the buyers' countries by Heimat plc.

(a) Buys goods from a UK supplier for £12,000

(b) Sells goods to an Italian customer for £7,300. The customer's VAT registration number is shown on the invoice

(c) Sells goods to a Danish customer for £470. The customer is not registered for VAT, and the relevant Danish VAT rate is 25%

(d) Sells goods to an Australian customer for £2,500

(e) Buys goods from a VAT registered German supplier for £3,000. The invoice shows Heimat plc's VAT registration number and the goods are transferred to the UK

Task

Compute the VAT payable to or recoverable from HM Customs & Excise for the period.

Key points in this chapter

- VAT is computed on the price after discounts.

- Mixed supplies are split, but composite supplies are not.

- Some supplies are taxable at either the standard or zero rate, while others are exempt.

- Input VAT on some supplies, including many cars, is not recoverable.

- If a trader makes some exempt supplies, only a proportion of his input VAT may be recoverable.

- VAT bad debt relief is available after six months.

- VAT is generally due on imports, but exports are zero rated.

- Special schemes include the cash accounting scheme and the annual accounting scheme.

- Returns are sent to the VAT Central Unit, but a trader may have dealings with his local VAT office or with a VAT tribunal.

- The most important penalties are the default surcharge and the misdeclaration penalty.

Quick quiz

1   David runs a grocery business. Every week his wife does the weekly shop for the family at the business premises and does not pay David for the groceries taken. How should this situation be treated for VAT?

2   What type of VAT supply is each of the following.

   (a)   sale of child's anorak (age 4-5)
   (b)   supply of life assurance policy
   (c)   supply of 10 first class stamps by Jesmond Post Office
   (d)   sale of hot meat pie by Joe's takeaway
   (e)   sale of pullover for man size 40 inch chest

3   Jonah runs a plumbing business in Brighton. He owns a Vauxhall Astra 2.8L petrol car which he uses for business and private purposes. He reclaims the input VAT on all petrol purchases. For the VAT quarter to 31 December 2000 how much output VAT must Jonah pay to Customs in respect of the car?

4   What are the turnover limits for the cash accounting and annual accounting schemes?

5   Where are completed VAT returns sent to?

6   What is the time limit for lodging an appeal against a disputed Custom's decision?

7   Peter was 2 months late registering his business for VAT. The first VAT return completed was for this 2 month period and showed VAT due of £4,200. What penalty, if any, is also due?

8   X Ltd submitted the return for 31 March 2000 on time but it contained an error in it which the company notified Customs of 6 months later when a new accountant discovered it. The extra £18,000 of VAT due was also paid at this time which was 2 October 2000. What penalties or interest will X Ltd suffer in respect of this error?

Answers to quick quiz

1   This situation is 'goods taken from a business for non-business use' and VAT should be accounted for on their market value (see 1.7).

2   (a)   zero rated (children's clothing)
    (b)   exempt (insurance)
    (c)   exempt (postal services provided by post office)
    (d)   standard rated (**hot** food so not zero rated)
    (e)   standard rated

3   Due to private use of the car and full recovery of petrol input VAT Johah must account for output VAT of £71.19 in the 3 month period to 31 December 2000 using the VAT scale charges.

4   Cash accounting   £350,000 (see 5.1).

      Annual accounting £300,000 (see 5.5).

5   VAT Central Unit at Southend (see 6.5).

6   Within 30 days of the date of Custom's decision (see 6.14).

7   A 5% penalty totalling £210 (£4,200 × 5%) is payable by Peter (see 7.3).

8   Since the error was notified as a voluntary disclosure to Customs no misdeclaration penalty will apply. However, interest will run from the due date for the return (30 April 2000) until the date the VAT was paid (2 October 2000). Custom's set the interest rate used.

Answer to activities

Answer 13.1

Tutorial note. There were two standard rated, two zero rated and two exempt supplies, and totals were needed for each category and for the invoice as a whole. Note that the total including VAT need not be shown, but in practice it always is shown. Note also that the VAT is computed on the net amount after the 4% cash discount.

PIPPA LIMITED
32 Hurst Road, London NE20 4LJ
VAT reg no 730 4148 37

To: Gold Ltd   Date: 12 May 20X2
       75 Link Road   Tax point: 12 May 20X2
       London NE25 3PQ   Invoice no. 2794

Item	Quantity	VAT rate %	Net £	VAT £
Sales of goods				
Personal computer	1	17.5	980	
Microscopes	3	17.5	360	
Total of standard rated (17.5%) supplies			1,340	225.12
Books	20	0.0	200	
Periodicals	500	0.0	450	
Total of zero rated (0%) supplies			650	0.00
Supplies of services				
Insurance		Exempt	1,200	
Medical treatment services		Exempt	400	
Total of exempt supplies			1,600	
Total invoice price excluding VAT			3,590	
Total VAT				225.12

	£
Total payable within 30 days	3,815.12
Less cash discount for payment within 10 days	143.60
Total payable if paid within 10 days	3,671.52

Terms: 30 days, 4% discount if paid within 10 days.

Answer 13.2

Tutorial note. Because Worth plc makes some exempt supplies, not all the VAT on purchases can be recovered. The VAT on purchases which is not attributable to either taxable supplies or exempt supplies must be apportioned.

(a)   Box 1: VAT due on outputs
        The figure is £450,000 × 17.5% = £78,750.00

(b)   Box 2: VAT due on acquisitions
        None.

(c)   Box 3: sum of Boxes 1 and 2

        £78,750.00

(d)   Box 4: VAT reclaimed on inputs

        The figure is £86,520.00, as follows.

        Apportionment percentage = (450 + 237)/(450 + 237 + 168) = 80.35%, rounded up to 81%.

	£
Tax on purchases attributable to taxable supplies £300,000 × 17.5%	52,500.00
Tax on unattributable purchases	
£240,000 × 17.5% × 81%	34,020.00
	86,520.00

(e)   *Box 5: net VAT to be paid or reclaimed*

The amount reclaimable is £(86,520.00 - 78,750.00) = £7,770.00.

Answer 13.3

Tutorial note. You first had to compute the relevant totals, then you had to check the position on partial exemption.

Date cash received	Standard rated turnover	Zero rated turnover	Exempt turnover	VAT at 7/47
	£	£	£	£
2.6.X4	270.35			40.26
15.6.X4	420.00			62.55
2.6.X4	620.74			92.45
7.6.X4		540.40		
22.6.X4		680.18		
14.6.X4	200.37			29.84
4.7.X4			180.62	
12.7.X4		235.68		
12.7.X4	429.32			63.94
21.7.X4			460.37	
20.8.X4			390.12	
3.8.X4		220.86		
23.8.X4	350.38			52.18
	2,291.16	1,677.12	1,031.11	341.22

Total taxable turnover is £(2,291.16 - 341.22 + 1,677.12) = £3,627.06. Total turnover is £(3,627.06 + 1,031.11) = £4,658.17.

The output VAT in respect of fuel is £325.00 × 7/47 = £48.40, so total output VAT is £(341.22 + 48.40) = £389.62.

The scale charge net of VAT is £(325.00 - 48.40) = £276.60, so the Box 6 figure is £(4,658.17 + 276.60) = £4,934.77, rounded down to £4,934.

Date cash paid	Purchase	VAT at 7/47
	£	£
4.6.X4	521.44	77.66
3.6.X4	516.13	76.87
1.7.X4	737.48	
4.7.X4	414.68	61.76
12.7.X4	280.85	
	2,470.58	216.29

The purchases net of VAT (Box 7) are £(2,470.58 - 216.29) = £2,254.29, rounded down.

Input VAT attributable to exempt supplies is 1,031.11/4,934.77 = 20.89%, rounded to 20% (*exempt percentage down*) × £216.29 = £43.26. As this is not more than £625 a month on average and not more than half of all input VAT, all input VAT is recoverable.

Value Added Tax Return
For the period
01 06 X4^{to}31 08 X4

Registration number	Period
483 8611 98	08 X4

You could be liable to a financial penalty if your completed return and all the VAT payable are not received by the due date.

MS S SMITH
32 CASE STREET
ZEDTOWN
ZY4 3JN

Due date: 30 09 X4

For official use	

Your VAT Office telephone number is 0123-4567

Before you fill in this form please read the notes on the back and the VAT Leaflet *"Filling in your VAT return"*.
Fill in all boxes clearly in ink, and write 'none' where necessary. Don't put a dash or leave any box blank. If there are no pence write "00" in the pence column. Do not enter more than one amount in any box.

For official use			£	p
	VAT due in this period on sales and other outputs	1	389	62
	VAT due in this period on acquisitions from other EC Member States	2	None	
	Total VAT due (the sum of boxes 1 and 2)	3	389	62
	VAT reclaimed in this period on purchases and other inputs (including acquisitions from the EC)	4	216	29
	Net VAT to be paid to Customs or reclaimed by you (Difference between boxes 3 and 4)	5	173	33
	Total value of sales and all other outputs excluding any VAT. Include your box 8 figure	6	4,934	00
	Total value of purchases and all other inputs excluding any VAT. Include your box 9 figure	7	2,254	00
	Total value of all supplies of goods and related services, excluding any VAT, to other EC Member States	8	None	00
	Total value of all acquisitions of goods and related services, excluding any VAT, from other EC Member States	9	None	00

Retail schemes. If you have used any of the schemes in the period covered by this return, enter the relevant letter(s) in this box.

If you are enclosing a payment please tick this box. ✔

DECLARATION: You, or someone on your behalf, must sign below.
I, _ _ _ _ SUZANNE SMITH _ _ _ _ _ _ _ _ _ _ _ _ _ _ _ _ declare that the
(Full name of signatory in BLOCK LETTERS)
information given above is true and complete.

Signature_ _ _ _ _ _ *S Smith* _ _ _ _ _ _ _ _ Date 28 Sept 20 X4
A false declaration can result in prosecution.

Answer 13.4

Healthy Wholefoods
1 High Street
Newcastle

H M Customs & Excise
Newcastle Office
1 Low Street
Newcastle

24 March 2000

Dear Sir

Classification of Catha Edulis

I am writing to request guidance with regard to a new product which will be added to our product range next month. The product is a herbal remedy imported from Abyssinia with the Latin name 'Catha Edulis'. The product is used in a similar fashion as tea.

I enclose a sample of the original product and of the product newly packaged for sale in our shops for your information. You will see from the original product enclosed that in Abyssinia the product is called Khat.

If you require any further information (or samples) please do not hesitate to contact me.

Yours faithfully

Mrs J K Buffle

Enc.

Answer 13.5

Tutorial note. There must be an initial default before a surcharge liability period can start. However, once it has started it is extended by later defaults. In this case, there is a single surcharge liability period extending at least as far as 30 September 20X5. Because there is no break in the period, the percentage rate escalates right up to 15%.

Quarter ended	Working	Surcharge	
		£	
30.6.X3	£5,000 × 2% = £100	0	(under £200)
30.9.X3	£4,500 × 5%	225	
31.3.X4	£3,500 × 10%	350	
30.6.X4	£4,500 × 15%	675	
30.9.X4	£500 × 15%	75	(surcharges under £200 are collected when at 10% or 15%)

Answer 13.6

Tutorial note. Part of the VAT suffered on the self supply is irrecoverable, but all of the VAT on materials bought to make that supply is recoverable.

	£	£
Output VAT		
£3,100,000 x 17.5%		542,500
£40,000 x 17.5%		7,000
		549,500
Input VAT		
Attributable to taxable supplies	400,000	
Unattributable £37,000 x 67% (see below)	24,790	
Self supply £40,000 x 17.5% x 67% (see below)	4,690	
Purchases for self supply £9,400 x 7/47	1,400	
		430,880
Amount due to HM Customs & Excise		118,620

The partial exemption fraction is $\dfrac{3{,}100 + 670}{3{,}100 + 670 + 1{,}920}$ = 0.663, rounded up to 67%

Answer 13.7

Tutorial note. The current VAT system for trade with other European Community states is designed so that when goods will be resold by a VAT registered trader in the destination state, that trader will impose the local VAT rate on the final consumer; but where the sale between states is to the final consumer, VAT is charged by the seller at the rate applying in the seller's state.

		£
(a)	Input VAT £12,000 x 17.5%	(2,100.00)
(b)	Zero rated sale	0.00
(c)	Output VAT £470 x 17.5%	82.25
(d)	Zero rated export	0.00
(e)	VAT on taxable acquisition	525.00
(e)	Input VAT on taxable acquisition £3,000 x 17.5%	(525.00)
	Recoverable from HM Customs & Excise	(2,017.75)

List of
Key Terms
and Index

These are the terms which we have identified throughtout the text as being KEY TERMS. You should make sure that you can define what these terms mean; go back to the pages highlighted here if you need to check.

X axis, 50

Y axis, 50
Year to date, 188

Zero rated, 245
Zero rated supplies, 264, 265

BPP PUBLISHING

ORDER FORM

Any books from our AAT range can be ordered by telephoning 020-8740-2211. Alternatively, send this page to our address below, fax it to us on 020-8740-1184, or email us at **publishing@bpp.com.** Or look us up on our website: www.bpp.com

We aim to deliver to all UK addresses inside 5 working days; a signature will be required. Order to all EU addresses should be delivered within 6 working days. All other orders to overseas addresses should be delivered within 8 working days.

To: BPP Publishing Ltd, Aldine House, Aldine Place, London W12 8AW

Tel: 020-8740 2211   **Fax: 020-8740 1184**   **Email: publishing@bpp.com**

Mr / Ms (full name): _____

Daytime delivery address: _____

_____

Postcode: _____   Daytime Tel: _____

Please send me the following quantities of books.

	5/00 Interactive Text	8/00 DA Kit	8/00 CA Kit
FOUNDATION			
Unit 1 Recording Income and Receipts	☐	☐	
Unit 2 Making and Recording Payments	☐	☐	
Unit 3 Ledger Balances and Initial Trial Balance	☐	☐	
Unit 4 Supplying information for Management Control	☐	☐	
Unit 20 Working with Information Technology (8/00 Text)	☐		
Unit 22/23 Achieving Personal Effectiveness	☐		
INTERMEDIATE			
Unit 5 Financial Records and Accounts	☐	☐	
Unit 6 Cost Information	☐	☐	
Unit 7 Reports and Returns	☐		
Unit 21 Using Information Technology	☐		
Unit 22: see below			
TECHNICIAN			
Unit 8/9 Core Managing Costs and Allocating Resources	☐		☐
Unit 10 Core Managing Accounting Systems	☐	☐	☐
Unit 11 Option Financial Statements (Accounting Practice)	☐		☐
Unit 12 Option Financial Statements (Central Government)	☐		
Unit 15 Option Cash Management and Credit Control	☐	☐	
Unit 16 Option Evaluating Activities	☐	☐	
Unit 17 Option Implementing Auditing Procedures	☐	☐	
Unit 18 Option Business Tax FA00(8/00 Text)	☐	☐	
Unit 19 Option Personal Tax FA00(8/00 Text)	☐		
TECHNICIAN 1999			
Unit 17 Option Business Tax Computations FA99 (8/99 Text & Kit)	☐	☐	
Unit 18 Option Personal Tax Computations FA99 (8/99 Text & Kit)	☐	☐	

TOTAL BOOKS   ☐ + ☐ + ☐ = ☐

@ £9.95 each = £ ☐

Postage and packaging:

UK: £2.00 for each book to maximum of £10

Europe (inc ROI and Channel Islands): £4.00 for first book, £2.00 for each extra

Rest of the World: £20.00 for first book, £10 for each extra

P & P   £ ☐

Unit 22 Maintaining a Healthy Workplace Interactive Text (postage free)   ☐ @ £3.95   £ ☐

GRAND TOTAL £ ☐

I enclose a cheque for £ _____ (cheques to BPP Publishing Ltd) or charge to Mastercard/Visa/Switch

Card number ☐☐☐☐ ☐☐☐☐ ☐☐☐☐ ☐☐☐☐ ☐☐☐☐ ☐☐

Start date _____   Expiry date _____   Issue no. (Switch only)___

Signature _____

REVIEW FORM & FREE PRIZE DRAW

All original review forms from the entire BPP range, completed with genuine comments, will be entered into one of two draws on 31 January 2001 and 31 July 2001. The names on the first four forms picked out on each occasion will be sent a cheque for £50.

Name: _____   **Address**: _____

_____

_____

How have you used this Interactive Text?
(Tick one box only)

☐ Home study (book only)

☐ On a course: college _____

☐ With 'correspondence' package

☐ Other _____

Why did you decide to purchase this Interactive Text? *(Tick one box only)*

☐ Have used BPP Texts in the past

☐ Recommendation by friend/colleague

☐ Recommendation by a lecturer at college

☐ Saw advertising

☐ Other _____

During the past six months do you recall seeing/receiving any of the following?
(Tick as many boxes as are relevant)

☐ Our advertisement in *Accounting Technician* magazine

☐ Our advertisement in *Pass*

☐ Our brochure with a letter through the post

Which (if any) aspects of our advertising do you find useful?
(Tick as many boxes as are relevant)

☐ Prices and publication dates of new editions

☐ Information on Interactive Text content

☐ Facility to order books off-the-page

☐ None of the above

Have you used the companion Assessment Kit for this subject?   ☐ Yes   ☐ No

Your ratings, comments and suggestions would be appreciated on the following areas

	Very useful	Useful	Not useful
Introductory section (How to use this Interactive Text etc)	☐	☐	☐
Chapter topic lists	☐	☐	☐
Chapter learning objectives	☐	☐	☐
Key terms	☐	☐	☐
Assessment alerts	☐	☐	☐
Examples	☐	☐	☐
Activities and answers	☐	☐	☐
Key learning points	☐	☐	☐
Quick quizzes and answers	☐	☐	☐
List of key terms and index	☐	☐	☐
Icons	☐	☐	☐

	Excellent	Good	Adequate	Poor
Overall opinion of this Text	☐	☐	☐	☐

Do you intend to continue using BPP Interactive Texts/Assessment Kits? ☐ Yes ☐ No

Please note any further comments and suggestions/errors on the reverse of this page.

Please return to: Nick Weller, BPP Publishing Ltd, FREEPOST, London, W12 8BR

REVIEW FORM & FREE PRIZE DRAW (continued)

Please note any further comments and suggestions/errors below

FREE PRIZE DRAW RULES

1   Closing date for 31 January 2001 draw is 31 December 2000. Closing date for 31 July 2001 draw is 30 June 2001.

2   Restricted to entries with UK and Eire addresses only. BPP employees, their families and business associates are excluded.

3   No purchase necessary. Entry forms are available upon request from BPP Publishing. No more than one entry per title, per person. Draw restricted to persons aged 16 and over.

4   Winners will be notified by post and receive their cheques not later than 6 weeks after the relevant draw date.

5   The decision of the promoter in all matters is final and binding. No correspondence will be entered into.